BANKS AND BANKING DEVELOPMENTS

BANK HOLDING COMPANIES AND GOVERNMENT SUPPORT ISSUES

BANKS AND BANKING DEVELOPMENTS

Additional books in this series can be found on Nova's website
under the Series tab.

Additional e-books in this series can be found on Nova's website
under the e-book tab.

BANKS AND BANKING DEVELOPMENTS

BANK HOLDING COMPANIES AND GOVERNMENT SUPPORT ISSUES

COLLEEN ROYCE
EDITOR

nova publishers
New York

Library of Congress Cataloging-in-Publication Data

ISBN: 978-1-63463-687-2

Published by Nova Science Publishers, Inc. † New York

CONTENTS

PREFACE

During the 2007-09 financial crisis, the federal government's actions to stabilize the financial system provided funding support and other benefits to bank holding companies and their subsidiaries. Agencies introduced new programs with broad-based eligibility that provided funding support to eligible institutions, which included entities that were part of a bank holding company and others. Programs that provided the most significant support directly to bank holding companies or their subsidiaries included Department of the Treasury capital investment programs, Federal Reserve System lending programs, and Federal Deposit Insurance Corporation (FDIC) guarantee programs. The federal government extended unprecedented support to financial institutions to stabilize financial markets during the financial crisis. While these actions helped to avert a more severe crisis, they raised questions about the appropriate scope of government safety nets for financial institutions. This book examines actual government support for banks and bank holding companies during the financial crisis; and recent statutory and regulatory changes related to government support for banks and bank holding companies. It also examines how financial reforms have altered market expectations of government rescues and the existence or size of funding advantages the largest bank holding companies may have received due to perceived government support.

Chapter 1 – The federal government extended unprecedented support to financial institutions to stabilize financial markets during the financial crisis. While these actions helped to avert a more severe crisis, they raised questions about the appropriate scope of government safety nets for financial institutions. GAO was asked to review the benefits that large bank holding companies (those with more than $500 billion in assets) have received from actual and implied government support.

This is the first of two reports GAO will issue on this topic. This report examines (1) actual government support for banks and bank holding companies during the financial crisis, and (2) recent statutory and regulatory changes related to government support for banks and bank holding companies. GAO reviewed relevant statutes, regulations, and agency documents; analyzed program transaction data; and interviewed regulators, representatives of financial institutions, and academics. In a second report to be issued in 2014, GAO will examine any funding or other economic advantages the largest bank holding companies have received as a result of implied government support.

Chapter 2 – "Too big to fail" is a market notion that the federal government would intervene to prevent the failure of a large, complex financial institution to avoid destabilizing the financial sector and the economy. Expectations of government rescues can distort investor incentives to properly price the risks of firms they view as too big to fail, potentially giving rise to funding and other advantages for these firms.

GAO was asked to review the benefits that the largest bank holding companies (those with more than $500 billion in assets) have received from perceived government support. This is the second of two GAO reports on government support for bank holding companies. The first study focused on actual government support during the 2007-2009 financial crisis and recent statutory and regulatory changes related to government support for these firms. This report examines how financial reforms have altered market expectations of government rescues and the existence or size of funding advantages the largest bank holding companies may have received due to perceived government support.

GAO reviewed relevant statutes and rules and interviewed regulators, rating agencies, investment firms, and corporate customers of banks. GAO also reviewed relevant studies and interviewed authors of these studies. Finally, GAO conducted quantitative analyses to assess potential "too-big-to-fail" funding cost advantages.

In its comments, the Department of the Treasury generally agreed with GAO's analysis. GAO incorporated technical comments from the financial regulators, as appropriate.

In: Bank Holding Companies and Government Support Issues ISBN: 978-1-63463-687-2
Editor: Colleen Royce

Chapter 1

GOVERNMENT SUPPORT FOR BANK HOLDING COMPANIES: STATUTORY CHANGES TO LIMIT FUTURE SUPPORT ARE NOT YET FULLY IMPLEMENTED*

United States Government Accountability Office

WHY GAO DID THIS STUDY

The federal government extended unprecedented support to financial institutions to stabilize financial markets during the financial crisis. While these actions helped to avert a more severe crisis, they raised questions about the appropriate scope of government safety nets for financial institutions. GAO was asked to review the benefits that large bank holding companies (those with more than $500 billion in assets) have received from actual and implied government support. This is the first of two reports GAO will issue on this topic. This report examines (1) actual government support for banks and bank holding companies during the financial crisis, and (2) recent statutory and regulatory changes related to government support for banks and bank holding companies. GAO reviewed relevant statutes, regulations, and agency documents; analyzed program transaction data; and interviewed regulators, representatives of financial institutions, and academics. In a second report to be issued in 2014, GAO will examine any funding or other economic advantages the largest bank holding companies have received as a result of implied government support.

WHAT GAO RECOMMENDS

GAO recommends that the Federal Reserve Board establish timeframes for completing its process for drafting procedures related to its emergency lending authority to ensure timely

* This is an edited, reformatted and augmented version of the United States Government Accountability Office publication, GAO-14-18, dated November 2013.

compliance with Dodd-Frank Act requirements. The Federal Reserve Board accepted this recommendation.

WHAT GAO FOUND

During the 2007-09 financial crisis, the federal government's actions to stabilize the financial system provided funding support and other benefits to bank holding companies and their subsidiaries. Agencies introduced new programs with broad-based eligibility that provided funding support to eligible institutions, which included entities that were part of a bank holding company and others. Programs that provided the most significant support directly to bank holding companies or their subsidiaries included Department of the Treasury capital investment programs, Federal Reserve System lending programs, and Federal Deposit Insurance Corporation (FDIC) guarantee programs. Together these actions helped to stabilize financial conditions, while participating firms also accrued benefits specific to their own institutions, such as liquidity benefits from programs that allowed them to borrow at longer maturities and at interest rates that were below possible market alternatives. At the end of 2008, program use—measured for each institution as the percentage of total assets supported by the programs—was higher on average for banks and bank holding companies with $50 billion or more in total assets than for smaller firms. The six largest bank holding companies were significant participants in several emergency programs but exited most by the end of 2009. Differences in program use were driven in part by how institutions funded themselves. For example, while smaller banks relied more on deposit funding, larger bank holding companies relied more on short-term funding markets and participated more in programs that assisted these markets. In addition to these programs, the Board of Governors of the Federal Reserve System (Federal Reserve Board) granted several regulatory exemptions to allow banks to provide liquidity support to their nonbank affiliates and for other purposes. Finally, government assistance to individual troubled firms benefited these firms, their counterparties, and the financial system.

The Dodd-Frank Wall Street Reform and Consumer Protection Act (Dodd-Frank Act) contains provisions that aim to modify the scope of federal safety nets, restrict future government support and strengthen regulatory oversight for the banking sector, but implementation is incomplete and the effectiveness of some provisions remains uncertain. Agencies have finalized certain changes to traditional safety nets for insured banks, but impacts of provisions to limit the scope of transactions that benefit from these safety nets will depend on how they are implemented. The act also places restrictions on emergency authorities used by regulators during the crisis to assist financial firms. For example, it prohibits the use of these authorities to rescue a specific failing firm. The Federal Reserve Board is required by the act to establish policies and procedures implementing changes to its emergency authority under Section 13(3) of the Federal Reserve Act, but it has not completed its process for drafting the required procedures or set time frames for doing so. Setting time frames could help ensure more timely completion of these procedures. FDIC has made progress toward implementing its new authority under the Dodd-Frank Act to resolve a large failing firm. FDIC continues to work to address potential obstacles to the viability of its resolution process as an alternative to bankruptcy, such as challenges that could arise when resolving more than one failing firm. Finally, the Federal Reserve Board has finalized certain enhanced prudential standards for the largest financial firms intended to reduce the risks these firms could pose to the financial system.

ABBREVIATIONS

ABCP	asset-backed commercial paper
ABS	asset-backed securities
AMLF	Asset-Backed Commercial Paper Money Market Mutual Fund Liquidity Facility
BEA	Bureau of Economic Analysis
CBO	Congressional Budget Office
CDCI	Community Development Capital Initiative
CDS	credit default swaps
COP	Congressional Oversight Panel
CPFF	Commercial Paper Funding Facility
CPP	Capital Purchase Program
DGP	Debt Guarantee Program
EESA	Emergency Economic Stabilization Act of 2008
FDIC	Federal Deposit Insurance Corporation
FHLB	Federal Home Loan Bank
FOMC	Federal Open Market Committee
FRBNY	Federal Reserve Bank of New York
FSOC	Financial Stability Oversight Council
GSE	government-sponsored enterprise
IDI	insured depository institution
ILC	industrial loan corporation
LIBOR	London Interbank Offered Rate
MBS	mortgage-backed securities
MMMF	money market mutual fund
NIC	National Information Center
OCC	Office of the Comptroller of the Currency
OIS	overnight indexed swap
OLA	Orderly Liquidation Authority
PDCF	Primary Dealer Credit Facility
SPOE	Single Point-of-Entry
TAF	Term Auction Facility
TAGP	Transaction Account Guarantee Program
TALF	Term Asset-Backed Securities Loan Facility
TARP	Troubled Asset Relief Program
TIP	Targeted Investment Program
TLGP	Temporary Liquidity Guarantee Program
TSLF	Term Securities lending Facility

November 14, 2013

The Honorable Sherrod Brown
Chairman
Financial Institutions and Consumer Protection Subcommittee
Committee on Banking, Housing, and Urban Affairs
United States Senate

The Honorable David Vitter
United States Senate

During the financial crisis of 2007-2009, the federal government extended unprecedented amounts of assistance to financial institutions to stabilize financial markets and the broader economy. This support included the creation of temporary programs that extended more than $1 trillion in loans, provided hundreds of billions of dollars of capital, and guaranteed hundreds of billions of dollars of other liabilities for participating financial institutions. On a few occasions, the federal government provided additional capital and other support to individual large troubled institutions to prevent a bankruptcy that could have further destabilized markets. While these government interventions helped to avert a more severe crisis, they raised questions about moral hazard and the appropriate scope of government safety nets for financial institutions.[1] In particular, extraordinary support for troubled financial institutions led to debate about how to decrease the likelihood of future rescues of failing institutions and limit the potential for federal safety nets intended for insured depository institutions to provide a backstop for activities conducted outside these institutions.

The Dodd-Frank Wall Street Reform and Consumer Protection Act (Dodd- Frank Act) includes provisions intended to prevent government rescues of individual financial institutions, place new restrictions on emergency authorities used by regulators to assist financial institutions during the last financial crisis, and subject a designated group of large financial institutions to stricter regulatory oversight, among other changes.[2]

Nevertheless, market observers have continued to debate whether some of the largest and most complex financial institutions—including bank holding companies with more than $500 billion in total consolidated assets—may continue to benefit from expectations of extraordinary government support that could potentially give them funding and other economic advantages relative to smaller competitors.

You asked us to review the economic benefits that the largest bank holding companies (those with more than $500 billion in total consolidated assets) have received as a result of actual or perceived government support. This is the first of two reports we will issue on this topic. In this report, we review (1) support banks and bank holding companies received as a result of government efforts to stabilize financial markets during the financial crisis of 2007-2009, and (2) recent statutory and regulatory changes related to government support for banks and bank holding companies and factors that could impact the effectiveness of these changes. In terms of scope, the first section of this report addresses benefits that bank holding companies and their subsidiaries received *during the crisis* from *actual* government support provided through emergency actions taken. It does not address benefits that some institutions may have received and may continue to receive from *perceived* government support—that is, support that market participants may expect the federal government to provide to these institutions in the event that they face large losses that threaten them with failure. In a second report to be issued in 2014, we will address questions about whether the largest bank holding companies have received funding or other economic advantages as a result of expectations that the government would not allow them to fail. That report will include the results of our original empirical analysis of funding costs for large bank holding companies.

To address the objectives for this report, we reviewed relevant statutes, regulations, agency documents and data, related studies, and prior GAO work. To describe government actions that extended support for banks and bank holding companies during the crisis, we included information and analyses from prior GAO work on the Troubled Asset Relief Program (TARP), the emergency programs of the Board of Governors of the Federal Reserve System (Federal Reserve Board), and other emergency assistance provided to the banking sector. To obtain perspectives on the benefits that bank holding companies and their subsidiaries received from emergency government actions, we reviewed papers by staff of financial regulators and other experts and interviewed federal financial regulators, representatives of bank holding companies that received emergency government assistance, trade associations, and academics. To describe the amount of funding support that institutions of various sizes received from emergency government programs, we obtained and analyzed program transaction data for the programs introduced by the Department of the Treasury (Treasury), the Federal Reserve Board, and the Federal Deposit Insurance Corporation (FDIC) that provided the most significant funding support directly to bank holding companies or their subsidiaries. For selected programs, we compared the terms of this assistance (such as interest rates and fees) to indicators of pricing for market alternatives that might have been available to program participants. While this analysis provides a measure of program pricing versus potential market alternatives, it does not produce a precise quantification of the benefits that accrued to participating financial institutions. To compare the extent to which banking organizations of various sizes used these emergency programs, we calculated the percentage of banking organization assets that were supported by emergency programs—either through capital injections, loans, or guarantees—at quarter-end dates for 2008 through 2012. Finally, we obtained and analyzed Federal Reserve Board documentation of Federal Reserve Board decisions to grant exemptions to Section 23A of the Federal Reserve Act and approve applications from financial companies to convert to bank holding company status.[3]

Our scope did not include an analysis of any benefits that banks or bank holding companies may have received from any expectations of future government support. As discussed earlier, we will cover any benefits to banking entities from perceived government support in our second report. For parts of our work that involved the analysis of computer-processed data, such as transaction data for the agencies' emergency programs, we assessed the reliability of these data and determined that they were sufficiently reliable for our purposes. Appendix I contains additional information about the data sources used and our assessment of the reliability of these data. Appendices III and IV contain additional information about our methodology for the data analyses in our first objective.

To address our second objective, we reviewed information on statutory and regulatory changes related to the authority to provide government support for banks and bank holding companies, including prior GAO work on implementation of the Dodd-Frank Act. To update the status of agencies' efforts to implement these changes, we reviewed agencies' proposed and final rules, and interviewed staff from FDIC, the Federal Reserve Board, the Office of the Comptroller of the Currency (OCC), and Treasury. We identified statutory provisions or requirements that agencies had not fully implemented and interviewed agency staff about planned steps to complete implementation. We also reviewed relevant congressional testimonies and other public statements by agency officials. To describe factors that could impact the effectiveness of these provisions, we reviewed prior GAO work on the potential impacts of Dodd-Frank Act provisions. To obtain additional perspectives on factors that could impact the effectiveness of these provisions, we interviewed and reviewed the public statements and analyses of agency officials, academics, and market experts. Appendix I contains additional information on our scope and methodology.

We conducted this performance audit from January 2013 through November 2013 in accordance with generally accepted government auditing standards. Those standards require that we plan and perform the audit to obtain sufficient, appropriate evidence to provide a reasonable basis for our findings and conclusions based on our audit objectives. We believe that the evidence obtained provides a reasonable basis for our findings and conclusions based on our audit objectives.

BACKGROUND

Bank Holding Companies

Bank holding companies are companies that own or control one or more banks. In the United States, most banks insured by FDIC are owned or controlled by a bank holding company. In addition to bank subsidiaries engaged in traditional banking activities of deposit-taking and lending, many U.S. bank holding companies also own or control nonbank subsidiaries, such as broker-dealers and insurance companies. The Bank Holding Company Act of 1956, as amended, establishes the legal framework under which bank holding companies operate and establishes their supervision, with the Federal Reserve Board having authority over bank holding companies and their banking and nonbanking interests.[4]

The Bank Holding Company Act also limits the types of activities that bank holding companies may conduct, either directly or through their nonbank affiliates. The restrictions, which are designed to maintain the general separation of banking and commerce in the United States, allow bank holding companies to engage only in banking activities and those activities that the Federal Reserve Board has determined to be "closely related to banking," such as extending credit, servicing loans, and performing appraisals of real estate and tangible and intangible personal property, including securities.[5] Under amendments to the Bank Holding Company Act made by the Gramm-Leach-Bliley Act, also known as the Financial Services Modernization Act of 1999, a bank holding company can elect to become a financial holding company that can engage in a broader range of activities that are financial in nature.[6] The Gramm- Leach-Bliley Act defined a set of activities as financial in nature and authorized the Federal Reserve Board, with the agreement of Treasury, to determine whether an additional activity is financial in nature or incidental or complementary to a financial activity.[7] For example, financial holding companies are permitted to engage in securities underwriting and dealing, but would be prohibited, for example, from selling commercial products. Large U.S. bank holding companies typically are registered as financial holding companies and own a number of domestic bank subsidiaries, as well as nonbank and foreign subsidiaries.

The largest U.S. bank holding companies have grown substantially in size and scope in recent decades. Since 1990, in part due to waves of mergers, the share of total bank holding company assets controlled by the largest 10 firms increased from less than 30 percent to more than 60 percent, as of July 2012.[8] Some bank holding companies grew to become large financial conglomerates that offer a wide range of products that cut across the traditional financial sectors of banking, securities, and insurance. Following the enactment of the Gramm-Leach-Bliley Act in 1999, the assets held in nonbank subsidiaries or at the holding company level grew to account for a progressively larger share of total bank holding company assets. Greater involvement by bank holding companies in nontraditional banking businesses has been accompanied by an increase in the proportion of bank holding company income that is generated by fee income, trading, and other noninterest activities. As large bank holding companies have broadened the scope of their activities and their geographic reach, they have become more organizationally complex. A simple indicator of organizational complexity is the number of separate legal entities within the bank holding company; the largest four U.S. bank holding companies each had at least 2,000 as of June 30, 2013.[9]

The 2007-2009 financial crisis raised concerns that some U.S. bank holding companies—as well as some nonbank financial institutions—had grown so large, interconnected, and leveraged that their failure could threaten the stability of the U.S. financial system and the global economy. The Dodd-Frank Act includes several provisions intended to reduce the risk of a failure of a large, complex financial institution, the damage that such a failure could do to the economy, and the likelihood that a failing institution would receive government support. For example, the act directs the Federal Reserve Board to impose enhanced prudential standards and oversight on bank holding companies with $50 billion or more in total consolidated assets and nonbank financial companies designated by the Financial Stability Oversight Council (FSOC) for supervision by the Federal Reserve Board.[10]

Federal Safety Net Programs for the Banking Sector

The federal government maintains programs—frequently referred to as safety nets—to reduce the vulnerability of depository institutions to runs that could threaten the health of the banking system and the broader economy.[11] Following a series of banking crises in the early 1900s, the government created two programs generally considered to form the core of these safety nets: the Federal Reserve System's discount window and FDIC deposit insurance. By making emergency liquidity available to solvent depository institutions through the discount window and reducing incentives for depositors to withdraw their funds, these safety nets were intended to help ensure that depository institutions could continue to lend and provide other important services, even during turbulent economic conditions. In addition to the discount window and deposit insurance, the Federal Reserve Board and FDIC have other emergency authorities related to maintaining financial stability. Moreover, the Federal Home Loan Bank System serves to provide liquidity to the banking system that helps to foster stability. In part because access to federal safety nets potentially reduced incentives for insured depositors to monitor and restrain the risk-taking of banks, banks were also subjected to federal supervision and regulation.

Discount Window

The Federal Reserve System, in its role as the lender of last resort, operates discount window programs, which provide a backup source of liquidity through collateralized loans for depository institutions to help ensure the stable flow of credit to households and businesses.[12] During normal market conditions, banks and other depository institutions in generally sound financial condition can obtain discount window loans to address short-term funding needs arising from unexpected funding pressures. In a financial crisis, discount window lending can provide broader liquidity support to the banking system that can help mitigate strains in financial markets. The Federal Reserve Board authorizes the Reserve Banks to offer three discount window programs to depository institutions: primary credit, secondary credit, and seasonal credit, each with its own terms.[13] The primary credit program is the principal discount window program and extends credit to depository institutions in generally sound condition on a very short-term basis (usually overnight). The secondary credit program is available to extend credit on a very short- term basis for depository institutions that are not eligible for primary credit, with the purpose of helping institutions to return to market sources of funds. The seasonal credit program generally extends loans to small depository institutions that face seasonal fluctuations in their funding needs. Section 10B of the Federal Reserve Act provides the statutory framework for these programs and, among other things, requires all discount window loans to be secured to the satisfaction of the lending Reserve Bank.[14]

Deposit Insurance

FDIC deposit insurance covers deposit accounts—including checking and savings accounts, money market deposit accounts, and certificates of deposit—at insured depository institutions up to the insurance limit and is backed by the full faith and credit of the U.S. government. Federal deposit insurance was created to reduce the incentive for depositors to withdraw funds from banks during a financial panic and maintain stability and confidence in the nation's banking system. During the 1800s and early 1900s, a number of states adopted different versions of deposit insurance to insure bank obligations in response to a wave of bank failures. However, these state insurance funds were later unable to cope with economic events during the 1920s, which led to calls for a system of federal deposit insurance to maintain financial stability. The Banking Act of 1933, which created FDIC by an amendment to the Federal Reserve Act, authorized FDIC to provide deposit insurance to banks and went into effect on January 1, 1934.[15] The deposit insurance fund, administered by FDIC to resolve failed banks and thrifts, protects depositors from losses due to institution failures up to a limit. The deposit insurance fund is primarily funded by fees from assessments on insured depository institutions. If necessary, FDIC can borrow from Treasury, the Federal Financing Bank, and the Federal Home Loan Banks. As discussed later in this report, the Dodd-Frank Act permanently increased the deposit insurance limit from $100,000 to $250,000 and changed the base used to determine an insured depository institution's risk-based assessment to be paid into the deposit insurance fund.[16]

Emergency Authorities

In addition to the discount window and deposit insurance, during the 2007-2009 financial crisis the Federal Reserve Board and FDIC used their emergency authorities to assist individual failing institutions.

As discussed later in this report, the Dodd-Frank Act changed these authorities so that emergency lending can no longer be provided to assist a single and specific firm but rather can only be made available through a program with broad-based eligibility—that is, a program that provides funding support to institutions that meet program requirements and choose to participate.[17]

- *Federal Reserve emergency lending authority.* Prior to the Dodd- Frank Act, emergency lending authority under Section 13(3) of the Federal Reserve Act permitted the Federal Reserve Board, in unusual and exigent circumstances, to authorize a Reserve Bank to extend credit to individuals, partnerships, or corporations, if the Reserve Bank determined that adequate credit was not available from other banking institutions, and if the extension of credit was secured to the satisfaction of the lending Reserve Bank.[18] During the financial crisis of 2007-2009, the Federal Reserve Board invoked this authority on a number of occasions to authorize one or more Reserve Banks to provide emergency assistance to particular institutions or to establish new programs to provide liquidity support to important credit markets.
- *FDIC open bank assistance.* The FDIC Improvement Act of 1991 included a systemic risk exception to the requirement that FDIC resolve failed banks using the least costly method.[19] Under this exception, FDIC could provide assistance to a failing bank if compliance with its requirements to resolve the bank using the least costly approach would have "serious adverse effects on economic conditions and financial stability"—that is, would cause systemic risk—and if such assistance would "avoid or mitigate such adverse effects."[20] FDIC could act under the exception only under a process that included recommendations from the FDIC Board of Directors and Federal Reserve Board and approval by the Treasury Secretary.[21] The agencies invoked this authority during the crisis to authorize FDIC to provide guarantees to particular banks and to introduce new guarantee programs with broad-based eligibility. As discussed later in this report, the Dodd-Frank Act effectively removed FDIC's authority to provide assistance to failing banks outside of a receivership.

Federal Home Loan Bank System

The Federal Home Loan Bank (FHLB) System also serves to provide funding support to depository institutions during normal and strained market conditions. The FHLB System is a government-sponsored enterprise (GSE) that consists of 12 Federal Home Loan Banks (FHLB) and is cooperatively owned by member financial institutions, which include banks, thrifts, insurance companies, and credit unions. The primary mission of the FHLB System is to promote housing and community development by making loans, known as advances, to member financial institutions. These institutions are required to secure FHLB advances with high-quality collateral (such as single-family mortgages) and may use FHLB advances to fund mortgages.

To raise the funds necessary to carry out its activities, the FHLB System issues debt in the capital markets at favorable rates compared to commercial borrowings due to market perceptions that the federal government would intervene to support the FHLB System in a crisis, thereby reducing its risk of default.

When credit markets become strained, as they did during the most recent crisis, the FHLB System can serve as an important backup source of liquidity for member institutions that meet the FHLBs' collateral and other requirements.

2007-2009 Financial Crisis

The 2007-2009 financial crisis was the most severe that the United States has experienced since the Great Depression. The dramatic decline in the U.S. housing market that began in 2006 precipitated a decline in the price of financial assets that were associated with housing, particularly mortgage-related assets based on subprime loans. Some institutions found themselves so exposed to declines in the values of these assets that they were threatened with failure—and some failed—because they were unable to raise the necessary capital as the value of their lending and securities portfolios declined. Uncertainty about the financial condition and solvency of financial entities led banks to dramatically raise the interest rates they charged each other for funds and, in late 2008, interbank lending effectively came to a halt. The same uncertainty also led money market funds, pension funds, hedge funds, and other entities that provide funds to financial institutions to raise their interest rates, shorten their terms, and tighten credit standards. As their funding became increasingly difficult to obtain, financial institutions responded by raising the prices and tightening their credit standards for lending to households and nonfinancial businesses. The liquidity and credit crisis made the financing on which businesses and individuals depend increasingly difficult to obtain as cash-strapped banks tightened underwriting standards, resulting in a contraction of credit to the economy. By late summer of 2008, the potential ramifications of the financial crisis included the continued failure of financial institutions, increased losses of individual wealth, reduced corporate investments, and further tightening of credit that would exacerbate the emerging global economic slowdown that was beginning to take shape.

Because financial crises can result in severe damage to the economy and the road to recovery can be long, governments and monetary authorities have historically undertaken interventions, even though some of the resulting actions raise concerns about moral hazard and can pose a risk of losses to taxpayers.[22] Given its severity and systemic nature, the recent global financial crisis prompted substantial interventions starting in late 2007, after problems in the subprime mortgage market intensified. As discussed further in the next section of this report, these interventions included the creation of temporary government programs to support important credit markets and financial institutions that intermediate credit in the economy by channeling funds from savers to borrowers.

Government Actions to Stabilize Markets Resulted in Significant Support to Bank Holding Companies

From 2007 through 2009, the federal government's actions to stabilize the financial system provided funding support and other benefits to bank holding companies and their bank and nonbank financial subsidiaries.

The Federal Reserve Board, Treasury, and FDIC introduced new programs with broad-based eligibility that provided funding support to institutions that met program requirements and chose to participate.[23] Selected programs—for which eligibility was not restricted exclusively to institutions that were part of a bank holding company—included Federal Reserve System lending programs, Treasury capital investment programs, and FDIC programs that guaranteed uninsured deposits and new debt issues. Isolating the impact of individual interventions is difficult, but collectively these actions likely improved financial conditions by enhancing confidence in financial institutions and the financial system. Bank holding companies and their subsidiaries also accrued benefits specific to their own institutions, including liquidity benefits from programs that allowed them to borrow at lower interest rates and at longer maturities than might have been available in the markets. Programs generally were made available to institutions of various sizes, and differences in the use of programs by institutions of various sizes were driven in part by differences in how institutions funded themselves. For example, compared to smaller bank holding companies, larger bank holding companies relied less on deposits as a source of funding and more on short-term credit markets and participated more in programs created to stabilize these markets. At the end of 2008, use of these programs—measured for each institution as the percentage of total assets supported by the programs—was larger on average for larger banking organizations—those with $50 billion or more in total assets— than for smaller banking organizations. The six largest bank holding companies were significant participants in several emergency programs but exited most of the programs by the end of 2009. Differences in program use across banking organizations of various sizes diminished as institutions exited the programs. In addition to programs that provided broad-based support, the Federal Reserve Board granted a number of regulatory exemptions to allow banks to provide liquidity support to their nonbank affiliates and for other purposes. Finally, some large bank holding companies benefitted from individual institution assistance or regulatory relief. For example, government assistance to prevent the failures of large institutions benefited recipients of this assistance and other market participants.

Crisis Programs with Broad-Based Eligibility Provided Funding Support to Bank Holding Companies and Their Subsidiaries

During the financial crisis, the Federal Reserve System, Treasury, and FDIC introduced new programs with broad-based eligibility to provide general funding support to the financial sector and to stabilize the financial system. Given this report's focus on bank holding companies, this section focuses on the financial stability programs that provided the most significant funding support directly to bank holding companies or their bank or nonbank subsidiaries. Table 1 provides an overview of the size, purpose, terms, and conditions of these programs, which included:

Table 1. Overview of Largest Emergency Programs That Provided General Funding Support to Bank Holding Companies or Their Subsidiaries

Programs	Peak dollar amount	Purpose	Key terms
Dollars in billions			
Federal Reserve System			
TAF – Term Auction Facility[a] (Dec. 12, 2007–Mar. 8, 2010)	$493	Auctioned 1 and 3-month discount window loans to depository institutions to address strains in term interbank lending markets.	*Eligible Institutions*. Depository institutions eligible for the primary credit discount window program and expected to remain so over the TAF loan term.[b] *Interest rate*. The interest rate was determined by auction. For each auction, winning bidders were awarded loans at the same interest rate. *Collateral eligibility*. Based on discount window requirements.[c]
PDCF - Primary Dealer Credit Facility (Mar. 16, 2008–Feb. 1, 2010)	$130	Provided overnight cash loans to primary dealers against eligible collateral to address strains in the repurchase agreement markets.	*Eligible institutions*. Primary dealers, a designated group ofbroker-dealers and banks that transacted with the Federal Reserve Bank of New York in its conduct of open market operations.[d] *Interest rate and fees*. The interest rate was equal to the primary credit rate - the rate charged on discount window loans in the primary credit program. The Federal Reserve Bank of New York charged a frequency-based fee, rangingfrom 10 to 40 basis points, to dealers who accessed the facility on more than 45 out of 180 business days. *Collateral eligibility*. Initially limited to collateral eligible for open market operations (e.g., Treasury and agency securities) as well as investment-grade corporate securities, municipal securities, and asset-backed securities (ABS); later expanded to include all securities eligible to be pledged in the triparty repurchase agreements system, including noninvestment grade securities and equities
TSLF - Term Securities Lending Facility (Mar. 11, 2008–Feb. 1, 2010)	$236	Auctioned loans of U.S. Treasury securities to primary dealers against eligible collateral to address strains in the repurchase agreement markets.	*Eligible institutions*. Primary dealers (same as PDCF) *Interest rate*. The interest rate was determined by auction (similar to TAF). For each auction, winning bidders were awarded loans at the same interest rate. *Collateral eligibility*. TSLF auctioned loans of securities against two schedules of collateral. Schedule 1 included allcollateral eligible for open market operations. Schedule 2 collateral initially included Schedule 1 collateral as well as highly-rated mortgage-backed securities(MBS). Schedule 2 collateral was later expanded to include investment grade corporate and municipal securities, MBS, and ABS.

Programs	Peak dollar amount	Purpose	Key terms
CPFF - Commercial Paper Funding Facility (Oct. 7, 2008–Feb. 1, 2010)	$348	Purchased asset-backed commercial paper (ABCP) and unsecured commercial paper from eligible issuers.	*Eligible issuers*. All U.S. issuers (including those with a foreign parent) with eligible commercial paper. To be eligible, commercial paper was required to have received the highest rating from at least one major credit rating agency. *Interest rate*. The interest rate was set at a fixed spread above the daily 3-month overnight indexed swap (OIS) rateto control for changes in short-term interest rates.[e] This spread was 100 basis points for unsecured commercial paper and 300 basis points for ABCP. *Credit surcharge*. To provide additional loss protection, issuers of unsecured paper were required to pay a credit surcharge of 100 basis points. Commercial paper issues guaranteed by TLGP were exempt from the surcharge.
Department of the Treasury (Treasury)			
CPP - Capital Purchase Program (Oct. 14, 2008–Dec. 31, 2009)	$205	The first and largest initiative under Treasury's Troubled Asset Relief Program; provided capital to eligible financial institutions by purchasing preferred shares and subordinated debt.	*Eligible institutions*. Qualifying institutions generally included U.S.-controlled depository institutions, bank holding companies, and most savings and loan holding companies. *Dividends*. Senior preferred shares paid dividends at a rateof 5 percent annually for the first 5 years and 9 percent annually thereafter. Treasury also received warrants to purchase shares of stock or a senior debt instrument. *Interest on subordinated debt*. For certain issuers, Treasury received subordinated debt rather than preferred shares to protect these institutions' special tax status. Interest rates for this debt were set at 7.7 percent for the first 5 years and 13.8 percent for the remaining years.
Federal Deposit Insurance Corporation (FDIC)			
TLGP – Temporary Liquidity Guarantee Program[f] (Announced Oct. 14, 2008) • DGP – Debt Guarantee Program (Guarantees expired Dec. 31, 2012) • TAGP – Transaction Account Guarantee Program (Expired Dec. 31, 2010)[g]	Approx. $346 debt and approx. $835 deposits	DGP guaranteed certain newly-issued senior unsecured debt of eligible institutions to improve liquidity in term funding markets. TAGP temporarily extended an unlimited deposit guarantee to domestic noninterest-bearing transaction accounts at	*Eligible institutions*. FDIC insured depository institutions (IDI); U.S. bank and savings and loan holding companies; and affiliates of IDIs upon application. *DGP fees*. FDIC assessed fees on each DGP-guaranteed debt issuance based on time to maturity. Following extensions of the DGP, FDIC also assessed surcharges. Surcharges for holding companies and affiliates of IDIs were twice as high as those for IDIs. *TAGP fees*. FDIC assessed a fee of 10 basis points on the quarter-end balance of eligible deposits over $250,000. Beginning in 2010, FDIC instead assessed risk-based fees of 15, 20, or 25 basis points of quarter-end balances over $250,000.

Table 1. (Continued)

Programs	Peak dollar amount	Purpose	Key terms
		participating insured depository institutions to limit further outflows of these deposits.	

Source: FDIC, Federal Reserve System, and Treasury documents.

Note: This table includes the emergency programs that provided the most significant funding support directly to bank holding companies and their subsidiaries. Bank holding companies and their subsidiaries benefited from other emergency government programs, such as programs that assisted money market mutual funds. Dates in parentheses are the program announcement dates, and where relevant, the date the program or assistance was closed or terminated. The peak dollar amount shown for CPP represents the total dollar amount invested through CPP. For all other programs, the peak dollar amount shown represents the peak dollar amount outstanding.

[a] 12 C.F.R. § 201.4(e).

[b] U.S. branches and agencies of foreign institutions that met program requirements were eligible to participate in TAF. The Reserve Banks extend discount window credit to U.S. depository institutions (including U.S. branches and agencies of foreign banks) under three programs, one of which is the primary credit program. Primary credit is available to generally sound depository institutions, typically on an overnight basis. To assess whether a depository institution is in sound financial condition, its Reserve Bank can regularly review the institution's condition, using supervisory ratings and data on adequacy of the institution's capital.

[c] TAF loans were collateralized based on haircut requirements for the discount window program. For TAF loans, Reserve Banks accepted as collateral any assets that were eligible to secure discount window loans.

[d] Several primary dealers were subsidiaries of large U.S. bank holding companies or large foreign banking organizations. U.S. bank holding companies with primary dealer subsidiaries included Citigroup Inc., Bank of America Corporation, Goldman Sachs Group, Inc., JP Morgan Chase & Co., and Morgan Stanley. Goldman Sachs Group, Inc. and Morgan Stanley were not bank holding companies when PDCF and TSLF launched in March 2008, but both firms participated in these programs after they converted to bank holding companies in September 2008.

[e] The OIS rate is an interest rate that tracks expectations of the future federal funds rate.

[f] 12 C.F.R. § 370.

[g] The Dodd-Frank Act provided temporary unlimited deposit insurance coverage for noninterest- bearing transaction accounts at all FDIC-insured institutions from December 31, 2010 through December 31, 2012. This coverage essentially was similar to that offered by TAGP. Pub. L. No. 111-203, § 343, 124 Stat. 1376, 1544 (2010).

- the Federal Reserve System's Term Auction Facility (TAF); Primary Dealer Credit Facility (PDCF); Term Securities Lending Facility (TSLF); and Commercial Paper Funding Facility (CPFF);
- Treasury's Capital Purchase Program (CPP); and
- FDIC's Temporary Liquidity Guarantee Program (TLGP), which had two components: the Debt Guarantee Program (DGP) guaranteed certain newly issued senior unsecured debt, and the Transaction Account Guarantee Program (TAGP) guaranteed certain previously uninsured deposits.

Institutions eligible for these programs included both entities that were part of a bank holding company structure and entities that were not. The Federal Reserve System designed its emergency programs to address disruptions to particular credit markets and to assist participants in these markets. For example, the Federal Reserve System's programs that targeted support to repurchase agreement markets provided assistance to securities firms that were subsidiaries of bank holding companies and securities firms that were not. The Federal Reserve System's CPFF purchased commercial paper from participating bank holding companies and other financial and nonfinancial firms that met the program's eligibility requirements. Treasury's CPP and FDIC's TLGP provided support primarily to insured depository institutions (banks and thrifts) and bank and savings and loan holding companies.

Bank holding companies also benefited from other government programs, such as programs that targeted support to other market participants. For example, in the absence of Treasury and Federal Reserve System programs to guarantee and support money market mutual funds, respectively, such funds may have reduced their purchases of money market instruments issued by subsidiaries of bank holding companies and other firms, thereby exacerbating funding pressures on these firms. Other significant government programs included the Term Asset-Backed Securities Loan Facility (TALF), which was created by the Federal Reserve System to support certain securitization markets, and other programs created by Treasury under TARP authority.[24]

While the Federal Reserve System and FDIC provided expanded support through traditional safety net programs for insured banks during the crisis, some of the emergency government programs provided funding support at the bank holding company level—where it could be used to support both bank and nonbank subsidiaries—or directly to nonbank entities. In late 2007, the Federal Reserve Board took a series of actions to ease strains in interbank funding markets, including lowering the target federal funds rate, easing terms at the discount window, and introducing a new program—TAF—to auction term loans to banks.[25] However, in part due to statutory and regulatory restrictions on the ability of insured banks to provide funding support to their nonbank affiliates, agencies determined that emergency government support to insured banks was not sufficient to stem disruptions to important credit markets. Nonbank credit markets—such as repurchase agreement and debt securities markets—had grown to rival the traditional banking sector in facilitating loans to consumers and businesses, and agencies determined that actions to address disruptions to these markets were needed to avert adverse impacts to the broader economy. For example, in March 2008, the Federal Reserve Board authorized PDCF and TSLF to address strains in repurchase agreement markets by providing emergency loans to broker-dealers, a few of whom were owned by U.S. bank holding companies.[26] When the crisis intensified in September 2008 following the failure of Lehman Brothers Holdings Inc.—a large broker-dealer holding company—the

Federal Reserve Board modified terms for its existing programs and took other actions to expand funding support for both bank and nonbank entities.[27]

In September 2008, Treasury and the Federal Reserve System introduced new temporary programs to address liquidity pressures on money market funds and to help ensure that these funds could continue to purchase money market instruments issued by bank holding companies and other firms.[28] In addition, in October 2008, Congress enacted legislation under which Treasury provided capital investments to banks, bank holding companies, and other institutions; the legislation also temporarily increased FDIC's deposit insurance limit from $100,000 to $250,000.[29] Also that month, the Federal Reserve System created CPFF to support commercial paper markets, and FDIC introduced TLGP, under which it guaranteed previously uninsured transaction accounts and certain newly issued senior unsecured debt for participating insured depository institutions, bank and savings and loan holding companies, and approved affiliates of insured depository institutions. For a more detailed discussion of the circumstances surrounding the creation of these programs, see appendix II.

Isolating the impact of individual government interventions is difficult, but collectively these interventions helped to improve financial conditions by enhancing confidence in financial institutions and the financial system overall.[30] Bank holding companies and their subsidiaries, in addition to the financial sector and the economy as a whole, benefited from improved financial conditions. Bank holding companies and their subsidiaries also experienced individual benefits from participating in particular programs.

Individually and collectively, government lending, guarantee, and capital programs provided important liquidity and other benefits to bank holding companies and their subsidiaries including:

- **Access to funding in quantities and/or at prices that were generally not available in the markets**. Government entities generally sought to set prices for assistance through these programs to be less expensive than prices available during crisis conditions but more expensive than prices available during normal market conditions.[31] In some credit markets assisted by government programs—such as commercial paper and repurchase agreement markets—conditions had deteriorated such that many institutions faced substantially reduced access to these markets or had no access at all. As discussed below, we compared program pricing to relevant indicators of market pricing where available and found that emergency lending and guarantee programs generally were priced below market alternatives that may have been available. The availability of funding support at this pricing in predictable quantities was also beneficial. Even at times when eligible institutions did not access the available programs, these programs diversified the sources of funds that could be available to them if they faced increased funding pressures.
- **Access to funding at longer maturities**. By providing and standing ready to provide funding support for terms of 1 month or longer, government programs helped to reduce rollover risk—the risk that an institution would be unable to renew or "rollover" funding obligations as they came due—for individual institutions and their counterparties. At times during the crisis, bank holding companies and their subsidiaries faced difficulties borrowing at terms of 1 month or longer in several important credit markets, including interbank, repurchase agreement, and commercial paper markets. Government programs mitigated funding pressures for

borrowers in these markets by reducing the risk that funding sources would rapidly disappear for an institution or its counterparties. Because participants in these programs were also lenders of funds, these programs helped to encourage these institutions to continue to lend funds to support the economy.

- **Stabilizing deposit funding**. FDIC's TAGP, which temporarily insured certain previously uninsured deposits for a fee, helped to stabilize deposit funding by removing the risk of loss from deposit accounts that were commonly used to meet payroll and other business transaction purposes and allowing banks, particularly smaller ones, to retain these accounts. Deposits are the primary source of funding for most banks, and smaller banks tend to fund themselves to a greater extent with deposits.
- **Funding support for a broad range of collateral types**. A few Federal Reserve System programs provided important liquidity benefits to individual institutions and credit markets by allowing institutions to obtain liquidity against a broad range of collateral types. TAF provided 1-month and 3-month loans to eligible banks against collateral types that could also be used to secure discount window loans. While TAF collateral requirements were based on discount window requirements, TAF provided emergency credit on a much larger scale, with TAF loans outstanding peaking at nearly $500 billion, compared to peak primary credit outstanding during the crisis of just over $100 billion.[32] In March 2008, the Federal Reserve System began providing liquidity support to certain nonbank financial firms—the primary dealers—for less liquid collateral types through PDCF and TSLF. Through PDCF, the Federal Reserve Bank of New York (FRBNY) allowed primary dealers to obtain overnight cash loans against harder-to-value collateral types, such as mortgage-backed securities. Through TSLF, FRBNY auctioned loans of Treasury securities to primary dealers in exchange for less-liquid collateral types to increase the amount of high-quality collateral these dealers had available to borrow against in repurchase agreement markets. When pressures in repurchase agreement markets intensified in September 2008, the Federal Reserve Board expanded the types of collateral it accepted for both PDCF and TSLF.

Although imperfect, one indicator of the extent to which an institution directly benefited from participation in an emergency program is the relative price of estimated market alternatives to the program. To determine how pricing of the emergency assistance compared to market rates, we compared pricing for programs to the pricing for market alternatives that might have been available to program participants. First, we compared the interest rates and fees charged by the Federal Reserve System and FDIC for participation in the emergency lending and guarantee programs with available market alternatives. We considered a number of potential indicators of market interest rates available to financial institutions, including a survey of interbank interest rates (the London Interbank Offered Rate or LIBOR), commercial paper interest rates published by the Federal Reserve Board, spreads on bank credit default swaps (CDS) and interest rates on repurchase agreements. These interest rates provide a general indication of market alternatives that could have been available to participants, but for a number of reasons the rates are unlikely to reflect available alternatives for all participants at all points in time during the crisis and cannot be used to produce a precise quantification of the benefits that accrued to participating financial institutions.[33] For example, participants' access to market alternatives may have been limited, data on the relevant private market may be limited, or market alternatives could vary across participants in ways that we do not observe in the data. The markets targeted by emergency programs had experienced significant strains, such as a substantial drop in liquidity, a sharp increase in prices, or lenders restricting access only to the most credit worthy borrowers or accepting only the safest collateral. Also, our indicators do not capture all of the benefits associated with participation in the relevant programs. Furthermore, once programs were introduced, they probably influenced the price of market alternatives, making it difficult to interpret differences between emergency program and market prices while programs were active. Second, to determine the extent to which Treasury capital investment programs were priced more generously than market alternatives, we reviewed estimates of the expected budget cost associated with equity funding support programs as well as a valuation analysis commissioned by the Congressional Oversight Panel. For more details on our methodology for these analyses, see appendix III.

Based on our analysis, we found that emergency assistance provided through these programs was often priced below estimated market alternatives that might have been available to program participants. This result is consistent with a policy goal of these programs to stabilize financial markets and restore confidence in the financial sector. The pricing of emergency assistance below estimated market alternatives is also evidenced by the significant participation in these programs. Specifically, we found that emergency lending and guarantee programs were generally priced below certain indicators of market alternatives that could have been available. In addition, based on analyses we reviewed, Treasury paid prices above estimated market prices for emergency equity support programs. For selected programs that we analyzed, we also found that program pricing would likely have become unattractive in comparison to market pricing during normal and more stable credit conditions.

Federal Reserve System programs. Federal Reserve System emergency lending programs during the crisis provided sources of both secured and unsecured funding at rates that were often below those of potential market alternatives and at terms that reduced rollover risk for participants. These characteristics are consistent with a policy goal to stabilize financial conditions by providing funding support for financial institutions that relied on wholesale funding markets. At the time, the markets targeted by the Federal Reserve emergency programs had experienced strains, such as a drop in volume or a significant increase in prices or collateral standards.

- *TAF.* Interest rates on TAF loans, on average, were between 22 and 39 basis points lower than three market interest rates that could have represented alternatives for participants. TAF auctioned collateralized loans—generally at terms of either 28 or 84 days—to insured banks to help alleviate strains in term funding markets. We compared interest rates for 28-day TAF loans with 1-month LIBOR, 30-day asset-backed commercial paper (ABCP) rates, and interest rates on very large 1- month unsecured certificates of deposit.[34] We chose these interest rates because they are all indicators of the cost of borrowing for financial institutions in term funding markets. However each differs from TAF in important ways. For example, LIBOR is based on unsecured loans (TAF loans were secured by collateral) and ABCP, despite being secured, has other features that differ from TAF, including the mix of underlying collateral.[35] We found that LIBOR exceeded TAF interest rates by an average of 22 basis points. ABCP interest rates exceeded TAF interest rates by on average 39 basis points and interest rates on very large certificates of deposit exceeded TAF interest rates by on average 29 basis points while the program was active. Because of differences between TAF and these measures of market interest rates, these spreads are an imperfect measure of the extent to which banks derived benefits from participating in TAF.

- *PDCF.* Our analysis suggests that PDCF provided secured overnight funding on more favorable terms for some types of collateral (such as corporate debt) than market alternatives that some primary dealers might have relied upon in the absence of PDCF. Because PDCF operated in a similar manner to repurchase agreement markets, we compared PDCF terms to available data for triparty and bilateral repurchase agreement transactions.[36] One important term for repurchase agreement loans is the haircut, which is the amount of additional collateral the lender requires over the value of the loan.[37] Repurchase agreement lenders generally require higher haircuts on riskier and less liquid collateral types. PDCF offered loans at the same interest rate (the discount rate charged on discount window loans) for all collateral types and applied a haircut schedule that assigned progressively higher haircuts to riskier assets. We compared PDCF haircuts to market haircuts for selected asset classes in the triparty repurchase agreement market. We found that the haircut required by PDCF was consistently greater than the median haircut in the triparty repurchase agreement market for comparable asset classes. Thus, borrowers who faced the median haircut on their collateral in the triparty market were better off borrowing in the triparty market than through PDCF, all else being equal. However, the PDCF haircut was smaller than the 75th percentile haircut in the triparty market for a variety of collateral types. This implies that higher-risk borrowers were better off borrowing through PDCF than through the triparty market, at least for certain types of collateral. Smaller haircuts would have allowed these PDCF participants to borrow more against the same collateral than in private repurchase agreement markets.
- *TSLF.* TSLF allowed primary dealers to obtain funding for the most commonly pledged collateral types at 32 basis points below an estimated market alternative. When TSLF was created in March 2008, repurchase agreement lenders were requiring higher interest rates and haircuts for loans against a range of less-liquid collateral types and were reluctant to lend against mortgage-related securities.[38] Through TSLF, primary dealers paid an auction-determined interest rate to exchange harder-to-finance collateral for more liquid Treasury securities—which were easier to borrow against in repurchase agreement markets—generally for a term of 28 days. TSLF held separate auctions of Treasury securities against two different schedules of collateral to apply a higher interest rate to riskier collateral. Schedule 1 collateral included higher quality assets, such as agency debt and agency mortgage-backed securities (MBS), and Schedule 2 collateral included Schedule 1 collateral and a broader range of asset types, such as highly-rated private-label MBS. We compared TSLF interest rates to the difference between lower interest rates primary dealers might have paid on repurchase agreements secured by Treasury securities and the higher interest rates they could have paid on repurchase agreements secured by TSLF-eligible collateral. Due to limited availability of interest rate data for

repurchase agreements collateralized by other lower-quality collateral eligible for TSLF, such as private-label MBS, we compared TSLF interest rates to the difference or spread between interest rates on repurchase agreements collateralized by agency MBS and repurchase agreements collateralized by Treasury securities.[39] We found that the spread between repurchase agreement interest rates on agency MBS (the most commonly-pledged collateral for TSLF) and Treasury securities exceeded TSLF interest rates by on average 32 basis points while the program was active.[40]

- *CPFF.* CPFF purchased 3-month commercial paper at prices that were lower than market rates during the crisis on instruments that could have represented alternative funding sources but were more expensive than average commercial paper rates during normal market conditions. CPFF controlled for changes in short-term interest rates by setting the price of commercial paper issuance to CPFF at a fixed spread above the daily 3-month overnight indexed swap rate, a rate that tracks investor expectations about the future federal funds rate. Table 2 summarizes the pricing structure for CPFF. We compared all- in borrowing costs (an interest rate plus a credit surcharge for unsecured borrowing) for CPFF borrowers with 3-month LIBOR. To determine how CPFF pricing compared to borrowing costs in crisis conditions, we compared CPFF pricing terms to 3-month LIBOR for the period from the failure of Lehman Brothers Holdings Inc. (Sept. 14, 2008) through the date on which CPFF became operational (Oct. 27, 2008). We found that average CPFF pricing terms were lower than the average LIBOR rate by 92 basis points and 44 basis points for CPFF purchases of unsecured commercial paper and collateralized ABCP, respectively. To determine how unsecured CPFF rates compared to benchmarks for borrowing costs in normal market conditions, we applied the CPFF pricing rule for unsecured commercial paper to a 2-month period in 2006 and found that CPFF pricing would have been more expensive than AA unsecured commercial paper interest rates by roughly 200 basis points and LIBOR by over 190 basis points. This analysis suggests that CPFF would have become less attractive to participants as market conditions improved.

Treasury capital investments. Analyses we reviewed suggest that the prices Treasury paid for equity in financial institutions participating in TARP exceeded estimated market prices that private investors might have paid for comparable investments in these institutions during the crisis. This pricing is consistent with a policy goal to stabilize financial conditions by improving the equity capitalization of banks. In late 2008, before CPP was announced, banks had difficulty issuing sufficient new equity to investors. We reviewed estimates of the expected budget cost associated with Treasury's equity funding support programs under TARP, CPP and the Targeted Investment Program (TIP), as well as a valuation analysis commissioned by the Congressional Oversight Panel.[41] Some of the benefits that accrued to banks from participation in equity funding support programs are likely to be proportional to the expected budgetary cost (also known as subsidy rates) estimated for accounting purposes. Treasury and Congressional Budget Office estimates of subsidy rates are based on a net present value analysis—the price and terms which are offered by a federal agency are compared to the lifetime expected cost (net present value) of the equity, and the difference is known as a subsidy. [42] The valuation analysis commissioned by the Congressional Oversight Panel explicitly compared the prices received by Treasury with market-based valuations of securities it determined to be comparable. Estimates of subsidy rates by Treasury, the Congressional Budget Office, and the Congressional Oversight Panel were generally similar for CPP, while the Congressional Budget Office's estimates for TIP were substantially lower than those of Treasury and the Congressional Oversight Panel (see figure 1). Based on these three analyses, these estimated subsidy rates suggest that the prices Treasury paid for equity in financial institutions were 18 to 27 percent over estimated market prices for CPP and 26 to 50 percent over estimated market prices for TIP equity. Estimates reflect differences in timing, methodology, and institutions included in the analyses, which we discussed previously and in the note to figure 1.[43]

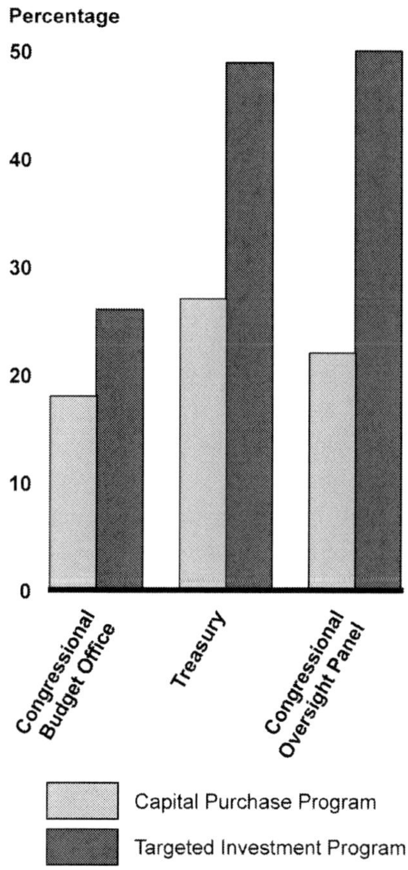

Source: GAO analysis of CBO, Treasury, and COP data.

Note: Analysis by the Congressional Budget Office is as of December 31, 2008, and the Targeted Investment Program (TIP) estimate includes only Citigroup. Treasury financial statement information is as of September 30, 2009. Analysis commissioned by the Congressional Oversight Panel includes valuations based on data from October 2008 through November 2008 and the TIP estimate includes only Citigroup, and the CPP estimate is based on a sample of 8 relatively large financial institutions. We used the earliest available estimates from the Congressional Budget Office and Treasury as they were closest to market conditions at the time that programs were initiated. Estimates of these subsidy rates depended on timing and market conditions and the size of these subsidy rates likely fell over time as market conditions improved.

Figure 1. Emergency Capital Program Subsidy Estimates.

Table 2. Pricing Terms for Commercial Paper Funding Facility

Rates and fees	Unsecured commercial paper	ABCP
Interest rate	3-month OIS + 100 basis points	3-month OIS + 300 basis points
Credit surcharge	100 basis points	None
All-in-cost	3-month OIS + 200 basis points	3-month OIS + 300 basis points

Source: Federal Reserve Board.

FDIC's DGP. For the DGP guarantees that we analyzed, the fees for FDIC's DGP were on average 278 basis points below the private cost of similar guarantees during crisis conditions, but more expensive than similar guarantees that were available in the private market during normal credit conditions. This pricing is consistent with a policy goal to promote financial stability by improving access to sources of debt funding. FDIC's DGP provided guarantees for certain newly issued senior unsecured debt for banks, bank holding companies, and other eligible institutions. When DGP was created in October 2008, lending to financial institutions in public debt markets had dropped dramatically. The fees for participation in DGP were based on the maturity of guaranteed liabilities (the longer the maturity the higher the fee) and the type of financial institution. We analyzed the 100-basis point fee that DGP charged to guarantee debt with a maturity of 1 year, plus the 10-basis point premium charged to bank holding companies.[44] We compared the total DGP fee with the weighted average price of 1-year bank CDS for certain bank holding companies because the guarantee is essentially similar to a private party insuring against the risk of default using a CDS.[45] Our analysis covered the period from the failure of Lehman Brothers (in September 2008) through the date DGP became operational (in October 2008). We found that the cost of insuring against bank default on the private market exceeded the FDIC fee terms by on average 278 basis points, with considerable variation across users—varying from over 1,000 basis points above the DGP fee terms to a few basis points below. We also applied the DGP pricing rule for guaranteeing bank holding company debt to a 2-month period in 2006, before the crisis, and found that DGP pricing would have exceeded the private cost of guarantees by roughly 100 basis points. This pricing suggests that DGP would have become less attractive to participants as market conditions improved. For more detail on our analysis of the prices and terms of all of the emergency programs, please see appendix III.

Programs Provided Support to Banking Organizations of Various Sizes and Some Programs Supported Funding Sources Used More by Larger Firms

Emergency government programs to stabilize financial markets provided funding support to bank holding companies and insured depository institutions (collectively, banking organizations) of various sizes.[46] This section also focuses on the programs that provided the most significant funding support directly to bank holding companies and their subsidiaries (listed previously in table 1). Agencies made these programs available to specific types of institutions regardless of their size, and institutions of various sizes participated in these programs. Differences in the level of program use by institutions of various sizes were driven in part by differences in how institutions funded themselves. For example, compared to smaller bank holding companies, larger bank holding companies relied to a greater extent on short-term credit markets that were the most severely disrupted during the crisis and participated more in programs intended to address disruptions in these markets. Smaller banking organizations relied more on deposits to fund their activities.

To compare the extent to which banking organizations of various sizes used emergency programs, we calculated the percentage of banking organization assets that were supported by emergency programs—either through capital injections, loans, or guarantees—at quarter-end dates for 2008 through 2012. Capital provided by emergency programs includes capital investments by Treasury under CPP and TIP. Loans provided by emergency programs include TAF, TSLF, PDCF, and CPFF loans from the Federal Reserve System. Funding guaranteed by emergency programs includes deposits guaranteed by FDIC through TAGP and debt guaranteed by FDIC through DGP. We then calculated each of these three types of liabilities as a percentage of assets for banking organizations by size for quarter-end dates from mid-2008 to the end of 2012. Finally, for each of the three types of liabilities, we decomposed average liabilities as a percentage of assets for banking organizations of different sizes into two components: (1) the rate of participation in emergency programs by banking organizations of different sizes and (2) the average liabilities as a percentage of assets for those participants.

We found that the extent to which banking organizations of different sizes used emergency programs varied over time and across programs. For example, the largest bank holding companies—those with more than $500 billion in assets as of June 30, 2013—used the programs to varying degrees but had exited most of the programs by the end of 2009. Moreover, as of December 31, 2008, average use of emergency programs generally was higher for banking organizations with $50 billion or more in assets than it was for banking organizations with less than $50 billion in assets. Total loans outstanding from Federal Reserve System programs (TAF, TSLF, PDCF, and CPFF) combined were at least 2 percent of assets on average for banking organizations with $50 billion or more in assets but less than 1 percent of assets on average for smaller banking organizations. CPP and TIP capital investments were at least 1.5 percent of assets on average for banking organizations with $50 billion or more in assets and less than 1 percent of assets on average for smaller organizations. Finally, DGP-guaranteed debt and TAGP-guaranteed deposits together were at least 6 percent of assets on average for banking organizations with $50 billion or more in assets and were less than 4 percent of assets on average for smaller banking organizations. However, by December 31, 2010, the Federal Reserve System's loan programs had closed, and differences in use of remaining programs by banking organizations of different sizes had diminished. For a more detailed discussion of our analysis of utilization of these programs by banking organizations of various sizes, see appendix IV.

Several factors influenced the extent to which eligible institutions used emergency programs. As explained above, one factor driving an institution's level of participation in a program was the extent to which it relied on the type of funding assisted by the program. In addition, market conditions and the speed with which eligible firms recovered affected the amount and duration of use of the programs by different firms. Agencies generally designed program terms and conditions to make the programs attractive only for institutions facing liquidity strains. Use of several of the programs peaked during the height of the financial crisis and fell as market conditions recovered. Federal Reserve Board officials told us that even as markets recovered, funding conditions improved for certain borrowers but not others. As a result, in PDCF, TSLF, and CPFF, several participants remained in the programs while others exited. Participants in CPP required the approval of their primary federal regulator before exiting the program. In addition, several of the programs included limits on the amount of assistance an entity could receive. Under CPP, qualified financial institutions were eligible to receive an investment of between 1 and 3 percent of their risk-weighted assets, up to a maximum of $25 billion. To prevent excessive use of CPFF that would be inconsistent with its role as a backstop, the Federal Reserve Board limited the maximum amount a single issuer could have outstanding at CPFF to the greatest amount of U.S.-dollar-denominated commercial paper the issuer had had outstanding on any day between January 1 and August 31, 2008. The Federal Reserve Board also set limits on the maximum amount that institutions could bid in each TAF and TSLF auction.[47] Finally, in some cases, institutions accepted emergency government assistance at the encouragement of their regulators. For example, several institutions accepted TARP capital investments at the encouragement of Treasury or their regulator.[48] However, participation in other programs appears to have been driven by market conditions and other factors.

The Federal Reserve Board Granted Exemptions to Allow Banks to Provide Liquidity Support to the Nonbanking Sector and for Other Purposes

During the financial crisis, the Federal Reserve Board granted a number of exemptions to requirements under Section 23A of the Federal Reserve Act for a range of purposes, such as allowing banks to provide greater liquidity support to the nonbank sector. The number of exemptions granted increased significantly during the crisis, and the majority of these exemptions were granted to U.S. bank holding companies and other firms with $500 billion or more in total assets (see figure 2). Section 23A of the Federal Reserve Act imposes quantitative limits on certain transactions between an insured depository institution and its affiliates, prohibits banks from purchasing low-quality assets from their nonbank affiliates, and imposes collateral requirements on extensions of credit to affiliates.[49] In letters documenting its approval of exemptions to Section 23A, the Federal Reserve Board has indicated that the twin purposes of Section 23A are (1) to protect against a depository institution suffering losses in transactions with its affiliates, and (2) to limit the ability of a depository institution to transfer to its affiliates the subsidy arising from the institution's access to the federal safety net.[50] In other words, these restrictions are intended to protect the safety and soundness of banks and to prevent them from subsidizing the activities of nonbank affiliates by passing on any benefits they may receive through access to deposit insurance and the discount window. The Federal Reserve Act granted the Federal Reserve Board authority to exempt transactions and relationships from Section 23A restrictions if such exemptions were in the public interest and consistent with statutory purposes.[51] Prior to the Dodd-Frank Act, the Federal Reserve Board had exclusive authority to grant exemptions to Section 23A.

During the financial crisis, the Federal Reserve Board granted a number of exemptions from the requirements of Section 23A, for a range of purposes that included, but were not limited to, the following:

- *Facilitating Liquidity Support for Holders of Mortgage-Related Assets.* In August 2007, the Federal Reserve Board issued three similar exemption letters granting Section 23A exemptions to three of the largest U.S. bank holding companies

(Citigroup Inc., Bank of America Corporation, and JP Morgan Chase & Co.) to allow their bank subsidiaries (Citibank, N.A.; Bank of America, N.A.; and JPMorgan Chase Bank, N.A.) to engage in securities financing transactions with their affiliated broker-dealers. The purpose of these exemptions was to allow each of these banks to extend up to $25 billion of credit (using their broker-dealer affiliates as conduits) to unaffiliated market participants in need of short-term liquidity to finance their holdings of certain mortgage loans and other assets.[52] The Federal Reserve Board's letters noted that these exemptions would provide significant public benefits by allowing banks to provide a substantial amount of liquidity into the market for these mortgage-related assets.

- *Facilitating Liquidity Support for Holders of Auction-Rate Securities*. In December 2008 and January 2009, the Federal Reserve Board granted exemptions to allow four large banks (Fifth Third Bank, BB&T Company, Northern Trust Company, and Wachovia Bank, N.A.) to purchase auction-rate securities and variable rate demand notes from their securities affiliates or parent company.[53] The Federal Reserve Board's letters noted that these exemptions were intended to facilitate the provision of liquidity by these banks to customers of their affiliates that were holding illiquid auction-rate securities or variable rate demand notes.[54] The securities affiliates of banks had been active in underwriting and selling auction-rate securities and when these securities became illiquid, the affiliates repurchased them from clients that sought to liquidate their positions. In this case, 23A exemptions allowed banks to provide financing for these purchases. The size of transactions permitted under these exemptions ranged from $600 million for The Northern Trust Company to approximately $7 billion for Wachovia Bank, N.A.
- *Facilitating Liquidity Support to Money Market Funds and Repurchase Agreement Markets*. In addition to exemptions granted to individual institutions, the Federal Reserve Board granted broad-based exemptions from Section 23A to enable banks to provide liquidity support to repurchase agreement markets and money market mutual funds (MMMF). First, on September 14, 2008, concurrent with the decision to expand eligible collateral types for PDCF and TSLF, the Federal Reserve Board adopted an interim final rule granting a temporary exemption to allow banks to provide their securities affiliates with short-term financing for assets that they ordinarily would have financed through the repurchase agreements markets. The purpose of this exemption was to improve the ability of broker-dealers to continue financing their securities and other assets despite the liquidity shortage in the triparty repurchase agreement market. Several days later, on September 19, the Federal Reserve Board amended Regulation W to grant a temporary exemption from Section 23A requirements for member banks' purchases of ABCP from affiliated money market funds, subject to certain conditions.[55] The purpose of this exemption was to enable banks to take full advantage of the Asset-Backed Commercial Paper Money Market Mutual Fund Liquidity Facility (AMLF), a program authorized by the Federal Reserve Board to provide loans to banks to fund the purchase of ABCP from MMMFs.
- *Facilitating Acquisitions of Failing Firms*. The Federal Reserve Board also granted Section 23A exemptions in connection with its efforts to facilitate private acquisitions of firms whose failure could have destabilized financial markets. Such

acquisitions included JP Morgan Chase & Co.'s acquisition of Bear Stearns and Wells Fargo & Company's acquisition of Wachovia Corporation. JP Morgan Chase & Co. received exemptions that allowed JP Morgan Chase Bank, N.A. to, among other things, extend credit to, and issue guarantees on behalf of, former Bear Stearns entities and to purchase a derivatives portfolio valued at approximately $44 billion from Bear Stearns. In November 2008, the Federal Reserve Board granted an exemption to allow Wells Fargo Bank, N.A., to extend up to $17 billion in credit to Wachovia Bank, N.A. to assist it in meeting its short-term funding obligations until the merger was completed.

For many of these cases, the Federal Reserve Board granted an exemption to help facilitate liquidity support to nonbank entities as part of its actions to reduce systemic risk and promote financial stability. In granting exemptions, the Federal Reserve Board imposed conditions that were intended to mitigate risks to the bank that would be providing credit, purchasing assets, or engaging in other transactions with affiliates.[56] However, one expert has raised concerns that such conditions might not offer sufficient protection for an insured depository institution during crisis conditions and that these exemptions in aggregate resulted in a large- scale transfer of safety net benefits created for banks to the nonbank, or "shadow banking," system.[57] As discussed in the next section of this report, the Dodd-Frank Act made changes to Section 23A of the Federal Reserve Act.

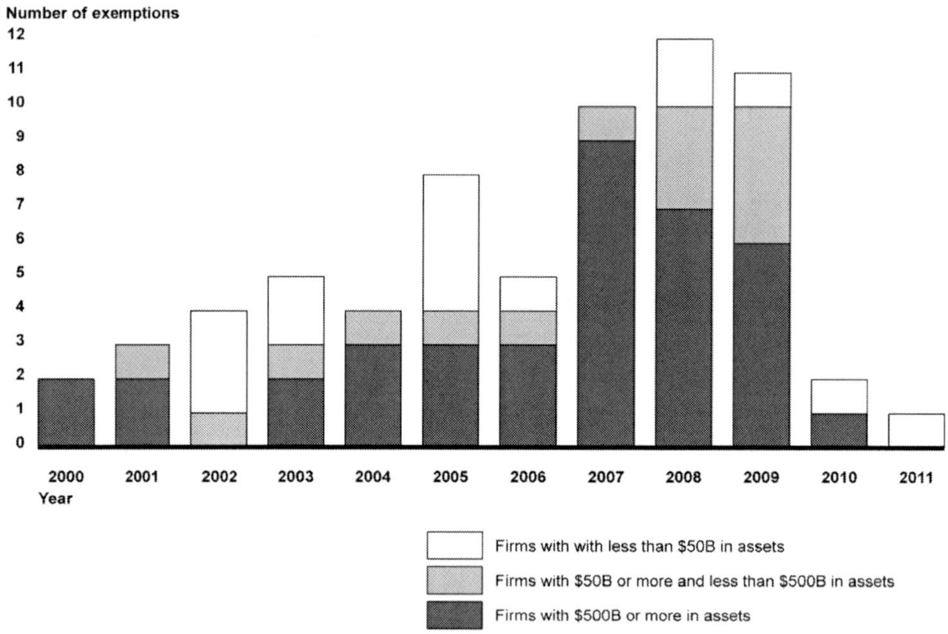

Source: GAO analysis of Federal Reserve Board documents.

Figure 2. Section 23A Exemptions for Firms by Total Assets, 2000-2011.

Some Large Bank Holding Companies Benefited from Individual Institution Assistance or Regulatory Relief

In addition to introducing emergency programs with broad-based eligibility, federal government agencies took special actions with respect to individual financial institutions on several occasions in 2008 and 2009. While these actions were intended to benefit a range of market participants and the broader financial system, some large U.S. bank holding companies received substantial direct benefits from these actions. Such actions included (1) assistance from multiple agencies to rescue or facilitate the acquisition of troubled firms whose failures posed significant risks to the financial system, and (2) the Federal Reserve Board granting bank holding company status to several nonbank financial companies and providing liquidity support to the London broker-dealers of a few of the largest bank holding companies.

Individual Institution Assistance

On several occasions in 2008 and early 2009, the federal government provided extraordinary support to or facilitated the acquisition of large financial institutions, which benefitted recipients of this assistance and other market participants, such as firms that had large risk exposures to these institutions.

- *Assistance to Facilitate JP Morgan's Acquisition of Bear Stearns*. In 2008, the Federal Reserve Board authorized emergency assistance to avert the failure of Bear Stearns Companies, Inc. (Bear Stearns) and facilitate the acquisition of the firm by JP Morgan Chase & Co.[58] On Friday, March 14, 2008, the Federal Reserve Board voted to authorize FRBNY to provide a $12.9 billion loan to Bear Stearns to enable the firm to avoid bankruptcy and to provide time for potential acquirers, including JP Morgan Chase & Co, to assess its financial condition. On Sunday, March 16, 2008, the Federal Reserve Board announced that FRBNY would lend up to $30 billion against certain Bear Stearns assets to facilitate JP Morgan Chase & Co's acquisition of Bear Stearns. During the following week, the terms of this assistance were renegotiated, resulting in the creation of a new lending structure under which a $28.82 billion FRBNY senior loan and a $1.15 billion JP Morgan Chase & Co subordinated loan funded the purchase of certain Bear Stearns's assets. FRBNY also provided certain regulatory exemptions to JP Morgan Chase & Co. in connection with its agreement to acquire Bear Stearns. For example, the Federal Reserve Board granted an 18-month exemption to allow JP Morgan Chase & Co to exclude certain Bear Stearns assets from its risk- weighted assets for purposes of applying risk-based capital requirements.
- *Assistance to Government-Sponsored Enterprises*. Extraordinary government support to Fannie Mae and Freddie Mac helped to stabilize mortgage markets and the broader financial markets and provided specific benefits to bank holding companies and other firms that likely would have incurred losses if the federal government had allowed these government-sponsored enterprises to fail. On September 6, 2008, the Federal Housing Finance Agency placed Fannie Mae and Freddie Mac into conservatorship out of concern that their deteriorating financial condition threatened their safety and

soundness and their ability to fulfill their public mission.[59] Treasury's investments in Fannie Mae and Freddie Mac under the Senior Preferred Stock Purchase Agreements program represent the federal government's single largest risk exposure remaining from its emergency actions to assist the financial sector.[60] As of June 30, 2013, cumulative cash draws by the GSEs under this program totaled $187.4 billion and cumulative dividends paid by the GSEs to Treasury totaled $131.6 billion.

- *Assistance to AIG.* Federal government actions to prevent the failure of AIG benefitted AIG and its counterparties—which included some of the largest U.S. and foreign financial institutions—and were intended to benefit the broader financial system.[61] In September 2008, the Federal Reserve Board and Treasury determined that market events could have caused AIG to fail, which would have posed systemic risk to financial markets. The Federal Reserve Board and Treasury collaborated to make available up to $182.3 billion in assistance to AIG. This assistance, which began with a revolving credit facility of up to $85 billion from FRBNY, was provided in several stages and was restructured over time.[62] In November 2008, the Federal Reserve Board authorized the creation of two special-purpose vehicles—Maiden Lane II LLC and Maiden Lane III LLC—to purchase certain AIG-related assets. Maiden Lane II was created to alleviate capital and liquidity pressures arising from a securities lending portfolio operated by certain AIG subsidiaries by purchasing residential MBS held in this portfolio. Maiden Lane III helped to fund the purchase of collateralized debt obligations from AIG counterparties that had purchased CDS from AIG to protect the value of those assets. AIG repaid all loans and capital investments it received from government entities during the crisis. In December 2012, Treasury sold its remaining investments in AIG, resulting in a total positive return of $22.7 billion for Treasury and FRBNY.
- *Extraordinary Assistance to Citigroup.* On November 23, 2008, Treasury, the Federal Reserve Board, and FDIC announced a package of additional assistance to Citigroup Inc. (Citigroup) that included $20 billion of capital from TIP and a loss-sharing agreement with the government entities that was intended to assure market participants that Citigroup would not fail in the event of larger-than- expected losses on certain of its assets. As discussed in our April 2010 report on Treasury's use of the systemic risk determination, Treasury, FDIC, and the Federal Reserve Board said they provided emergency assistance to Citigroup because they were concerned that a failure of a firm of Citigroup's size and interconnectedness would have systemic implications.[63] As of September 30, 2008, Citigroup was the second largest banking organization in the United States, with total consolidated assets of approximately $2 trillion. In June 2009, Treasury entered into an agreement to exchange the $25 billion in Citigroup preferred shares purchased in its initial CPP investment for Citigroup common shares to help improve Citigroup's capital position.[64] In December 2009, Citigroup repaid the $20 billion TIP investment. On December 23, 2009, Citigroup announced that it had entered into an agreement with FDIC, FRBNY, and Treasury to terminate the loss- sharing agreement. As part of the termination agreement, Citigroup agreed to pay a $50 million termination fee to FRBNY.
- *Extraordinary Assistance to Bank of America.* On January 16, 2009, Treasury, the Federal Reserve Board, and FDIC announced a similar package of assistance to Bank of America Corporation (Bank of America). The additional assistance included

capital through TIP and a loss-sharing agreement that was similar to the one executed for Citigroup. While Bank of America received $20 billion in capital through TIP, the government entities never finalized the announced loss-sharing agreement with Bank of America. In September 2009, the agencies agreed to terminate the loss-sharing agreement with Bank of America. As part of the agreement to terminate the agreement-in-principle, Bank of America paid fees of $276 million to Treasury, $57 million to the Federal Reserve Board, and $92 million to FDIC. Bank of America repaid its $20 billion TIP investment in December 2009.

Bank Holding Company Status and Liquidity Support for London Subsidiaries

In late 2008, at the height of the financial crisis, the Federal Reserve Board approved applications by several large nonbank financial firms to convert to bank holding company status. Becoming bank holding companies provided these firms with greater access to emergency government funding support, while subjecting them to oversight by the Federal Reserve System and other requirements under the Bank Holding Company Act.[65] Eligibility for TARP capital investments under CPP and debt guarantees through TLGP were generally restricted to depository institutions and their holding companies, and several large firms that became bank holding companies in late 2008 subsequently participated in one or both of these programs. Among the largest firms converting to bank holding companies during the crisis were two investment banks (Goldman Sachs Group, Inc. and Morgan Stanley), two companies that were large providers of credit card products and other services (American Express Company and Discover Financial Services), and two other financial firms (CIT Group Inc. and GMAC LLC). In many cases, obtaining bank holding company status involved firms converting an industrial loan corporation (ILC) into a bank.[66] Federal Reserve Board officials noted that these firms already had access to the discount window through their ILCs and converting these ILCs to banks did not change their access to the discount window, but their access to discount window liquidity was limited by the amount of assets these subsidiaries—first as ILCs and later as banks—could pledge to the discount window as collateral. According to Federal Reserve Board documents, deposits held by these firms were a small fraction of their total consolidated assets at the time they became bank holding companies. While bank holding companies are subject to restrictions on nonbanking activities under the Bank Holding Company Act, Federal Reserve Board orders approving bank holding company applications described nonbanking activities of the companies that were permissible under the act and noted that the act provides each newly formed bank holding company 2 years to conform its existing nonbanking investments and activities to the act's requirements.

On September 21, 2008, the Federal Reserve Board announced that FRBNY would extend credit—on terms similar to those applicable for PDCF loans—to the U.S. and London broker-dealer subsidiaries of Goldman Sachs Group, Inc., Morgan Stanley, and Merrill Lynch & Co. to provide support to these subsidiaries as they became part of bank holding companies that would be regulated by the Federal Reserve System.[67] On November 23, 2008, in connection with other actions taken by Treasury, FDIC, and the Federal Reserve Board to assist Citigroup, the Federal Reserve Board authorized FRBNY to extend credit to the London-based broker-dealer of Citigroup on terms similar to those applicable to PDCF loans.

DODD-FRANK AIMS TO RESTRICT FUTURE GOVERNMENT SUPPORT, BUT IMPLEMENTATION IS INCOMPLETE AND EFFECTIVENESS REMAINS UNCERTAIN

Enacted in July 2010, the Dodd-Frank Act contains provisions intended to modify the scope of federal safety nets for financial firms, place limits on agency authorities to provide emergency assistance, and strengthen regulatory oversight of the largest firms, among other things.[68] FDIC and the Federal Reserve Board have finalized certain changes to traditional safety nets for insured banks, but impacts of the act's provisions to limit the scope of financial transactions that benefit from these safety nets will depend on how they are implemented. The act also prohibits regulators' use of emergency authorities to rescue an individual institution and places other restrictions on these authorities. For example, the act effectively removes FDIC's authority to provide assistance to a single, specific failing bank outside of receivership and grants FDIC new authority to resolve a large failing institution outside of bankruptcy.[69] FDIC has made progress toward implementing its new resolution authority and continues to work to address potential obstacles to the viability of its resolution process as an alternative to bankruptcy, such as challenges that could arise when resolving more than one large institution concurrently. The act also places new restrictions and requirements on the Federal Reserve Board's emergency lending authority. However, the Federal Reserve Board has not yet completed its process for drafting policies and procedures required by the act to implement these changes or set timeframes for doing so. Finalizing such procedures would help ensure that any future use of this authority complies with Dodd-Frank Act requirements. Finally, the Federal Reserve Board has made progress towards implementing certain enhanced regulatory standards that are intended to reduce the risks that the largest financial institutions pose to the financial system.

Agencies Have Finalized Changes to Traditional Safety Nets, but Have Not Fully Implemented Provisions to Limit the Scope of Transactions That Have Access

The Dodd-Frank Act instituted a series of reforms related to the traditional safety nets for insured banks, including changes to deposit insurance and discount window reporting requirements. In addition, the act contains provisions intended to limit the scope of financial transactions that benefit from access to these traditional safety nets. These provisions include revisions to the Federal Reserve Board's authority to permit certain transactions between banks and their affiliates under Section 23A of the Federal Reserve Act, restrictions on the ability of bank holding companies to engage in proprietary trading; and restrictions on the ability of insured banks to engage in certain derivatives transactions.

Deposit Insurance

FDIC has implemented Dodd-Frank Act provisions that increased the deposit insurance limit and required FDIC to change the calculation for premiums paid by insured depository institutions. Section 335 of the Dodd-Frank Act permanently raised the standard maximum deposit insurance amount from $100,000 to $250,000 for individual deposit accounts, as previously discussed.[70] FDIC issued and made effective a final rule instituting the increase in August 2010 and required insured depository institutions to comply by January 2011.[71] Section 343 of the act provided temporary unlimited deposit insurance coverage for certain uninsured deposits from December 2010 through December 2012.[72] This coverage expired on December 31, 2012, and transaction accounts can now only be insured to the $250,000 ceiling.[73] Section 331 of the Dodd- Frank Act required FDIC to amend its regulation and modify the definition of an insured depository institution's assessment base, which can affect the amount of deposit insurance assessment the institution pays into the deposit insurance fund. Under the Dodd-Frank Act, the assessment base changed from total domestic deposits to average consolidated total assets minus average tangible equity (with some possible exceptions).[74] FDIC issued a final rule changing the assessment base in February 2011, and the rule became effective in April 2011.[75] According to FDIC, the change in the assessment base calculation shifted some of the overall assessment burden from community banks to larger institutions that rely less on domestic deposits for their funding than smaller institutions, but without affecting the overall amount of assessment revenue collected.[76] In the quarter after the rule became effective, those banks with less than $10 billion in assets saw a 33 percent drop in their assessments (from about $1 billion to about $700 million), while those banks with over $10 billion in assets saw a 17 percent rise in their assessments (from about $2.4 billion to about $2.8 billion).

Discount Window Reporting Requirements

The Dodd-Frank Act made changes to the Federal Reserve Board's reporting requirements to increase the transparency for discount window transactions. During and after the crisis, some members of Congress and others expressed concern that certain details of the Federal Reserve System's discount window and emergency lending activities, including the names of borrowers receiving loans, were kept confidential. Section 1103 of the Dodd-Frank Act requires the Federal Reserve Board to disclose transaction-level details for discount window loans and open market transactions on a quarterly basis after a 2-year delay.[77] The Dodd-Frank Act established similar reporting requirements for the Federal Reserve Board's Section 13(3) authority, as discussed later. No rulemaking was required, and the Federal Reserve Board began to post the data publicly on its website in September 2012. The first set of releases covered loans made between July and September 2010, and data for subsequent periods are being published quarterly with a 2-year lag. The Dodd-Frank Act also grants GAO authority to audit certain aspects of discount window transactions occurring after July 21, 2010.

Section 23A

The Dodd-Frank Act made numerous changes to Section 23A of the Federal Reserve Act that both significantly expanded the scope of activities covered by Section 23A's restrictions and created new requirements for participation by FDIC and the OCC in granting exceptions.[78] As previously discussed, the Federal Reserve Board granted a number of exemptions to Section 23A during the crisis. Some observers have raised concerns that these exemptions in aggregate resulted in a large scale transfer of federal safety net benefits to the nonbank, or "shadow banking," system. The changes listed below, with the exception of changes related to investments in private funds, did not require rulemakings and became effective on July 21, 2012.

- The Dodd-Frank Act gave FDIC and OCC, jointly with the Federal Reserve Board, the authority to grant Section 23A exemptions by order for institutions they supervise. The Dodd-Frank Act requires the regulators to notify FDIC of any proposed exemption and give FDIC 60 days to object in writing, should FDIC determine the proposed exemption constitutes an unacceptable risk to the deposit insurance fund.[79] The Federal Reserve retains the authority to grant exemptions by regulation.
- The Dodd-Frank Act expanded the scope of activities that are covered by Section 23A by amending the definition of covered transactions to include derivatives transactions with affiliates and transactions with affiliates that involve securities lending and borrowing that may cause a bank to face credit exposure to an affiliate.[80] The Dodd-Frank Act also removed the exception from the 10 percent quantitative limit for certain covered transactions between a bank and its financial subsidiary and extended section 23A and 23B to cover permitted investments in certain private funds.
- The Dodd-Frank Act changed the collateral requirements for 23A transactions by requiring banks to maintain the correct level of collateral at all times for covered transactions subject to collateralization.[81] Previously, banks only had to post collateral at the time of entrance into the covered transaction. This change was designed to strengthen the protection granted to banks extending credit to their affiliates by ensuring that the collateral remains correctly valued and simultaneously shields the bank's interest from fluctuations in market prices of collateralized assets.

As of October 2013, the Federal Reserve Board has granted only two exemptions since the enactment of the Dodd-Frank Act, according to available information on its website. How the Federal Reserve Board, FDIC, and OCC might respond to requests for exemptions in the future is uncertain. Representatives from one large bank told us that their primary regulator advised them that that because of FDIC's required approval, they should not expect exemptions to be available going forward. However, one academic has expressed concern about how exemptions might be applied under different circumstances, such as in periods of economic stress.

Proprietary Trading (Volcker Rule)

Agencies have not yet issued final rules to implement the Dodd-Frank Act's restrictions on proprietary trading—trading activities conducted by banking entities for their own account as opposed to those of their clients. A number of market participants and researchers with whom we spoke maintain that the ability of banking entities to use federally insured deposits to seek profits for their own account provides incentives for them to take on excessive risk. To address these concerns, Section 619 of the Dodd-Frank Act (also known as the Volcker Rule) generally prohibits proprietary trading by insured depository institutions and their affiliates and places restrictions on sponsorship or investment in hedge and private equity funds. An FSOC study noted that implementing the act's restrictions on proprietary trading will be challenging because certain trading activities exempted from the act's restrictions may appear very similar to proprietary trading activities that the act seeks to restrict. While regulators issued proposed rules in November 2011 and February 2012, no final or interim final rules have been issued.[82]

Restrictions on Some Derivatives Transactions

Section 716 of the Dodd-Frank Act requires banks that are registered dealers of derivatives known as swaps to transfer certain swap activities to nonbank affiliates, or lose access to deposit insurance and the Federal Reserve System liquidity provided through the discount window for certain activities taken in connection with the swap entity's swap business.[83] Section 716's prohibition on federal assistance to swaps entities became effective in July 2013, but the law allowed for an initial 2- year extension as well as an additional 1-year extension. Several banks applied for and were granted 2-year extensions by the Federal Reserve Board and OCC, and those financial institutions now have until July 2015 to comply, with the additional option of applying for another 1-year exemption.

Dodd-Frank Restricts Certain FDIC Authorities but Provides New Resolution Authority

The Dodd-Frank Act restricts emergency authorities used by financial regulators during the most recent financial crisis, such as FDIC's open bank assistance authority; provides FDIC with new resolution authority to resolve a large, complex failing firm in a manner that limits the disruption to the financial system; and establishes a requirement for certain firms to develop and submit to regulators resolution plans (known as living wills) for their resolution under bankruptcy.

Open Bank Assistance

The Dodd-Frank Act restricts FDIC's authority to provide open bank assistance to an individual failing bank outside of receivership and replaces it with a new authority, subject to certain restrictions and a joint resolution of congressional approval, to create a debt-guarantee program with broad-based eligibility.[84] Previously, FDIC could provide open bank assistance upon a joint determination by FDIC, the Federal Reserve Board, and the Secretary of the Treasury that compliance with certain cost limitations would result in serious adverse effects on economic conditions or financial stability and that such assistance could mitigate these systemic effects.[85] Sections 1104 through 1106 of the Dodd-Frank Act provide permanent authority for FDIC to establish a widely available program to guarantee certain debt obligations of solvent insured depository institutions or solvent bank holding companies during times of severe economic distress, upon a liquidity event finding. In addition, institutions would have to pay fees for these guarantees as they did under TLGP during the crisis.[86] In order for FDIC to exercise the authority, the Dodd-Frank Act requires the Secretary of the Treasury (in consultation with the President) to determine the maximum amount of debt outstanding that FDIC can guarantee, and the guarantee authority requires congressional approval.[87] Furthermore, the Dodd-Frank Act amendments to the Federal Deposit Insurance Act that provided for temporary unlimited deposit insurance for noninterest-bearing transaction accounts were repealed as of January 1, 2013. The FDIC may not rely on this authority or its former systemic risk exception authority to provide unlimited deposit insurance for transaction accounts in a future crisis.

Resolution Authority

The Dodd-Frank Act includes two key reforms intended to facilitate the orderly resolution of a large failing firm without a taxpayer-funded rescue: (1) the Orderly Liquidation Authority (OLA), through which FDIC can liquidate large financial firms outside of the bankruptcy process; and (2) requirements for bank holding companies with $50 billion or more in assets and nonbank financial companies designated by FSOC to formulate and submit to regulators resolution plans (or "living wills") that detail how the companies could be resolved in bankruptcy in the event of a material financial distress or failure.[88]

OLA gives FDIC the authority, subject to certain constraints, to liquidate large financial firms, including nonbanks, outside of the bankruptcy process.[89] This authority allows for FDIC to be appointed receiver for a financial firm if the Secretary of the Treasury determines that the firm's failure and its resolution under applicable federal or state law, including bankruptcy, would have serious adverse effects on U.S. financial stability and no viable private sector alternative is available to prevent the default of the financial company.[90] While the Dodd-Frank Act does not specify how FDIC must exercise its OLA resolution authority and while a number of approaches have been considered, FDIC's preferred approach to resolving a firm under OLA is referred to as Single Point-of-Entry (SPOE). Under the SPOE approach, FDIC would be appointed receiver of a top- tier U.S. parent holding company of the financial group determined to be in default or in danger of default following the completion of the appointment process set forth under the Dodd-Frank Act. Immediately after placing the parent holding company into receivership, FDIC would transfer some assets (primarily the equity and investments in subsidiaries) from the receivership estate to a bridge financial holding company. By taking control of the firm at the holding company level, this approach is intended to allow subsidiaries (domestic and foreign) carrying out critical services to remain open and operating. One key factor for the success of the SPOE approach is ensuring that the holding company builds up sufficient loss-absorbing capacity to enable it to recapitalize its subsidiaries, if necessary.

In a SPOE resolution, at the parent holding company level, shareholders would be wiped out, and unsecured debt holders would have their claims written down to reflect any losses that shareholders cannot cover. Under the Dodd-Frank Act, officers and directors responsible for the failure cannot be retained.[91] FDIC expects the well-capitalized bridge financial company and its subsidiaries to borrow in the private markets and from customary sources of liquidity. The new resolution authority under the Dodd- Frank Act provides a back-up source for liquidity support, the Orderly Liquidation Fund, which could provide liquidity support to the bridge financial company if customary sources of liquidity are unavailable.[92] The law requires FDIC to recover any losses arising from a resolution by assessing bank holding companies with $50 billion or more in consolidated assets, nonbank financial holding companies designated for supervision by the Federal Reserve System, and other financial companies with $50 billion or more in consolidated assets.[93]

Progress has been made to implement the reforms related to resolving large, complex financial institutions. FDIC has largely completed the core rulemakings necessary to carry out its systemic resolution responsibilities. For example, FDIC approved a final rule implementing OLA that addressed the priority of claims and the treatment of similarly situated creditors.[94] The FDIC plans to seek public comment on its resolution strategy by the end of 2013. In addition, FDIC has worked with other financial regulatory agencies, both domestic and foreign, to make extensive preparations and to conduct planning exercises in order to be as prepared as possible to successfully resolve a firm whose failure could threaten the stability of the financial system.

Although progress has been made, FDIC and others have acknowledged that OLA is new and untested, and several challenges to its effectiveness remain. For example, FDIC could face difficulties in effectively managing the failure of one or more large bank holding companies or credibly imposing losses on the creditors of those holding companies. These challenges include the following:

- *Financial stability concerns.* FDIC may find it difficult to impose losses on all creditors of failing financial institutions because of concerns about financial stability. FDIC could in principle transfer certain bank holding company liabilities to a bridge holding company in order to protect those creditors. This concern has been subject to debate. For example, a report by the Bipartisan Policy Center, a think-tank, emphasized the importance of protecting short-term creditors of systemically important firms, while an industry association report emphasized the importance of imposing losses on short-term creditors in order to maintain market discipline.[95] While the Dodd-Frank Act allows FDIC to treat similarly situated creditors differently, it places restrictions on FDIC's ability to do so. Any transfer of liabilities from the receivership to the bridge financial company that has a disparate impact upon similarly situated creditors will only be made if such a transfer will maximize the return to those creditors left in the receivership and if such action is necessary to initiate and continue operations essential to the bridge financial company.[96]
- *Global cooperation.* Some experts have questioned how FDIC would handle issues related to the non-U.S. subsidiaries of a failed firm. For example, if a global U.S. firm were at risk of being placed in receivership under OLA, foreign regulators might act to ring-fence assets of a non-U.S. subsidiary to prevent these assets from being transferred abroad where they would not be available to protect counterparties in their jurisdiction. Such a development could increase financial instability by reducing the assets available to a U.S. firm to satisfy creditors' claims. Because SPOE involves losses borne only by holding company creditors, some observers have suggested this approach would avoid potential challenges associated with the failure of foreign subsidiaries or actions of foreign regulators to ring-fence the assets of a subsidiary. For example, if subsidiary liabilities were guaranteed under SPOE, foreign regulators would not need to ring- fence foreign subsidiaries in order to protect foreign customers or creditors.
- *Multiple, simultaneous insolvencies.* Experts have questioned whether FDIC has sufficient capacity to use OLA to handle multiple failures of systemically important firms and thus prevent further systemic disruption. In addition, FDIC may find it more difficult to impose losses on creditors when multiple large institutions are failing at once, which could reduce the credibility of OLA. According to a survey of investors, few respondents believed that FDIC could effectively use OLA to handle the resolution of multiple firms simultaneously.[97]

Living Wills

Title I of the Dodd-Frank Act requires bank holding companies with $50 billion or more in consolidated assets and nonbank financial companies designated by FSOC to formulate and submit to FDIC, the Federal Reserve Board, and FSOC resolution plans (or "living wills") that detail how the companies could be resolved in the event of material financial distress or failure.[98] The Federal Reserve Board and FDIC finalized rules relating to resolution plans, and the large financial institutions that were the first firms required to prepare such plans submitted these to regulators as expected in July 2012.[99] Regulators reviewed these initial plans and developed guidance on what information should be included in 2013 resolution plan submissions.[100]

Experts have expressed mixed views on the usefulness of the living wills. Some experts have noted that resolution plans may provide regulators with critical information about a firm's organizational structure that could aid the resolution process or motivate complex firms to simplify their structures, and this simplification could help facilitate resolution. However, other experts have told us that resolution plans may provide limited benefits in simplifying firm structures, in part because tax, jurisdictional, and other considerations may outweigh the benefits of simplification. Furthermore, some experts commented that although resolution plans may assist regulators in gaining a better understanding of the structures and activities of complex financial firms, the plans may not be useful guides during an actual liquidation—in part because the plans could become outdated or because the plans may not be helpful during a crisis.

Dodd-Frank Restricts Emergency Lending Authority, but the Federal Reserve Board Has Not Completed its Process for Drafting Required Procedures

The Dodd-Frank Act creates new restrictions and requirements associated with the Federal Reserve Board's Section 13(3) authority.[101] Generally, the act prohibits use of Section 13(3) authority to assist an individual institution (as the Federal Reserve Board did with Bear Stearns and AIG). While the act continues to allow the Federal Reserve Board to use 13(3) authority to authorize programs with broad-based eligibility, it sets forth new restrictions and requirements for such programs. For example, the act prohibits a Reserve Bank from lending to an insolvent firm through a broad-based program or creating a program designed to remove assets from a single and specific institution's balance sheet.[102] According to Federal Reserve Board staff, under its current Section 13(3) authority, the Federal Reserve Board could re-launch emergency programs to assist the repurchase agreement, commercial paper, and other credit markets, if these markets became severely strained and if the program is broad-based and meets the other requirements imposed by the Dodd-Frank Act. The Dodd-Frank Act also includes additional transparency and reporting requirements should the Federal Reserve Board exercise its Section 13(3) authority.[103]

Although the Dodd-Frank Act requires the Federal Reserve Board to promulgate regulations that establish policies and procedures governing any future lending under Section 13(3) authority, Federal Reserve Board officials told us that they have not yet completed the process for drafting these policies and procedures.[104] Federal Reserve Board staff have made progress in drafting these policies and procedures by regulation, but have not set time frames for completing and publicly proposing a draft regulation. While there is no mandated deadline for completion of the procedures, the Dodd-Frank Act does require the Federal Reserve Board to establish the policies and procedures "as soon as is practicable."[105] According to a Federal

Reserve Board official, in implementing its regulatory responsibilities under the Dodd-Frank Act, the Federal Reserve Board has focused first on the required regulations that have statutory deadlines and the regulations which are specifically directed at enhancing the safety and soundness of the financial system. Although the act did not set a specific deadline, the Federal Reserve Board can better ensure accountability for implementing rulemaking and more timely completion of these procedures by setting internal timelines for completing the rulemaking process. Furthermore, finalizing these policies and procedures could help the Federal Reserve Board to ensure that any future emergency lending does not assist an insolvent firm and complies with other Dodd-Frank Act requirements.

Completing these policies and procedures could also address prior recommendations we made with respect to the Federal Reserve System's emergency assistance programs.[106] For example, in our July 2011 report, we recommended that the Chairman of the Federal Reserve Board direct Federal Reserve Board and Reserve Bank staff to set forth the Federal Reserve Board's process for documenting its justification for each use of section 13(3) authority. We noted that more complete documentation could help the Federal Reserve Board ensure that it is complying with the Dodd-Frank Act's requirement on its use of this authority.[107] The Federal Reserve Board agreed that this prior report's recommendations would benefit its response to future crises and agreed to strongly consider how best to respond.

Enhanced Prudential Standards for Large Financial Firms Have Not been Fully Implemented

The Dodd-Frank Act also introduced a number of regulatory changes designed to reduce the risks that the largest financial institutions pose to the financial system. A notable change is a set of new prudential requirements and capital standards designed to strengthen the regulatory oversight and capital base of large financial institutions.[108] The Federal Reserve Board has made progress towards implementing these enhanced regulatory standards.

The Dodd-Frank Act requires the Federal Reserve Board to create enhanced capital and prudential standards for bank holding companies with $50 billion or more in consolidated assets and nonbank financial holding companies designated by FSOC.[109] The act's provisions related to enhanced prudential standards for these covered firms include the following:

- **Risk-based capital requirements and leverage limits.** The Federal Reserve Board must establish capital and leverage standards, which as proposed would include a requirement for covered firms to develop capital plans to help ensure that they maintain capital ratios above specified standards, under both normal and adverse conditions.[110] In addition, the Federal Reserve Board has announced its intention to apply capital surcharges to some or all firms based on the risks firms pose to the financial system.
- **Liquidity requirements.** The Federal Reserve Board must establish liquidity standards, which as proposed would include requirements for covered firms to hold liquid assets that can be used to cover their cash outflows over short periods.[111]

- **Single-counterparty credit limits.** The Federal Reserve Board must issue rules that, in general, limit the total net credit exposure of a covered firm to any single unaffiliated company to 25 percent of its total capital stock and surplus.[112]
- **Risk management requirements.** Publicly traded covered firms must establish a risk committee and be subject to enhanced risk management standards.[113]
- **Stress testing requirements.** The Federal Reserve Board is required to conduct an annual evaluation of whether covered firms have sufficient capital to absorb losses that could arise from adverse economic conditions.[114]
- **Debt-to-equity limits.** Certain covered firms may be required to maintain a debt-to-equity ratio of no more than 15-to-1.[115]
- **Early remediation.** The Federal Reserve Board is required to establish a regulatory framework for the early remediation of financial weaknesses of covered firms in order to minimize the probability that such companies will become insolvent and the potential harm of such insolvencies to the financial stability of the United States.[116]

Some of these rules have been finalized, while others have not. For example, in October 2012, the Federal Reserve Board issued a final rule implementing the supervisory and company-run stress test requirements.[117] In December 2012, the Federal Reserve Board issued proposed regulations designed to implement enhanced prudential standards and early remediation requirements for foreign banking organizations and foreign nonbank financial companies.[118]

The Federal Reserve Board intends to satisfy some aspects of the Dodd- Frank Act's heightened prudential standards rules for bank holding companies with total consolidated assets of $50 billion or more through implementation of the new Basel Committee on Banking Supervision standards, known as Basel III. The new standards seek to improve the quality of regulatory capital and introduce a new minimum common equity requirement. Basel III also raises the quantity and quality of capital required and introduces capital conservation and countercyclical buffers designed to better ensure that banks have sufficient capital to absorb losses in a future crisis. In addition, Basel III establishes for the first time an international leverage standard for internationally active banks.

Consistent with that intention, in July 2013 FDIC, the Federal Reserve Board, and OCC finalized a rule that revised risk-based and leverage capital requirements for banking organizations.[119] The interim final rule implements a revised definition of regulatory capital, a new common equity Tier 1 minimum capital requirement, a higher minimum Tier 1 capital requirement, and a supplementary leverage ratio that incorporates a broader set of exposures in the denominator.[120]

In addition, in July 2013 FDIC, the Federal Reserve Board, and OCC proposed a rule to establish a new leverage buffer.[121] Specifically, the proposed rule requires bank holding companies with more than $700 billion in consolidated total assets or $10 trillion in assets under custody to maintain a Tier 1 capital leverage buffer of at least 2 percent above the minimum supplementary leverage ratio requirement of 3 percent, for a total of 5 percent. In addition to the leverage buffer for covered bank holding companies, the proposed rule would require insured depository institutions of covered bank holding companies to meet a 6 percent supplementary leverage ratio to be considered "well capitalized" for prompt corrective action purposes.[122] The proposed rule would take effect beginning on January 1, 2018.

CONCLUSION

During the 2007-2009 financial crisis, federal agencies determined that expanding support to insured banks through traditional safety nets—the discount window and deposit insurance—would not be sufficient to stem disruptions to important credit markets. The Federal Reserve System, Treasury, and FDIC introduced new programs to provide general funding support to the financial sector, and some of these programs provided support at the bank holding company level or directly to nonbank financial institutions. These programs helped to improve financial conditions, and bank holding companies and their subsidiaries also experienced individual benefits from participating in particular programs, including liquidity benefits from programs that allowed them to borrow at lower interest rates and at longer maturities than might have been available in the markets. In addition, the Federal Reserve Board granted exemptions to allow banks to channel additional funding support to nonbank financial firms that lacked direct access to the federal safety nets for insured depository institutions. Government assistance to prevent the failures of large financial institutions—such as Fannie Mae, Freddie Mac, and AIG— also benefited bank holding companies, their subsidiaries, and other firms that had large risk exposures to these institutions. While these actions collectively helped to avert a more severe crisis, they raised concerns about moral hazard and the appropriate scope of federal safety nets for the financial sector.

The Dodd-Frank Act contains provisions that aim to restrict future government support for financial institutions, but the effectiveness of these provisions will depend in large part on how agencies implement them. Among other things, the act places new restrictions on the Federal Reserve Board and FDIC's emergency authorities and grants FDIC new resolution authority to resolve a large failing institution outside of the bankruptcy process. While the act continues to allow the Federal Reserve Board to use its authority under Section 13(3) of the Federal Reserve Act to authorize programs with broad-based eligibility, it sets forth new restrictions and requirements for such programs, including a requirement that lending not assist insolvent firms. The act also requires the Federal Reserve Board to establish policies and procedures governing future actions under this authority. As of the date of this report, the Federal Reserve Board has not yet completed its process for drafting these policies and procedures and has not set time frames for doing so. A Federal Reserve Board official indicated that the Board of Governors has focused first on completion of other required regulations that have statutory deadlines and the regulations that are specifically directed at enhancing the safety and soundness of the U.S. financial system. While the act did not set a specific deadline, setting time frames could help ensure more timely completion of these policies and procedures. Moreover, finalizing these procedures could help the Federal Reserve Board to ensure that any future emergency lending does not assist a failing firm and complies with other new requirements. Consistent with the changes to Federal Reserve Board authorities, the act removes FDIC's authority to provide open bank assistance under the systemic risk exception while allowing FDIC (subject to congressional approval) to provide certain assistance through a broadly available program. FDIC continues to work to implement its new resolution authority. The viability and credibility of its resolution process as an alternative to placing a systemically important firm into bankruptcy is a critical part of removing market expectations of future extraordinary government assistance. The act also contains provisions to limit the scope of financial transactions that benefit from access to federal safety nets, although it remains to be seen how these provisions will be implemented. For example, the act could result in fewer regulatory exemptions allowing banks to provide additional funding to their nonbank affiliates. Finally, certain provisions of the act that require the Federal Reserve Board to subject the largest financial firms to heightened prudential standards have not been fully implemented but could reduce the risks that those institutions pose to the financial system.

RECOMMENDATION FOR EXECUTIVE ACTION

To better ensure that the design and implementation of any future emergency lending programs comply with Dodd-Frank Act requirements in a timely manner, we recommend that the Chairman of the Board of Governors of the Federal Reserve System set timeframes for completing the process for drafting policies and procedures governing the use of emergency lending authority under Section 13(3) of the Federal Reserve Act.

AGENCY COMMENTS AND OUR EVALUATION

We provided copies of this draft report to the FDIC, the Federal Reserve Board, FSOC, OCC, and Treasury for their review and comment. We also provided excerpts of the draft report for technical comment to the Federal Housing Finance Agency. All of the agencies provided technical comments, which we have incorporated, as appropriate.

In its written comments the Federal Reserve Board accepted our recommendation and noted that it has made progress toward completing draft policies and procedures governing the use of its emergency lending authority under Section 13(3) of the Federal Reserve Act. The Federal Reserve Board's letter referred to its Chairman's July 2013 remarks on the status of these efforts. The Chairman said that he was hopeful that a final product would be completed relatively soon, perhaps by the end of this year. He further noted that in the meantime, the law is clear about what the Federal Reserve Board can and cannot do. Based on these remarks, we conducted further audit work at the Federal Reserve Board and revised our draft to include additional information about the Federal Reserve Board's progress towards drafting the required policies and procedures. While the Federal Reserve Board has made progress on a draft regulation, it has not set timeframes for completing the drafting process and issuing a final regulation. Setting timeframes for completing draft and final policies and procedures would help to ensure more timely completion of the rulemaking process. Furthermore, while certain restrictions outlined in the act may not require clarification by rulemaking, the Dodd-Frank Act explicitly directs the Federal Reserve Board to draft policies and procedures to help ensure that it complies with the full set of new restrictions and requirements the act imposes on its emergency lending authority.

In its response, the Federal Reserve Board also noted that Federal Reserve System and FDIC assistance was repaid with interest and suggested that it would be helpful for GAO, perhaps in a future report, to analyze the offsetting costs paid by financial institutions assisted through the emergency programs. We note that our draft report contained some information and analyses related to such offsetting costs. In table 1 on pages 14 through 16, we describe the key terms of selected broad-based programs, including interest, fees, and dividends that participating institutions were required to pay for this assistance. Furthermore, our draft report noted that one indicator of the extent to which an institution benefitted from participation in an emergency government program is the relative price of estimated market alternatives to the program. On pages 21 through 29, we report the results of our analyses of the pricing terms of some of the largest programs that provided funding support to bank holding companies and other eligible financial institutions. While past GAO reports have reported on the income earned by the Federal Reserve System, FDIC, and Treasury on their crisis interventions, this information is not relevant to this report's discussion of the support that bank holding companies received during the government's attempt to stabilize the financial system. As we discussed, these government interventions helped to avert a more severe crisis, but raised questions about moral hazard as market participants may expect similar emergency actions in future crises.

Treasury also provided written comments. Treasury noted that the emergency programs discussed in the report were necessary to prevent a collapse of the financial system and that they created economic benefits not only for individual firms, large and small, but also for the financial system and the broader economy.

Treasury also observed that the Dodd-Frank Act reforms discussed in our draft report were consistent with its commitment to ending "too big to fail." In separate comments provided via email, Treasury and FSOC provided suggestions related to the report's analyses of the pricing and utilization of selected emergency programs. In response to these suggestions, we added additional information about the exclusion of observations from our pricing analyses, and added data on average assets per institution to Table 3 in appendix IV, among other changes. Treasury and FSOC also suggested that GAO consider using different benchmarks for analyzing the pricing for the Federal Reserve System's CPFF and FDIC's DGP. While analyses of these suggested benchmarks (short-dated bond prices for CPFF and 2-3 year bond prices for DGP borrowers) could provide useful insights into the robustness of our results, these analyses also have limitations and would not necessarily improve on the analyses of the benchmarks that we conducted. We concluded that the analyses included in our report are appropriate. As noted in the report, while these analyses have limitations, we determined that they are sufficient for our purposes. We note that Federal Reserve System and FDIC staff with whom we discussed our selected benchmarks for these programs agreed that the benchmarks we used in our pricing analysis are appropriate.

Lawrance L. Evans, Jr.
Director, Financial Markets and Community Investment

APPENDIX I: OBJECTIVES, SCOPE AND METHODOLOGY

The objectives of our report were to examine: (1) support banks and bank holding companies received as a result of government efforts to stabilize financial markets during the financial crisis of 2007-2009; and (2) recent statutory and regulatory changes related to government support for banks and bank holding companies and factors that could impact the effectiveness of these changes. In terms of scope, the first section of this report addresses benefits that bank holding companies and their subsidiaries received during the crisis from actual government support provided through emergency actions. It does not address benefits that some financial institutions may have received and may continue to receive from perceived government support. In a second report to be issued in 2014, we will report the results of our examination into whether the largest bank holding companies have received funding cost or other economic advantages as a result of expectations that the government would not allow them to fail.

To address our first objective, we reviewed documents from financial regulatory agencies—the Board of Governors of the Federal Reserve System (Federal Reserve Board), the Federal Deposit Insurance Corporation (FDIC), and the Department of the Treasury (Treasury) and analyzed agency data on emergency government actions to stabilize financial markets. Our review focused on (1) emergency government programs that provided funding support to bank holding companies or their subsidiaries as well as other eligible financial institutions, (2) government actions that provided extraordinary assistance to individual financial institutions, and (3) regulatory exemptions that allowed banks to engage in certain transactions with their nonbank affiliates. To identify the programs that provided the most significant funding support directly to bank holding companies or their subsidiaries, we reviewed program eligibility rules and data on program participation for programs created during the 2007-2009 financial crisis by Treasury, FDIC, and the Federal Reserve System.[123] Specifically, we identified a set of emergency programs created during the crisis that provided at least $10 billion in direct funding support to bank holding companies or their subsidiaries.

We determined that these programs included Treasury's Capital Purchase Program (CPP); FDIC's Temporary Liquidity Guarantee Program (TLGP); and the Federal Reserve System's Term Auction Facility (TAF), Primary Dealer Credit Facility (PDCF), Term Securities Lending Facility (TSLF), and Commercial Paper Funding Facility (CPFF).[124] To describe the purpose, terms, and conditions of these programs and other emergency government actions discussed in our first objective, we reviewed agency documents and included information and analyses from prior GAO work on the Troubled Asset Relief Program (TARP), the Federal Reserve System's emergency programs, and other emergency assistance provided to the financial sector. To obtain perspectives on the benefits that bank holding companies received from emergency government actions, we reviewed papers by staff of regulators and other subject-matter experts and interviewed federal financial regulators, representatives of bank holding companies that received emergency government assistance, and academics. For the Federal Reserve System and FDIC programs that were among the programs that provided the most significant funding support, we compared the pricing and terms of this assistance (such as interest rates and fees) to indicators of funding market conditions during normal and crisis conditions. While this analysis provides a measure of program pricing versus potential market alternatives, it does not produce a precise quantification of the benefits that accrued to participating financial institutions. To determine the extent to which emergency equity support programs, CPP and the Targeted Investment Program (TIP), were priced more generously than estimated market alternatives, we reviewed estimates of the expected budget cost associated with equity funding support programs as well as a valuation analysis commissioned by the Congressional Oversight Panel (COP). For more information about the methodology for our analysis of the pricing and terms of these programs and associated limitations, see appendix III. For programs that provided the most significant direct funding support, to compare the extent to which banking organizations of various sizes used these emergency programs, we calculated the percentage of banking organization assets that were supported by emergency programs—either through capital injections, loans, or guarantees—at quarter-end dates for 2008 through 2012. For more information about our methodology for analyzing program utilization, see appendix IV. Finally, we obtained and analyzed Federal Reserve Board documentation of Federal Reserve Board decisions to grant exemptions to Section 23A of the Federal Reserve Act and approve applications from financial companies to convert to bank holding company status.[125]

To address our second objective, we identified and reviewed relevant statutory provisions, regulations, and agency documents. To identify recent statutory and regulatory changes related to government support for banks and bank holding companies, we reviewed sections of the Dodd- Frank Wall Street Reform and Consumer Protection Act (Dodd-Frank Act) that change rules or create new requirements for safety net programs for insured depository institutions; further restrict the types of financial activities that can be conducted by insured depository institutions or their holding companies; make changes to agencies' emergency authorities to assist or resolve financial institutions; and subject the largest bank holding companies to enhanced regulatory oversight and standards.[126] To corroborate our selection of Dodd-Frank Act provisions, we obtained the views of regulatory officials and financial markets experts on the provisions that are related to government support for banks and bank holding companies. To update the status of agencies' efforts to implement these provisions, we reviewed agencies' proposed and final rules, and interviewed staff from FDIC, the Federal Reserve Board, the Office of the Comptroller of the Currency, and Treasury. We also reviewed relevant congressional testimonies and other public statements by agency officials. We identified statutory provisions or requirements that agencies had not fully implemented and interviewed agency staff about planned steps to complete implementation. To describe factors that could impact the effectiveness of relevant provisions, we reviewed prior GAO work on the potential impacts of Dodd-Frank Act provisions. To obtain additional perspectives on factors that could impact the effectiveness of these provisions, we interviewed and reviewed the public statements and analyses of agency officials, academics, and market experts.

For parts of our work that involved the analysis of computer-processed data, we assessed the reliability of these data and determined that they were sufficiently reliable for our purposes. Data sets for which we conducted data reliability assessments include Federal Reserve Board transaction data for TAF, PDCF, TSLF, and CPFF; Treasury transaction data for CPP and TIP; and FDIC transaction data for TLGP programs (the Debt Guarantee Program and the Transaction Account Guarantee Program). We have relied on Federal Reserve Board and Treasury transaction data for their respective emergency programs for past reports, and we determined that these data were sufficiently reliable for the purpose of presenting and analyzing the pricing and utilization of these programs. To assess the reliability of FDIC's TLGP data, we interviewed FDIC staff about steps they took to maintain the integrity and reliability of program data. We also assessed the reliability of data sources used to provide indicators of the pricing and terms for market alternatives that could have been available to institutions that participated in these programs. These data sources were interbank interest rates (the London Interbank Offered Rate), additional interest rates from the Federal Reserve, credit default swap spreads from Bloomberg, repurchase agreement interest rates from IHS Global Insight, and repurchase agreement haircuts from the Federal Reserve

Bank of New York. To assess the reliability of these data we took a number of steps including inspecting data for missing observations, corroborating interest rate data with other sources, and discussing data with agency officials. We determined these data were sufficiently reliable for measuring market alternatives that might have been available to participants in emergency programs. To calculate the average percentage of assets supported by emergency programs for banking organizations of different sizes, in addition to the program transaction data discussed above, we used Y-9 data for bank holding companies from the Federal Reserve Bank of Chicago, demographic data for bank holding companies and other emergency program participants from the Federal Reserve System's National Information Center and SNL Financial, balance sheet and demographic data for depository institutions from FDIC, and gross domestic product price index data from the Bureau of Economic Analysis. To assess the reliability of these data, we reviewed relevant documentation. In addition, for the Y-9 data for bank holding companies from the Federal Reserve Bank of Chicago and the balance sheet data for depository institutions from FDIC, we conducted electronic testing of key variables.

We conducted this performance audit from January 2013 through November 2013 in accordance with generally accepted government auditing standards. Those standards require that we plan and perform the audit to obtain sufficient, appropriate evidence to provide a reasonable basis for our findings and conclusions based on our audit objectives. We believe that the evidence obtained provides a reasonable basis for our findings and conclusions based on our audit objectives.

Appendix II: Overview of Selected Federal Government Programs That Provided Emergency Funding Support to Banking Entities during the 2007-2009 Financial Crisis

During the financial crisis, the Federal Reserve System, Treasury, and FDIC introduced new programs with broad-based eligibility to provide general funding support to the banking sector and stabilize the financial system. Federal government interventions that provided the most significant direct funding support to U.S. bank holding companies or their subsidiaries were:

- the Federal Reserve System's credit and liquidity programs;[127]
- Treasury's capital investments through the Troubled Asset Relief Program; and
- FDIC's guarantees of certain newly issued debt and previously uninsured deposits through the Temporary Liquidity Guarantee Program (TLGP).

The first of these interventions occurred in late 2007 when the Federal Reserve System modified discount window terms and launched a new program to auction discount window loans to banks to address strains in interbank credit markets.

- *Discount window.* In August 2007, the cost of term funding (loans provided at terms of 1 month or longer) spiked suddenly—primarily due to investor concerns about banks' actual exposures to various mortgage-related securities—and commercial banks increasingly had to borrow overnight to meet their funding needs.[128] The Federal Reserve Board feared that the disorderly functioning of interbank lending markets would impair the ability of commercial banks to provide credit to households and businesses. To ease stresses in these markets, on August 17, 2007, the Federal Reserve Board approved two temporary changes to discount window terms: (1) a reduction of the discount rate—the interest rate at which the Reserve Banks extended collateralized loans at the discount window—by 50 basis points; and (2) an extension of the discount window lending term from overnight to up to 30 days, with the possibility of renewal.[129] This change initially resulted in little additional borrowing from the discount window. After subsiding in October 2007, tensions in term funding markets reappeared in late November, possibly driven by a seasonal contraction in the supply of year-end funding.

- *Term Auction Facility (TAF).* On December 12, 2007, the Federal Reserve Board announced the creation of TAF to address continuing disruptions in U.S. term interbank lending markets.[130] TAF provided term funding to depository institutions eligible to borrow from the discount window.[131] In contrast to the traditional discount window program, which loaned funds to individual institutions at the discount rate, TAF auctioned loans to many eligible institutions at once at a market-determined interest rate. Federal Reserve Board officials noted that one important advantage of this auction approach was that it could address concerns among eligible borrowers about the perceived stigma of discount window borrowing. TAF was the largest Federal Reserve System emergency program in terms of the dollar amount of funding support provided, with TAF loans outstanding peaking at $493 billion in March 2009.

In March 2008, the Federal Reserve Board invoked its emergency authority under Section 13(3) of the Federal Reserve Act to authorize two new programs to support repurchase agreement markets—large, short- term collateralized funding markets—that many financial institutions rely on to finance a wide range of securities.[132] The Federal Reserve Board limited eligibility for these programs to the primary dealers, a designated group of broker-dealers and banks that transact with the Federal Reserve Bank of New York (FRBNY) in its conduct of open market operations.[133] Many of the primary dealers are subsidiaries of U.S. bank holding companies or large foreign banking organizations.

- *Term Securities Lending Facility (TSLF).* On March 11, 2008, the Federal Reserve Board announced the creation of TSLF to auction 28-day loans of U.S. Treasury securities to primary dealers to increase the amount of high-quality collateral available for these dealers to borrow against in the repurchase agreement markets. In early March, the Federal Reserve Board found that repurchase agreement lenders were requiring higher haircuts for loans against a range of securities and were becoming reluctant to lend against mortgage-related securities. As a result, many financial institutions increasingly had to rely on higher-quality collateral, such as U.S. Treasury securities, to obtain cash in these markets, and a shortage of such high quality collateral emerged. Through competitive auctions that allowed dealers to bid a fee to exchange harder-to-finance collateral for easier-to-finance Treasury securities, TSLF was intended to promote confidence among lenders and to reduce the need for dealers to sell illiquid assets into the markets, which could have further depressed the prices of these assets. The market value of TSLF securities loans outstanding peaked at $236 billion in October 2008.

- *Primary Dealer Credit Facility (PDCF).* On March 16, 2008, the Federal Reserve Board announced the creation of PDCF to provide overnight collateralized cash loans to the primary dealers. In the days following the March 11 announcement of TSLF, one of the primary dealers, Bear Stearns, experienced a run on its liquidity.[134] Because the first TSLF auction would not be held until later that month, Federal Reserve Board and FRBNY staff worked to ready PDCF for launch by Monday, March 17, 2008, when Federal Reserve Board officials feared a Bear Stearns bankruptcy announcement might trigger runs on the liquidity of other primary dealers. Although the Bear Stearns bankruptcy was averted, PDCF commenced operation on March 17, 2008.[135] Eligible PDCF collateral initially included collateral eligible for open-market operations as well as investment-grade corporate securities, municipal securities, and asset-backed securities, including private label mortgage-backed securities. The Federal Reserve Board later expanded eligible collateral types for both TSLF and PDCF.

In late 2008, the bankruptcy of Lehman Brothers triggered an intensification of the crisis and the Federal Reserve System, Treasury and FDIC took a range of new actions to provide additional support to financial institutions and key credit markets.

- Federal Reserve System actions. In September and October 2008, the Federal Reserve Board modified its existing programs, launched new programs, and took other actions to address worsening market conditions.
- *Modifications to TSLF, PDCF, and TAF.* On September 14, 2008, shortly before Lehman Brothers announced it would file for bankruptcy, the Federal Reserve Board announced changes to TSLF and PDCF to provide expanded liquidity support to primary dealers. Specifically, the Federal Reserve Board announced that TSLF-eligible collateral would be expanded to include all investment-grade debt securities and PDCF-eligible collateral would be expanded to include all securities eligible to be pledged in the tri-party repurchase agreements system, including noninvestment grade securities and equities.[136] On September 29, 2008, the Federal Reserve Board also announced expanded support through TAF by doubling the amount of funds that would be available in each TAF auction cycle from $150 billion to $300 billion.
    - *Commercial Paper Funding Facility (CPFF).* On October 7, 2008, the Federal Reserve Board announced the creation of CPFF under its Section 13(3) authority to provide a liquidity backstop to U.S. issuers of commercial paper. Commercial paper is an important source of short-term funding for U.S. financial and nonfinancial businesses.[137] CPFF became operational on October 27, 2008, and was operated by FRBNY. In the weeks leading up to CPFF's announcement, the commercial paper markets showed signs of strain: the volume of commercial paper outstanding declined, interest rates on longer-term commercial paper increased significantly, and increasing amounts of commercial paper were issued on an overnight basis as money-market funds and other investors became reluctant to purchase commercial paper at longer-dated maturities. By standing

ready to purchase eligible commercial paper, CPFF was intended to eliminate much of the risk that commercial paper issuers would be unable to issue new commercial paper to replace their maturing commercial paper obligations.

- *Other actions*. The Federal Reserve System launched other new programs that provided liquidity support for other market participants, but did not serve a major source of direct support for U.S. bank holding companies or their subsidiaries.[138]

- *Troubled Asset Relief Program*. On October 3, 2008, the Emergency Economic Stabilization Act of 2008 (EESA) was signed into law to help stem the financial crisis.[139] EESA provided Treasury with the authority to create the Troubled Asset Relief Program (TARP), under which it could buy or guarantee up to almost $700 billion of the "troubled assets" that it deemed to be at the heart of the crisis, including mortgages, mortgage-backed securities, and any other financial instruments, such as equity investments. Treasury created the Capital Purchase Program (CPP) in October 2008 to provide capital to viable financial institutions by using its authority to purchase preferred shares and subordinated debt. In return for its investments, Treasury received dividend or interest payments and warrants.[140] On October 14, 2008, Treasury allocated $250 billion of the original $700 billion in overall TARP funds for CPP. The allocation was subsequently reduced in March 2009 to reflect lower estimated funding needs, as evidenced by actual participation rates. The program was closed to new investments on December 31, 2009. Smaller capital infusion programs included the Targeted Investment Program (TIP) and the Community Development Capital Initiative (CDCI).
- *Temporary Liquidity Guarantee Program*. In October 2008, FDIC created TLGP to complement the Federal Reserve and Treasury programs in restoring confidence in financial institutions and repairing their capacity to meet the credit needs of American households and businesses.[141] TLGP's Debt Guarantee Program (DGP) was designed to improve liquidity in term-funding markets by guaranteeing certain newly issued senior unsecured debt of financial institutions and their holding companies. By guaranteeing payment of these debt obligations, DGP was intended to address the difficulty that creditworthy institutions were facing in replacing maturing debt because of risk aversion in the markets. TLGP's Transaction Account Guarantee Program (TAGP) also was created to stabilize an important source of liquidity for many financial institutions. TAGP temporarily extended an unlimited deposit guarantee to certain noninterest-bearing transaction accounts to assure holders of the safety of these deposits and limit further outflows. By facilitating access to borrowed funds at lower rates, Treasury, FDIC, and the Federal Reserve expected TLGP to free up funding for banks to make loans to creditworthy businesses and consumers. Furthermore, by promoting stable funding sources for financial institutions, they intended TLGP to help avert bank and thrift failures that would impose costs on the insurance fund and taxpayers and potentially contribute to a worsening of the crisis.

Appendix III: Methodology for Analysis of Pricing and Terms for Financial Stability Programs

Although imperfect, one indicator of the extent to which an institution benefited from participation in an emergency program is the relative price of estimated market alternatives to the program. To determine how pricing of the emergency assistance compared to market rates, we compared the interest rates and fees charged by the Federal Reserve and FDIC for participation in the emergency lending and guarantee programs with market alternatives that might have been available to program participants. We considered a number of potential indicators of market interest rates available to financial institutions, including a survey of interbank interest rates (the London Interbank Offered Rate or LIBOR), commercial paper interest rates published by the Federal Reserve Board, spreads on bank credit default swaps (CDS), and interest rates on repurchase agreements. These interest rates and spreads provide a general indication of market alternatives available to participants but are imperfect and hence unlikely to reflect available alternatives for all participants at all points in time. For example, participants' access to market alternatives may have been limited, there may be only limited data on the relevant private market, or market alternatives could vary across participants in ways that we do not observe in the data. Furthermore, once programs were introduced, they probably influenced the price of market alternatives, making it difficult to interpret differences between program pricing to contemporary market pricing while programs were active. Where possible—when programs had pricing rules (PDCF, CPFF, and DGP)—we applied program pricing rules during time periods that were not influenced by the program itself to compare program pricing with counterfactual market prices. By choosing high and low financial stress time periods, we can estimate the extent to which participants may have benefitted from program pricing during the financial crisis as well as the extent to which program pricing became less attractive as financial conditions returned to normal.

Programs with auction-based pricing (TAF and TSLF) raise particular challenges in interpreting differences between program pricing and market pricing. Under certain assumptions, bidders would bid program pricing up to their market alternatives, which could limit potential benefits from the program as well as eliminate any difference between program and market pricing.[142] In addition, without a pricing rule we cannot apply pricing for auction-based programs to high or low financial stress time periods not influenced by the program itself—in other words, contemporaneous pricing is contaminated by the program itself, making it difficult to determine the true market alternative. As a result, deviations between program and market pricing could indicate differences in terms rather than a benefit to participating financial institutions. These challenges suggest that our estimates of the difference between program and market pricing for auction-based programs should be interpreted with caution. TAF and TSLF also had minimum pricing determined by the Federal Reserve that was prescribed when auctions were undersubscribed. In these instances prices were no longer auction- determined in the traditional sense although the outcome of the auction (undersubscription) determined when the minimum pricing would apply.

It is important to note that, among other limitations, our indicators do not capture all the benefits associated with program participation. Because our proxies for market alternatives are imperfect, market prices appear on occasion to be lower than emergency program pricing despite significant participation by financial institutions at these times. Participation by itself suggests that program prices and/or terms were relatively attractive in comparison to available alternatives—benefits could arise from price, quantity available, or other nonprice characteristics of the assistance (loan term, eligible collateral, etc.). Therefore, we discarded values of spreads between program pricing and market alternatives when they were zero or negative since negative spreads are unlikely to capture the benefits that accrued to participants. If these truly reflected market alternatives for the pool of potential participants, then there would be no participation or the participation would have been based on other nonprice considerations. We assume that the true (unobserved) market alternatives overlap at times with our observed proxies. At other times the market alternatives we are able to observe and measure may not overlap with the true market alternatives for participants (including when observed market alternatives indicate programs are more expensive than market rates).

Because PDCF operated similarly to repurchase agreement markets, we compared collateral haircuts in PDCF with select asset classes in the triparty (intermediated by a clearing bank) repurchase agreement markets. We selected those asset classes where we were able to draw clear parallels between categories of collateral allowed under PDCF and categories identified in data based on private repurchase agreement market we received from the Federal Reserve Bank of New York. The haircut is an important loan term in repurchase agreement contracts and collateralized lending, the amount of additional collateral required over the value of the loan that is required to secure the loan. Securities with greater risk or less liquidity generally have larger haircuts (i.e., more collateral is required). PDCF borrowers might have utilized triparty repurchase agreement markets for alternative sources of secured borrowing during the 2007-2009 financial crisis.

To determine the extent to which emergency equity support programs, CPP and TIP, were priced more generously than estimated market alternatives, we reviewed estimates of the expected budget cost associated with equity funding support programs as well as a valuation analysis commissioned by the Congressional Oversight Panel (COP). The benefits that accrued to banks from participation in equity funding support programs are likely to be proportional to the subsidy rates estimated for accounting purposes. Estimates of subsidy rates are based on a net present value analysis—the price and terms which are offered by a federal agency are compared to the lifetime expected cost (net present value) of the equity and the difference is known as a subsidy. Because private market participants might have charged a price based on a comparable net present value analysis, banks would have benefitted to the extent that the prices offered by Treasury for their equity exceed what they were likely to receive based on the net present value. The valuation analysis commissioned by COP explicitly compared the prices received by Treasury with market-based valuations of similar securities. We assume that the net present values estimated for accounting purposes by Treasury and CBO are reasonable proxies for the market valuations that are more directly estimated in the COP analysis. We used the earliest available estimates from the Congressional Budget Office (CBO) and Treasury as they were closest to market conditions at the time that programs were initiated. Estimates of these subsidy rates depended on timing and market conditions and the size of these subsidy rates likely fell over time as market conditions improved.

APPENDIX IV: USE OF FINANCIAL STABILITY PROGRAMS BY BANKING ORGANIZATIONS OF DIFFERENT SIZES

Data

Emergency government programs to stabilize financial markets resulted in funding support to bank holding companies and insured depository institutions (collectively, banking organizations) of various sizes.[143] To compare use of emergency funding programs by banking organizations of different sizes, we analyzed quarterly data on bank holding companies and depository institutions for the period from 2008 to 2012 along with data on emergency program transactions that occurred during that period. We used quarterly balance sheet and demographic data on bank holding companies for the period from the first quarter of 2008 through the fourth quarter of 2012 from the Federal Reserve Bank of Chicago and the Federal Reserve System's National Information Center (NIC), quarterly balance sheet and demographic data on depository institutions from FDIC for the period from the first quarter of 2008 through the fourth quarter of 2012, and quarterly data on the GDP price index from the Bureau of Economic Analysis (BEA) for the period from the first quarter of 2008 through the fourth quarter of 2012. We also used data on Debt Guarantee Program (DGP) and TAGP transactions from FDIC, data on Commercial Paper Funding Facility, Primary Dealer Credit Facility, TAF, and TSLF transactions from the Board of Governors of the Federal Reserve System, and data on CPP and TIP transactions from the U.S. Department of the Treasury. Finally, we used demographic data on emergency funding program participants obtained from NIC and from SNL Financial.

Methodology

We organized depository institutions and bank holding companies into groups—hereafter banking organizations—based on their regulatory high holder (the highest holding company in a tiered organization), where depository institutions or bank holding companies that did not indicate a high holder are assumed to be their own high holder. We calculated consolidated assets for each banking organization, excluding banking organizations for which we cannot reliably calculate consolidated assets. We excluded banking organizations with a high holder that was not in our data, e.g., banking organizations with foreign high holders. For banking organizations with a high holder that was in our data and that included at least one bank holding company, we excluded those for which the high holder did not report consolidated assets, those for which the high holder reported consolidated assets but they were less than its parent-only assets, those for which the high holder's consolidated assets were less than consolidated assets reported by some other bank holding company in the organization, those for which none of the bank holding companies reported consolidated assets, and those that did not contain any depository institutions. For all remaining banking organizations that contained at least one bank holding company, we set consolidated assets for the group equal to consolidated assets reported by the high holder. Note that consolidated assets for a bank holding company include the assets of all consolidated subsidiaries, which generally include all companies for which the bank holding company owns more than 50 percent of the outstanding voting stock. For banking organizations with a high holder in our data that did not include a bank holding company, such as standalone depository institutions, we set consolidated assets for the banking organization equal to the depository institution's consolidated assets.

Table 3. Numbers and average assets of banking organizations in analysis sample by size and quarter, June 30, 2008 to December 31, 2012

Quarter		Banking organization in analysis sample						
		Assets less than $500 million	Assets $500 million to 1 billion	Assets $1 to 10 billion	Assets $10 to 50 billion	Assets $50 to 250 billion	Assets $250 billion or more	organizations excluded from
2008q2	Number	5,824	686	536	59	20	8	256
	Average assets	$0.15	$0.69	$2.59	$19.91	$114.48	$1,089.51	—
2008q4	Number	5,746	674	546	61	15	8	269
	Average assets	$0.15	$0.69	$2.52	$19.29	$111.59	$1,134.68	—
2009q2	Number	5,687	676	554	60	18	9	264
	Average assets	$0.16	$0.69	$2.48	$18.12	$119.98	$1,184.69	—
2009q4	Number	5,595	681	540	57	19	9	264
	Average assets	$0.16	$0.69	$2.48	$18.05	$117.11	$1,183.91	—
2010q2	Number	5,520	671	528	53	20	9	261
	Average assets	$0.16	$0.69	$2.49	$18.25	$114.96	$1,207.20	—
2010q4	Number	5,448	648	520	53	20	10	262
	Average assets	$0.16	$0.69	$2.51	$18.42	$104.81	$1,123.85	—
2011q2	Number	5,377	644	512	54	19	10	255
	Average assets	$0.16	$0.69	$2.47	$19.31	$109.30	$1,144.96	—
2011q4	Number	5,287	628	514	54	18	10	256
	Average assets	$0.16	$0.69	$2.50	$19.81	$117.06	$1,119.79	—
2012q2	Number	5,215	632	506	55	17	11	251
	Average assets	$0.16	$0.69	$2.50	$19.86	$108.07	$1,055.56	—
2012q4	Number	5,076	634	505	55	16	10	248
	Average assets	$0.17	$0.69	$2.59	$20.92	$113.98	$1,091.00	—

Source: GAO analysis of BEA, FDIC, and Federal Reserve data.

Note: Assets are adjusted for inflation and expressed in fourth quarter 2012 dollars. We do not report average assets for banking organizations we excluded from the analysis sample because the banking organizations we excluded from the analysis sample are the ones for which we could not reliably calculate consolidated assets.

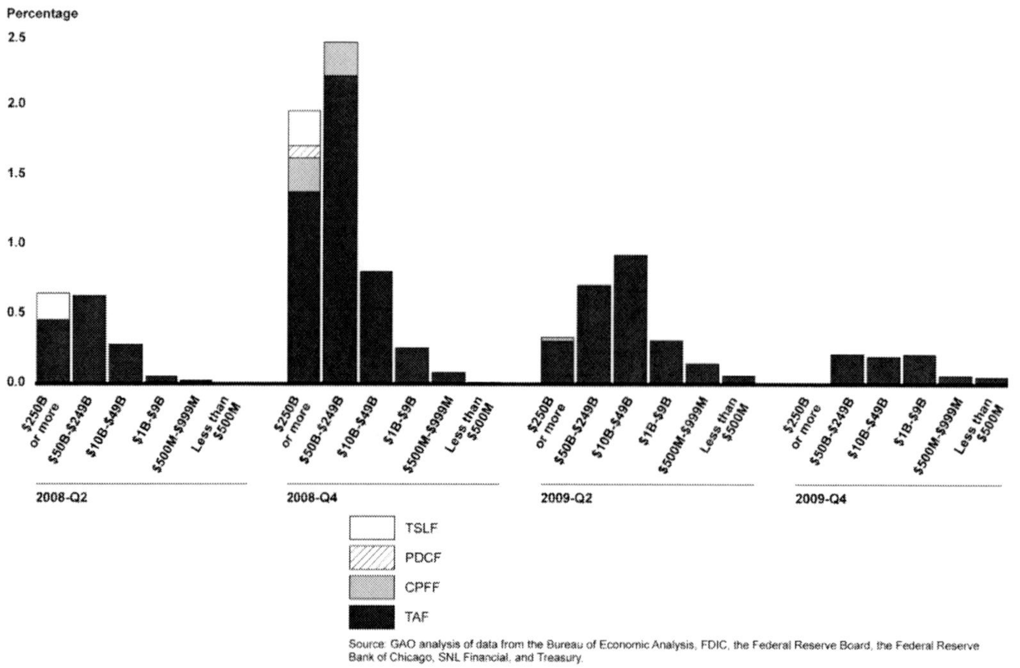

Source: GAO analysis of data from the Bureau of Economic Analysis, FDIC, the Federal Reserve Board, the Federal Reserve Bank of Chicago, SNL Financial, and Treasury.

Note: Banking organizations include consolidated top-tier U.S. bank holding companies and standalone depository institutions. Assets for bank holding companies are consolidated assets for the top-tier bank holding company, which include the assets of consolidated subsidiaries. Assets for standalone depository institutions are consolidated assets for the institution. We exclude banking organizations for which we could not reliably calculate consolidated assets. Banking organizations are divided into groups each quarter using consolidated assets that were first adjusted for inflation and measured in fourth quarter 2012 dollars. Size groups include banking organizations with assets equal to the lower bound but do not include banking organizations with assets equal to the upper bound. For example, banking organizations with $50 billion in assets would be in the "$50-250 billion" group, not the "$10-50 billion" group.

Figure 3. Average CPFF, PDCF, TAF, and TSLF Loan Amounts Outstanding as a Percentage of Assets at Quarter-End for Banking Organizations by Size, June 30, 2008, through December 31, 2012.

Banking organizations for which we could reliably calculate consolidated assets constitute our analysis sample. Small bank holding companies (those with assets less than $500 million) generally report their consolidated assets in the second and fourth quarters of each year, but they generally do not do so in the first and third quarters of each year. To maintain consistency in the composition of the analysis sample over time, we ultimately used results for only the second and fourth quarters of each year from 2008 to 2012. Companies that converted to bank holding companies during the crisis are included in our analysis only for the quarters for which they filed financial statements for bank holding companies with the Federal Reserve. For example, both Goldman Sachs Group, Inc. and Morgan Stanley became bank holding companies in September 2008 but neither filed form FR Y-9C, the source of our data on consolidated assets for large bank holding companies, until the first quarter of 2009. As a result, these two companies are not part of our analysis sample until 2009. We assigned banking organizations in our analysis sample to one of six size groups based on their consolidated assets, adjusted for inflation and expressed in fourth quarter 2012 dollars: less than $500 million; at least $500 million and less than $1 billion; at least $1 billion and less than $10 billion; at least $10 billion and less than $50 billion; at least $50 billion and less than $250 billion; and $250 billion or more. Table 3 shows the numbers of banking organizations in our analysis sample by size group and the numbers of banking organizations excluded from our analysis sample for the second and fourth quarters of each year from 2008 to 2012.

For each banking organization in our analysis sample, we calculated the percentage of assets funded by capital provided, loans provided, and liabilities guaranteed by emergency programs at quarter-end for the second and fourth quarters of 2008 through 2012. Capital provided by emergency programs includes capital investments by Treasury under CPP and TIP. Loans provided by emergency programs include TAF, TSLF, PDCF, and CPFF loans from the Federal Reserve System. Funding guaranteed by emergency programs includes deposits guaranteed by FDIC through TAGP and debt guaranteed by FDIC through DGP. To compare the extent to which banking organizations of various sizes used emergency programs, we calculated the percentage of banking organization assets that were supported by emergency programs—either through capital injections, loans, or guarantees—at quarter-end dates from mid-2008 through the end of 2012. In addition, for each of the three types of support, we decomposed average support as a percentage of assets for banking organizations of different sizes into its two components: (1) the rate of participation in emergency programs by banking organizations of different sizes as measured by the percentage of banking organizations using funds provided or guaranteed by the emergency programs and (2) average support as a percentage of assets for those participants.

Results

Federal Reserve System programs. TAF was established in December 2007, PDCF and TSLF were established in March 2008, and CPFF began purchasing commercial paper in October 2008. As of the end of 2008, combined CPFF, PDCF, TAF, and TSLF loans outstanding ranged from about 0.01 percent of assets on average for all banking organizations with less than $500 million in assets to about 2.5 percent of assets on average for all banking organizations with at least $50 billion but less than $250 billion in assets (see figure 3). For banking organizations with $250 billion or more in assets, combined CPFF, PDCF, TAF, and TSLF loans outstanding were about 2.0 percent of assets on average. As of mid-2009, loans outstanding for these four programs combined had declined to less than 1 percent of assets on average for banking organizations of all sizes, and as of the end of 2009, they had declined to less than half a percent of assets on average.

Through mid-2009, the larger banking organizations participated in the four Federal Reserve System programs we analyzed at higher rates than smaller banking organizations (see Panel A of table 4). However, by the end of 2009, banking organizations with $250 billion or more in assets had completely exited all of these programs, but of the remaining institutions, larger banking organizations continued to participate at higher rates than smaller banking organizations. These programs all closed in the first quarter of 2010.[144]

Table 4. Participation Rates and Average Loan Amounts Outstanding as a Percent of Assets at Quarter-End for Participating Banking Organizations for CPFF, PDCF, TAF, and TSLF, June 30, 2008 through December 31, 2009

A. Percent of banking organizations participating in CPFF, PDCF, TAF, or TSLF (%)						
Quarter	**Assets <\$500M**	**Assets ≥\$500M, <\$1B**	**Assets ≥\$1B, <\$10B**	**Assets ≥\$10B, <\$50B**	**Assets ≥\$50B, <\$250B**	**Assets ≥\$250B**
2008q2	0.03	0.58	2.24	11.86	30.00	75.00
2008q4	0.19	1.78	6.04	26.23	60.00	75.00
2009q2	0.83	3.25	8.48	25.00	38.89	44.44
2009q4	0.66	1.91	5.56	7.02	10.53	0
B. Average CPFF, PDCF, TAF, and TSLF loans outstanding as a percent of assets for participating banking organizations (%)						
Quarter	**Assets <\$500M**	**Assets ≥\$500M, <\$1B**	**Assets ≥\$1B, <\$10B**	**Assets ≥\$10B, <\$50B**	**Assets ≥\$50B, <\$250B**	**Assets ≥\$250B**
2008q2	8.46	4.30	2.41	2.39	2.11	0.87
2008q4	5.99	4.76	4.27	3.08	4.09	2.61
2009q2	7.56	4.60	3.69	3.70	1.83	0.76
2009q4	7.94	3.31	3.91	2.86	2.09	N/A

Source: GAO analysis of data from BEA, FDIC, the Federal Reserve Board, the Federal Reserve Bank of Chicago, SNL Financial, and Treasury.

Note: Banking organizations include consolidated top-tier U.S. bank holding companies and standalone depository institutions. Assets for bank holding companies are consolidated assets for the top-tier bank holding company, which include the assets of consolidated subsidiaries. Assets for standalone depository institutions are consolidated assets for the institution. We exclude banking organizations for which we could not reliably calculate consolidated assets. Banking organizations are divided into groups each quarter using consolidated assets that were first adjusted for inflation and measured in fourth quarter 2012 dollars. The participation rate is the percentage of banking organizations with CPFF, PDCF, TAF, or TSLF loans outstanding at quarter-end.

Among banking organizations that participated in at least one of the four Federal Reserve programs, average combined CPFF, PDCF, TAF, and TSLF loans outstanding as a percentage of assets were generally larger for smaller participants (see Panel B of table 4). As of the end of 2008, among participating banking organizations, combined CPFF, PDCF, TAF, and TSLF loans outstanding ranged from about 2.6 percent of assets on average for participants with \$250 billion or more in assets to about 6.0 percent of assets on average for participants with less than \$500 million in assets. As of the end of 2009, combined CPFF, PDCF, TAF, and TSLF loans outstanding ranged from about 2.1 percent of assets for participants with at least \$50 billion but less than \$250 billion in assets to about 7.9 percent of assets for banking organizations with less than \$500 million in assets, while banking organizations with \$250 billion or more in assets were no longer participating in these programs.

Treasury capital investments. Treasury began making equity investments in banking organizations through CPP in October 2008 and it established TIP in December 2008. As of the end of 2008, CPP investment amounts outstanding ranged from about 0.01 percent of assets on average for banking organizations with less than $500 million in assets to about 1.9 percent of assets on average for banking organizations with at least $50 billion but less than $250 billion in assets (see figure 4). CPP and TIP investment amounts outstanding for banking organizations with $250 billion or more were about 1.6 percent of assets on average.[145] As of mid-2010, banking organizations with $250 billion or more in assets had repaid Treasury and exited CPP and TIP. At the same time, CPP investment amounts had fallen to less than 1 percent of assets on average for banking organizations in all smaller size groups. As of the nd of 2012, banking organizations with at least $50 billion but less than $250 billion in assets had repaid Treasury and exited CPP, and CPP investment amounts had fallen to less than 0.25 percent of assets on average for banking organizations in all smaller size groups.[146]

Table 5. Participation Rates and Average Investment Amounts Outstanding as a Percentage of Assets at Quarter-End for Participating Banking Organizations for CPP and TIP, December 31, 2008 to December 31, 2012

A. Percent of banking organizations participating in CPP or TIP at quarter-end (%)						
Quarter	**Assets <$500M**	**Assets ≥$500M, <$1B**	**Assets ≥$1B, <$10B**	**Assets ≥$10B, <$50B**	**Assets ≥$50B, <$250B**	**Assets ≥$250B**
2008q4	0.49	4.30	14.65	37.70	80.00	87.50
2009q2	4.57	17.46	25.81	41.67	50.00	44.44
2009q4	5.20	16.89	25.93	36.84	52.63	11.11
2010q2	5.22	17.14	25.38	33.96	35.00	0.00
2010q4	4.75	16.98	23.46	18.87	35.00	0.00
2011q2	4.72	17.24	21.68	16.67	15.79	0.00
2011q4	3.42	10.03	14.59	12.96	16.67	0.00
2012q2	3.32	9.18	10.47	10.91	11.76	0.00
2012q4	2.36	5.68	6.53	5.45	0.00	0.00
B. Average CPP and TIP investment amounts outstanding as a percent of assets at quarter-end for participating banking organizations (%)						
Quarter	**Assets <$500M**	**Assets ≥$500M, <$1B**	**Assets ≥$1B, <$10B**	**Assets ≥$10B, <$50B**	**Assets ≥$50B, <$250B**	**Assets ≥$250B**
2008q4	2.25	2.08	2.22	2.33	2.38	1.79
2009q2	2.14	2.12	2.10	2.31	2.86	2.27
2009q4	2.32	2.11	2.09	2.25	2.88	2.81
2010q2	2.28	2.10	2.10	2.24	2.81	N/A
2010q4	2.32	2.10	2.16	2.39	2.71	N/A
2011q2	2.30	2.14	2.16	2.36	1.96	N/A
2011q4	2.42	2.35	2.28	2.34	1.96	N/A
2012q2	2.47	2.38	2.38	2.44	0.89	N/A
2012q4	2.65	2.56	2.66	2.86	N/A	N/A

Source: GAO analysis of data from BEA, FDIC, the Federal Reserve Board, the Federal Reserve Bank of Chicago, and Treasury.

Note: Banking organizations include consolidated top-tier U.S. bank holding companies and standalone depository institutions. Assets for bank holding companies are consolidated assets for the top-tier bank holding company, which include the assets of consolidated subsidiaries. Assets for standalone depository institutions are consolidated assets for the institution. We exclude banking organizations for which we could not reliably calculate consolidated assets. Banking organizations are divided into groups each quarter using consolidated assets that were first adjusted for inflation and measured in fourth quarter 2012 dollars. The participation rate is the percentage of banking organizations with CPP or TIP amounts outstanding at quarter-end.

At the end of 2008, participation rates in CPP and TIP were higher for larger banking organizations and ranged from about 0.5 percent for banking organizations with less than $500 million in assets to about 87.5 percent for banking organizations with $250 billion or more in assets (see Panel A of Table 5). As of the end of 2010, all banking organizations with $250 billion or more in assets had repaid Treasury and were no longer participating in CPP or TIP. For banking organizations that continued to participate in CPP, participation rates ranged from about 4.8 percent for banking organizations with less than $500 million in assets to 35 percent for banking organizations with at least $50 billion but less than $250 billion in assets. As of the end of 2012, all banking organizations with $50 billion or more had exited CPP and TIP. For banking organizations that continued to participate in CPP, participation rates ranged from about 2.4 percent for banking organizations with less than $500 million in assets to about 6.5 percent for banking organizations with $1-10 billion in assets (see Panel A of table 5). For participating banking organizations of all sizes, average CPP and TIP amounts outstanding were 2 to 3 percent of assets in most quarters (see Panel B of table 5).

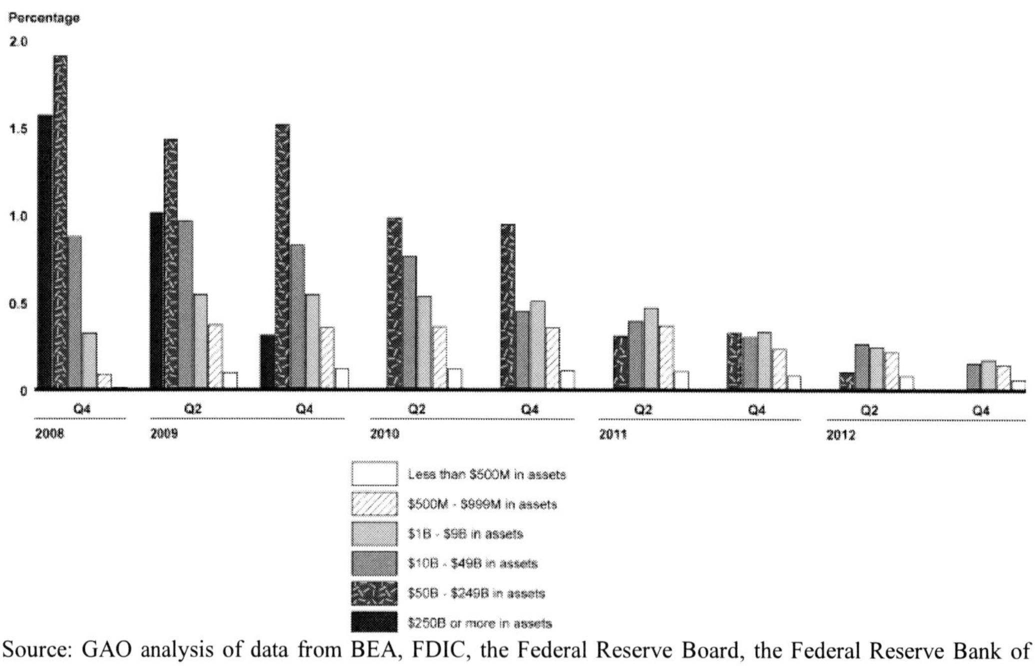

Source: GAO analysis of data from BEA, FDIC, the Federal Reserve Board, the Federal Reserve Bank of Chicago, SNL Financial and Treasury.

Note: Banking organizations include consolidated top-tier U.S. bank holding companies and standalone depository institutions. Assets for bank holding companies are consolidated assets for the top-tier bank holding company, which include the assets of consolidated subsidiaries. Assets for standalone depository institutions are consolidated assets for the institution. We exclude banking organizations for which we could not reliably calculate consolidated assets. Banking organizations are divided into groups each quarter using consolidated assets that were first adjusted for inflation and measured in fourth quarter 2012 dollars. Size groups include banking organizations with assets equal to the lower bound but do not include banking organizations with assets equal to the upper bound. For example, banking organizations with $50 billion in assets would be in the "$50-250 billion" group, not the "$10-50 billion" group.

Figure 4. Average CPP and TIP Investment Amounts Outstanding as a Percentage of Assets at Quarter-End for All Banking Organizations by Size, December 31, 2008 through December 31, 2012.

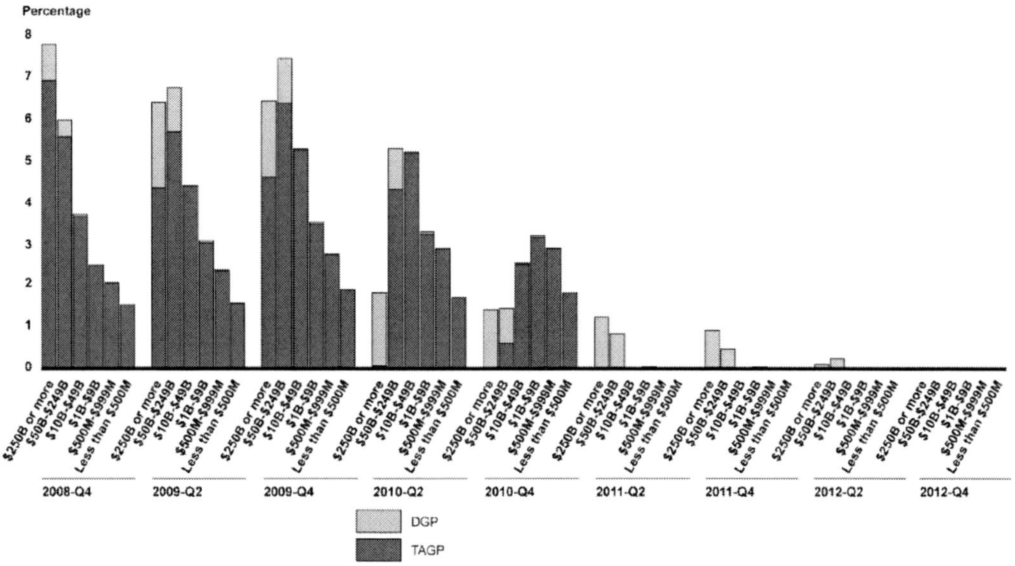

Source: GAO analysis of data from BEA, FDIC, the Federal Reserve Board, the Federal Reserve Bank of Chicago,SNL Financial and Treasury

Note: Banking organizations include consolidated top-tier U.S. bank holding companies and standalone depository institutions. Assets for bank holding companies are consolidated assets for the top-tier bank holding company, which include the assets of consolidated subsidiaries. Assets for standalone depository institutions are consolidated assets for the institution. We exclude banking organizations for which we could not reliably calculate consolidated assets. Banking organizations are divided into groups each quarter using consolidated assets that were first adjusted for inflation and measured in fourth quarter 2012 dollars. Size groups include banking organizations with assets equal to the lower bound but do not include banking organizations with assets equal to the upper bound. For example, banking organizations with $50 billion in assets would be in the "$50-250 billion" group, not the "$10-50 billion" group.

Figure 5. Average DGP-Guaranteed Debt and TAGP-Guaranteed Deposits Outstanding as a Percentage of Assets at Quarter- End for All Banking Organizations by Size, December 31, 2008, through December 31, 2012.

FDIC's TLGP. FDIC implemented DGP and TAGP, the two components of TLGP, in October 2008. As of the end of 2008, average DGP- guaranteed debt and TAGP-guaranteed deposit amounts outstanding altogether as a percentage of assets were higher for larger banking organizations than smaller banking organizations and ranged from about 1.5 percent of assets on average for banking organizations with less than $500 million in assets to 7.7 percent of assets on average for banking organizations with $250 billion or more in assets (see figure 5). By the end of 2010, differences in utilization of DGP and TAGP across banking organizations of different sizes had diminished somewhat, with DGP- guaranteed debt and TAGP-guaranteed deposit amounts outstanding altogether ranging from 1.4 percent for banking organizations with $250 billion or more in assets to about 3.2 percent for banking organizations with at least $1 billion but less than $10 billion in assets. TAGP expired on December 31, 2010, and by the end of 2011, DGP-guaranteed debt amounts outstanding were less than 1 percent of assets on average for banking organizations of all sizes. DGP expired on December 31, 2012, so none of the assets of any banking organization were funded using DGP-guaranteed debt after that date.

In general, 50 percent or more of the banking organizations in every size group were using either DGP-guaranteed debt or TAGP-guaranteed deposits (or both) as funding through the end of 2010 (see Panel A of table 6). At the end of 2008, participation rates ranged from about 66.3 percent for banking organizations with less than $500 million in assets to about 92.9 percent for banking organizations with at least $1 billion but less than $10 billion in assets. At the end of 2010, participation rates ranged from about 50 percent for banking organizations with at least $50 billion but less than $250 billion in assets to 100 percent for banking organizations with $250 billion or more in assets. Participation rates for banking organizations with less than $50 billion in assets fell after TAGP expired on December 31, 2010, and in mid-2011 ranged from about 0.04 percent for banking organizations with less than $500 million in assets to about 3.1 percent for banking organizations with at least $1 billion but less than $10 billion in assets. Participation rates were about 42.1 percent and 100 percent for banking organizations with at least $50 billion but less than $250 billion in assets and with $250 billion or more in assets, respectively, at that time. By mid-2012, only banking organizations with $50 billion or more were participating in DGP, which then expired at the end of 2012.

At the end of 2008, average DGP-guaranteed debt and TAGP- guaranteed deposit amounts outstanding were higher as a percentage of assets for larger participants than for smaller participants and ranged from about 2.3 percent for participants with less than $500 million in assets to about 8.8 percent for participants with $250 billion or more in assets (see Panel B of table 6). At the end of 2010, average DGP- guaranteed debt and TAGP-guaranteed deposit amounts outstanding as a percentage of assets had fallen for banking organizations with $50 billion or more in assets but not for smaller banking organizations. At that time, DGP-guaranteed debt and TAGP-guaranteed deposit amounts outstanding ranged from about 1.4 percent of assets on average for participants with $250 billion or more in assets to about 5.6 percent of assets on average for participants with $10-50 billion in assets. TAGP expired on December 31, 2010, and as of the end of 2011, DGP-guaranteed debt amounts outstanding were less than 2 percent of assets on average for banking organizations of all sizes. DGP expired on December 31, 2012.

Lastly, our analysis found that the six largest bank holding companies as of December 31, 2012—all with consolidated assets greater than $500 billion—used the emergency programs to varying degrees but had exited most by the end of 2009. Table 7 shows the percentage of consolidated assets funded by DGP-guaranteed debt, TAGP-guaranteed deposits, TAF loans, CPFF loans, PDCF loans, TSLF loans, and CPP and TIP equity investments for the largest bank holding companies at year-end from 2008 to 2012. For comparison purposes we also show the average percent of assets funded by the same programs for the six banking organization size groups over the same period.

Table 6. Participation Rates in DGP and TAGP and Average DGP-Guaranteed Debt and TAGP-Guaranteed Deposits Outstanding as a Percentage of Assets at Quarter-End for Participating Banking Organizations, December 31, 2008, through December 31, 2012

A. Percent of banking organizations participating in DGP, TAGP, or both at quarter-end (%).

Quarter	Assets <$500M	Assets ≥$500M, <$1B	Assets ≥$1B, <$10B	Assets ≥$10B, <$50B	Assets ≥$50B, <$250B	Assets ≥$250B
2008q4	66.27	84.87	92.86	86.89	86.67	87.50
2009q2	66.98	89.79	93.14	88.33	88.89	100.00
2009q4	70.46	90.60	93.89	87.72	89.47	100.00
2010q2	66.56	86.74	87.12	77.36	85.00	100.00
2010q4	65.33	81.48	80.77	45.28	50.00	100.00
2011q2	0.04	0.78	3.13	1.85	42.11	100.00
2011q4	0.04	0.64	2.92	1.85	33.33	100.00
2012q2	0.00	0.00	0.00	0.00	5.88	27.27
2012q4	0.00	0.00	0.00	0.00	0.00	20.00

B. Average DGP-guaranteed debt and TAGP-guaranteed deposit amounts outstanding as a percent of assets for participating banking organizations at quarter end (%).

Quarter	Assets <$500M	Assets ≥$500M, <$1B	Assets ≥$1B, <$10B	Assets ≥$10B, <$50B	Assets ≥$50B, <$250B	Assets ≥$250B
2008q4	2.30	2.42	2.66	4.22	6.82	8.81
2009q2	2.34	2.62	3.27	4.94	7.51	6.34
2009q4	2.67	3.01	3.71	5.96	8.25	6.37
2010q2	2.55	3.29	3.73	6.67	6.16	1.81
2010q4	2.75	3.51	3.93	5.56	2.88	1.41
2011q2	1.75	2.12	1.61	1.48	1.99	1.23
2011q4	1.72	1.72	1.58	0.21	1.37	0.91
2012q2	N/A	N/A	N/A	N/A	4.14	0.38
2012q4	N/A	N/A	N/A	N/A	N/A	<0.01

Source: GAO analysis of data from BEA, FDIC, the Federal Reserve Board, the Federal Reserve Bank of Chicago, and Treasury.

Note: Banking organizations include consolidated top-tier U.S. bank holding companies and standalone depository institutions. Assets for bank holding companies are consolidated assets for the top-tier bank holding company, which include the assets of consolidated subsidiaries. Assets for standalone depository institutions are consolidated assets for the institution. We exclude banking organizations for which we could not reliably calculate consolidated assets. Banking organizations are divided into groups each quarter using consolidated assets that were first adjusted for inflation and measured in fourth quarter 2012 dollars. The participation rate is the percentage of banking organizations with positive amounts of TAGP-guaranteed deposits or DGP-guaranteed debt outstanding at quarter-end.

Table 7. Average outstanding amounts of equity provided, loans provided, and liabilities guaranteed by emergency programs for select bank holding companies and for banking organizations by size at year end, 2008-2012

	DGP-guaranteed debt outstanding	TAGP-guaranteed deposits outstanding	TAF loans outstanding	CPFF loans outstanding	PDCF loans outstanding	Market value of TSLF loans outstanding	CPP and TIP investment amounts outstanding
Select banking organizations as of December 31, 2008:							
Bank of America Corporation							
% of assets	2.44	5.53	2.47	0.82	0	0	0.82
$ billions	44.55	100.69	45.00	14.93	0	0	15.00
Citigroup, Inc.							
% of assets	1.64	2.50	0.77	0.64	0.71	1.87	2.32
$ billions	31.87	48.41	15.00	12.39	13.80	36.19	45.00
Goldman Sachs Group, Inc.[a]							
% of assets	—	—	—	—	—	—	—
$ billions	—	—	—	—	—	—	—
% of assets	0.96	6.24	1.38	0	0	0.11	1.15
$ billions	20.93	135.73	30.00	0	0	2.46	25.00
Morgan Stanley[a]							
% of assets	—	—	—	—	—	—	—
$ billions	—	—	—	—	—	—	—
Wells Fargo & Company							
% of assets	0.46	4.85	5.54	0	0	0	1.91
$ billions	6.08	63.48	72.50	0	0	0	25.00
Average for banking organizations by size as of December 31, 2008:							
Assets ≥ $250 billion							
% of assets	0.86	6.85	1.38	0.24	0.09	0.25	1.57
$ billions	13.42	54.84	20.68	3.68	1.72	4.83	15.90
Assets $50-250 billion							
% of assets	0.40	5.52	2.21	0.24	0	0	1.91
$ billions	0.59	6.63	2.55	0.40	0	0	2.09
Assets $10-50 billion							
% of assets	0.05	3.61	0.81	0	0	0	0.88
$ billions	0.01	0.59	0.18	0	0	0	0.15
Assets $1-10 billion							
% of assets	<0.01	2.47	0.26	0	0	0	0.32
$ billions	<0.01	0.06	0.01	0	0	0	0.01
Assets $500 million to $1 billion							
% of assets	0.01	2.04	0.08	0	0	0	0.09

	DGP-guaranteed debt outstanding	TAGP-guaranteed deposits outstanding	TAF loans outstanding	CPFF loans outstanding	PDCF loans outstanding	Market value of TSLF loans outstanding	CPP and TIP investment amounts outstanding
$ billions	<0.01	0.01	<0.01	0	0	0	<0.01
Assets < $500 million							
% of assets	<0.01	1.52	0.01	0	0	0	0.01
$ billions	<0.01	<0.01	<0.01	0	0	0	<0.01
Select banking organizations as of December 31, 2009:							
Bank of America Corporation							
% of assets	1.99	7.22	0	0	0	0	0
$ billions	44.31	161.02	0	0	0	0	0
Citigroup, Inc.							
% of assets	3.52	2.71	0	0	0	0	0
$ billions	65.59	50.56	0	0	0	0	0
Goldman Sachs Group, Inc.							
% of assets	2.42	0.26	0	0	0	0	0
$ billions	20.57	2.19	0	0	0	0	0
JPMorgan Chase & Co.							
% of assets	1.99	5.53	0	0	0	0	0
$ billions	40.48	112.29	0	0	0	0	0
Morgan Stanley							
% of assets	3.08	1.01	0	0	0	0	0
$ billions	23.77	7.76	0	0	0	0	0
Wells Fargo & Company							
% of assets	0.77	7.38	0	0	0	0	0
$ billions	9.52	91.82	0	0	0	0	0
Average for banking organizations by size as of December 31, 2009:							
Assets ≥ $250 billion							
% of assets	1.81	4.56	0	0	0	0	0.31
$ billions	23.48	52.49	0	0	0	0	0.84
Assets $50-250 billion							
% of assets	1.07	6.32	0.22	0	0	0	1.52
$ billions	1.47	7.12	0.37	0	0	0	1.29
Assets $10-50 billion							
% of assets	0.03	5.20	0.20	0	0	0	0.83
$ billions	0.01	0.80	0.04	0	0	0	0.14
Assets $1-10 billion							
% of assets	0.05	3.43	0.22	0	0	0	0.54
$ billions	<0.01	0.08	0.01	0	0	0	0.01

Table 7. (Continued)

	DGP-guaranteed debt outstanding	TAGP-guaranteed deposits outstanding	TAF loans outstanding	CPFF loans outstanding	PDCF loans outstanding	Market value of TSLF loans outstanding	CPP and TIP investment amounts outstanding
Assets $500 million-1 billion							
% of assets	0.02	2.71	0.06	0	0	0	0.36
$ billions	<0.01	0.02	<0.01	0	0	0	<0.01
Assets <$500 million							
% of assets	<0.01	1.88	0.05	0	0	0	0.12
$ billions	<0.01	<0.01	<0.01	0	0	0	<0.01
Select banking organizations as of December 31, 2010:							
Bank of America Corporation							
% of assets	1.21	0	0	0	0	0	0
$ billions	27.45	0	0	0	0	0	0
Citigroup, Inc.							
% of assets	3.04	0	0	0	0	0	0
$ billions	58.25	0	0	0	0	0	0
Goldman Sachs Group, Inc.							
% of assets	2.07	0	0	0	0	0	0
$ billions	18.84	0	0	0	0	0	0
JPMorgan Chase & Co.							
% of assets	1.71	0	0	0	0	0	0
$ billions	36.13	0	0	0	0	0	0
Morgan Stanley							
% of assets	2.63	0	0	0	0	0	0
$ billions	21.27	0	0	0	0	0	0
Wells Fargo & Company							
% of assets	0.76	0	0	0	0	0	0
$ billions	9.50	0	0	0	0	0	0
Average for banking organizations by size as of December 31, 2010:							
Assets ≥ $250 billion							
% of assets	1.41	0	0	0	0	0	0
$ billions	17.90	0	0	0	0	0	0
Assets $50-250 billion							
% of assets	0.85	0.59	0	0	0	0	0.95
$ billions	1.19	0.30	0	0	0	0	0.92
Assets $10-50 billion							
% of assets	0.03	2.49	0	0	0	0	0.45
$ billions	0.01	0.42	0	0	0	0	0.08

	DGP-guaranteed debt outstanding	TAGP-guaranteed deposits outstanding	TAF loans outstanding	CPFF loans outstanding	PDCF loans outstanding	Market value of TSLF loans outstanding	CPP and TIP investment amounts outstanding
Assets $1-10 billion							
% of assets	0.05	3.12	0	0	0	0	0.51
$ billions	<0.01	0.08	0	0	0	0	0.01
Assets $500 million-1 billion							
% of assets	0.02	2.84	0	0	0	0	0.36
$ billions	<0.01	0.02	0	0	0	0	<0.01
Assets <$500 million							
% of assets	<0.01	1.80	0	0	0	0	0.11
$ billions	<0.01	<0.01	0	0	0	0	<0.01
Select banking organizations as of December 31, 2011:							
Bank of America Corporation							
% of assets	1.12	0	0	0	0	0	0
$ billions	23.85	0	0	0	0	0	0
Citigroup, Inc.							
% of assets	2.03	0	0	0	0	0	0
$ billions	38.00	0	0	0	0	0	0
Goldman Sachs Group, Inc.							
% of assets	0.92	0	0	0	0	0	0
$ billions	8.50	0	0	0	0	0	0
JPMorgan Chase & Co.							
% of assets	0.89	0	0	0	0	0	0
$ billions	20.18	0	0	0	0	0	0
Morgan Stanley							
% of assets	1.75	0	0	0	0	0	0
$ billions	13.09	0	0	0	0	0	0
Wells Fargo & Company							
% of assets	0.27	0	0	0	0	0	0
$ billions	3.50	0	0	0	0	0	0
Average for banking organizations by size as of December 31, 2011:							
Assets ≥ $250 billion							
% of assets	0.91	0	0	0	0	0	0
$ billions	11.38	0	0	0	0	0	0
Assets $50-250 billion							
% of assets	0.46	0	0	0	0	0	0.33
$ billions	0.65	0	0	0	0	0	0.29
Assets $10-50 billion							
% of assets	<0.01	0	0	0	0	0	0.30

Table 7. (Continued)

	DGP-guaranteed debt outstanding	TAGP-guaranteed deposits outstanding	TAF loans outstanding	CPFF loans outstanding	PDCF loans outstanding	Market value of TSLF loans outstanding	CPP and TIP investment amounts outstanding
$ billions	<0.01	0	0	0	0	0	0.06
Assets $1-10 billion							
% of assets	0.05	0	0	0	0	0	0.33
$ billions	<0.01	0	0	0	0	0	0.01
Assets $500 million-1 billion							
% of assets	0.01	0	0	0	0	0	0.24
$ billions	<0.01	0	0	0	0	0	<0.01
Assets <$500 million							
% of assets	<0.01	0	0	0	0	0	0.08
$ billions	<0.01	0	0	0	0	0	<0.01
Select banking organizations as of December 31, 2012:							
Bank of America Corporation							
% of assets	0	0	0	0	0	0	0
$ billions	0	0	0	0	0	0	0
Citigroup, Inc.							
% of assets	<0.01	0	0	0	0	0	0
$ billions	<0.01	0	0	0	0	0	0
Goldman Sachs Group, Inc.							
% of assets	0	0	0	0	0	0	0
$ billions	0	0	0	0	0	0	0
JPMorgan Chase & Co.							
% of assets	0	0	0	0	0	0	0
$ billions	0	0	0	0	0	0	0
Morgan Stanley							
% of assets	0	0	0	0	0	0	0
$ billions	0	0	0	0	0	0	0
Wells Fargo & Company							
% of assets	<0.01	0	0	0	0	0	0
$ billions	<0.01	0	0	0	0	0	0
Average for banking organizations by size as of December 31, 2012:							
Assets ≥ $250 billion							
% of assets	<0.01	0	0	0	0	0	0
$ billions	<0.01	0	0	0	0	0	0
Assets $50-250 billion							
% of assets	0	0	0	0	0	0	0

	DGP-guaranteed debt outstanding	TAGP-guaranteed deposits outstanding	TAF loans outstanding	CPFF loans outstanding	PDCF loans outstanding	Market value of TSLF loans outstanding	CPP and TIP investment amounts outstanding
$ billions	0	0	0	0	0	0	0
Assets $10-50 billion							
% of assets	0	0	0	0	0	0	0.16
$ billions	0	0	0	0	0	0	0.04
Assets $1-10 billion							
% of assets	0	0	0	0	0	0	0.17
$ billions	0	0	0	0	0	0	<0.01
Assets $500 million-1 billion							
% of assets	0	0	0	0	0	0	0.15
$ billions	0	0	0	0	0	0	<0.01
Assets <$500 million							
% of assets	0	0	0	0	0	0	0.06
$ billions	0	0	0	0	0	0	<0.01

Source: GAO analysis of data from BEA, FDIC, the Federal Reserve Board, the Federal Reserve Bank of Chicago, SNL Financial, and Treasury.

Note: Banking organizations include consolidated top-tier U.S. bank holding companies and standalone depository institutions. Assets for bank holding companies are consolidated assets for the top-tier bank holding company, which include the assets of consolidated subsidiaries. Assets for standalone depository institutions are consolidated assets for the institution. We exclude banking organizations for which we could not reliably calculate consolidated assets. Select bank holding companies are those with $500 billion or more in assets as of December 31, 2012. Banking organizations are divided into groups each quarter using consolidated assets that were first adjusted for inflation and measured in fourth quarter 2012 dollars.

[a] Goldman Sachs Group, Inc. and Morgan Stanley became bank holding companies in September 2008 but did not file form FR Y-9C, the source of our data on consolidated assets, for the fourth quarter of 2008.

End Notes

[1] Moral hazard can occur when market participants expect similar emergency actions in future crises, thereby weakening their incentives to properly manage risks.

[2] Pub. L. No. 111-203, 124 Stat. 1376 (2010).

[3] Pub. L. No. 63-43, § 23A, 38 Stat. 251, 272 (1913) (12 U.S.C. § 371c).

[4] Pub. L. No. 84-511, 70 Stat. 133 (codified at 12 U.S.C. §§ 1841-1852).

[5] § 4(c)(6), 70 Stat. at 137 (codified at 12 U.S.C. § 1843(k)(4)(F)).

[6] Pub. L. No. 106-102, 113 Stat. 1338 (1999) (codified in scattered sections of 12, 15 U.S.C). In order to be a financial holding company: (1) all depository institutions controlled by the bank holding company must be and remain well capitalized; (2) all depository institutions controlled by the bank holding company must be and remain well managed; and (3) the bank holding company must have made an effective election to become a financial holding company. 12 C.F.R. § 225.81(b).

[7] § 103(a), 113 Stat. at 1342 (codified at 12 U.S.C. § 1843(k)). The financial holding company can engage in activities that the Federal Reserve Board determines (1) are financial in nature or incidental to such financial activity, or (2) are complementary to a financial activity and do not pose a substantial risk to the safety and soundness of depository institutions or the financial system generally. *Id.*

[8] An important factor contributing to merger activity was a statutory change removing barriers to geographic expansion by banks. The Riegle-Neal Interstate Banking and Branching Efficiency Act of 1994 authorized interstate mergers between adequately capitalized and managed banks starting in June 1997, regardless of whether the transaction would be prohibited by state law, though states had the right to opt out of that arrangement if they passed legislation prior to June 1997 prohibiting merger transactions with out-of-state banks. Pub. L. No. 103-328, 108 Stat. 2338 (codified at scattered sections of 12 U.S.C.). Previously, most banks that wanted to operate across state lines had to establish a bank holding company and, with certain restrictions, acquire or charter a bank in each state in which they wanted to operate. With the advent of interstate branching, banks that previously were not permitted to expand across state lines could do so by acquiring existing banks, and some multistate bank holding companies could consolidate their operations into a single bank with multistate branches.

[9] One limitation of this indicator is that some legal entities may be vehicles for tax purposes and therefore may not result in a significant increase in organizational complexity.

[10] Pub. L. No. 111-203, § 165, 124 Stat. 1376, 1423 (2010) (codified at 12 U.S.C. § 5365).

[11] This inherent vulnerability arises from the role of banks in using deposits that are available upon demand to fund long-term, illiquid loans.

[12] The Federal Reserve System consists of the Federal Reserve Board—a federal agency—and 12 regional Reserve Banks. The Federal Reserve Board has delegated some of its responsibilities for supervision and regulation to the Reserve Banks. The Federal Reserve Act authorizes the Reserve Banks to make discount window loans to the extent authorized by the Federal Reserve Board. Pub. L. No. 63-43, §§ 10B, 13, 38 Stat. 251 (codified at of 12 U.S.C. §§ 347b(a), 343).

[13] 12 C.F.R. § 201.4(a)-(c).

[14] 12 U.S.C. § 347b(a).

[15] Pub. L. No. 73-66, 48 Stat. 162 (codified in scattered sections of 12 U.S.C.). The Banking Act of 1933 is also known as the Glass-Steagall Act.

[16] Pub. L. No. 111-203, §§ 331, 334-335, 124 Stat. 1376, 1538-40 (2010).

[17] §1101(a), 124 Stat. at 2113.

[18] Pub. L. No. 63-43, § 13(3), 38 Stat. 251 (codified at 12 U.S.C. § 343).

[19] Pub. L. No. 102-242, § 141, 105 Stat. 2236, 2275 (codified at 12 U.S.C. § 1823(c)(4)(G)).

[20] *Id.*

[21] *Id.* For more information about this the systemic risk exception, see GAO, *Federal Deposit Insurance Act: Regulators' Use of Systemic Risk Exception Raises Moral Hazard Concerns and Opportunities Exist to Clarify the Provision,* GAO-10-100 (Washington, D.C.: Apr. 15, 2010).

[22] For a more detailed discussion of the economic losses associated with the 2007-2009 financial crisis, see GAO, *Financial Regulatory Reform: Financial Crisis Losses and Potential Impacts of the Dodd-Frank Act*, GAO-13-180 (Washington, D.C.: Jan. 16, 2013).

[23] This report focuses on those emergency programs that provided the most significant direct funding support to bank holding companies or their subsidiaries. As a result, we do not include an analysis of the Term Asset-Backed Securities Loan Facility, or the Public- Private Investment Partnership, among others, because these programs did not provide significant *direct* support to bank holding companies or their subsidiaries.

[24] For more information about TALF, see GAO, *Troubled Asset Relief Program: Treasury Needs to Strengthen Its Decision-Making Process on the Term Asset-Backed Securities Loan Facility*, GAO-10-25 (Washington, D.C.: Feb. 5, 2010). For more information about CPP and other TARP programs, see GAO, *Troubled Asset Relief Program: One Year Later, Actions Are Needed to Address Remaining Transparency and Accountability Challenges*, GAO-10-16 (Washington, D.C.: Oct. 8, 2009).

[25] To ease stresses in these markets, on August 17, 2007, the Federal Reserve Board approved two temporary changes to discount window terms: (1) a reduction of the discount rate—the interest rate at which the Reserve Banks extended collateralized loans at the discount window—by 50 basis points; and (2) an extension of the discount window lending term from overnight to up to 30 days, with the possibility of renewal. One basis point is equivalent to 0.01 percent or 1/100th of a percent. On March 16, 2008, the Federal Reserve Board further reduced the spread of the primary credit rate over the target federal funds rate to 25 basis points and increased the maximum maturity of discount window loans to 90 days.

[26] In March 2008, U.S. bank holding companies with primary dealer subsidiaries included Citigroup, Inc., Bank of America Corporation, and JP Morgan Chase & Co. Morgan Stanley and Goldman Sachs Group Inc. also had subsidiaries that were primary dealers and in September 2008, both firms converted to bank holding companies.

[27] On September 14, 2008, the Federal Reserve Board announced that TSLF-eligible collateral would be expanded to include all investment-grade debt securities and PDCF- eligible collateral would be expanded to include all

securities eligible to be pledged in the triparty repurchase agreements system, including noninvestment-grade securities and equities. On September 29, 2008, the Federal Reserve Board also announced expanded support through TAF by doubling the amount of funds that would be available in each TAF auction cycle from $150 billion to $300 billion.

28 In September 2008, following the failure of Lehman Brothers Holdings Inc., many money market mutual funds faced severe liquidity pressures as redemption requests from their investors increased significantly. Treasury and Federal Reserve Board officials became concerned that pressures on these funds could further exacerbate turmoil in the markets, as these funds were significant investors in many money market instruments, such as commercial paper and certificates of deposit. On September 19, 2008, Treasury announced that it would insure the holdings of any publicly offered eligible money market mutual fund—both retail and institutional—that paid a fee to participate in the program. On the same day, the Federal Reserve Board authorized the creation of a new program—the AMLF—to provide liquidity support to money market mutual funds and to promote liquidity in the ABCP markets. AMLF provided loans to U.S. depository institutions, their holding companies, and affiliates that used the proceeds of these loans to purchase ABCP from money market mutual funds. For more information about AMLF, see GAO, *Federal Reserve System: Opportunities Exist to Strengthen Policies and Processes for Managing Emergency Assistance,* GAO-11-696 (Washington, D.C.: July 21, 2011).

29 Emergency Economic Stabilization Act of 2008, Pub. L. No. 110-343, Div. A, 122 Stat. 3765 (12 U.S.C. §§ 5201-5261).

30 In prior work, we found that TARP, along with other efforts by the Federal Reserve System and FDIC, made important contributions to helping stabilize credit markets. For example, the TED spread—a key indicator of credit risk that gauges the willingness of banks to lend to other banks—had narrowed to precrisis levels within a year of the October 2008 announcements of TARP, TLGP, CPFF, and other government actions.

31 This pricing was intended to encourage program participants to exit the programs as market conditions normalized.

32 Because of the perceived stigma associated with borrowing from the discount window, banks that participated in TAF might have been reluctant to turn to the discount window for funding support.

33 In our analysis, we discarded values of spreads between program pricing and market alternatives when they were zero or negative—negative spreads are unlikely to capture the benefits that accrued to participants. For example, we excluded 15 observations (or 40 percent of auctions) in our analysis of TSLF when the schedule 1 auction rate was equal to or above the private cost for similar borrowing but did not exclude any observations in our analysis of DGP because the DGP fee never exceeded the weighted-average private cost for similar guarantees during the time period we analyzed. If these truly reflected market alternatives for the pool of potential participants then there would be no participation, or the participation would have been based on other considerations. Participation by itself suggests that program prices and/or terms were relatively attractive in comparison to available alternatives—benefits could arise from price, quantity available, or other nonprice characteristics of the assistance (loan term, eligible collateral, etc.).

34 We are aware that concerns about LIBOR manipulation could affect its usefulness as an indicator of potential market alternatives for banks. We discussed this issue with Federal Reserve Bank of New York officials who indicated that it was still among the best available indicators despite these concerns. In addition, GAO has found in previous work that LIBOR reflected significant financial market stress during the 2007-2009 financial crisis. See GAO-10-16.

35 In addition, there can be uncertainty about the assets underlying ABCP or limited liquidity support from sponsors.

36 Triparty repurchase agreement transactions are intermediated by a third party (a clearing bank) that stands between the borrower and lender.

37 Interest rates are another important term for repurchase loans. However, we were unable to compare PDCF interest rates to market alternatives for all eligible collateral types because available data for repurchase agreement market interest rates are limited to higher quality and more liquid collateral types (such as Treasury securities). While repurchase agreement lenders generally require higher interest rates for riskier and less liquid collateral types, PDCF offered loans at the same interest rate for all collateral types.

38 As a result, many financial institutions increasingly had to rely on higher quality collateral, such as Treasury securities, to obtain cash in these markets, and a shortage of such high-quality collateral emerged.

39 As a result we could only compare market repurchase agreement interest rates with interest rates from the Schedule 1 auctions.

40 Researchers at the Federal Reserve Bank of New York also found that TSLF was priced below estimated market rates, although the size of the difference they estimated was smaller than our results.

41 Through TIP, Treasury sought to foster market stability and strengthen the economy by making case-by-case investments in institutions that it deemed critical to the functioning of the financial system. Bank of America Corporation and Citigroup Inc. were the only two institutions that participated in this program.

42 Because private market participants might have charged a price based on a comparable net present value analysis, banks would have benefitted to the extent that the prices offered by Treasury for their equity exceed what they were likely to receive based on the net present value. We used the earliest available estimates from the Congressional Budget Office and Treasury as they were closest to market conditions at the time that programs

were initiated. Estimates of these subsidy rates depended on timing and market conditions and the size of these subsidy rates likely fell over time as market conditions improved.

[43] For more details on their respective methodologies, see Congressional Budget Office, *The Troubled Asset Relief Program: Report on Transactions Through December 31, 2008* (Washington, D.C.: January 2009); GAOand Congressional Oversight Panel, *February Oversight Report: Valuing Treasury's Acquisitions* (Washington, D.C.: February 2009).

[44] For debt issued on or after April 1, 2009, FDIC included an additional surcharge of between 10 and 50 basis points for debt with a maturity of 1 year or more. Most DGP- guaranteed debt with a maturity of 1 year or more was issued prior to April 1, 2009.

[45] We created a weighted average of 1-year CDS prices with weights based on the largest bank holding company users of DGP. Our results may not reflect the relative price of DGP for DGP participants that were not included in the weighted average.

[46] Our analysis focuses on use of emergency programs by banking organizations. However, emergency programs also provided funding for some nonbank financial institutions, such as broker-dealers, and for some nonfinancial companies, such as McDonald's Corp. and Harley-Davidson.

[47] In addition, TAF program terms stated that a depository institution's TAF loans outstanding with terms greater than 28 days could not exceed 75 percent of the value of collateral it had pledged to the discount window.

[48] For example, in October 2008, nine of the largest financial institutions agreed to accept TARP capital investments in part to signal the importance of the program to the stability of the financial system.

[49] Pub. L. No. 63-43, § 23A, 38 Stat. 251, 272 (12 U.S.C. § 371c).

[50] Section 23A requirements—and the associated concerns about transfer of the subsidy arising from the depository institution's access to federal safety nets—apply to depository institutions of all sizes.

[51] 12 U.S.C. § 371c(f)(2).

[52] The Federal Reserve Board's letters granting these exemptions noted that these banks would channel these credit transactions through their affiliated broker-dealers "for operational reasons." The transactions between each bank and broker-dealer would take the form of either reverse repurchase agreements or securities borrowing transactions and would be on the same terms as each transaction between the broker-dealer and unaffiliated market participant.

[53] As of December 31, 2008, BB&T Corp., Fifth Third Bancorp, and Northern Trust Corp had total consolidated assets of $147.5 billion, $69.5 billion, and $70.4 billion, respectively. Wachovia Corporation was the fourth largest U.S. bank holding company, with total consolidated assets of $635.5 billion. On January 1, 2009, Wells Fargo & Company completed its acquisition of Wachovia Corporation.

[54] Auction-rate securities are long-term bonds or preferred stocks whose interest rates or dividends are periodically reset through auctions. Until its collapse, the auction-rate securities market had been an important and growing source of funds for municipalities and other issuers. Variable rate demand notes are floating-rate debt instruments with a maturity of usually 20 or 30 years.

[55] *Transactions Between Member Banks and Their Affiliates: Exemption for Certain Purchases of Asset-Backed Commercial Paper by a Member Bank from an Affiliate*, 73 Fed. Reg. 55708 (Sept. 26, 2008) (amending 12 C.F.R. § 223.42 and adding § 223.56).

[56] Section 23B of the Federal Reserve Act generally requires that certain transactions between a bank and its affiliates occur on market terms—that is, on terms and under circumstances that are substantially the same, or at least as favorable to the bank, as those prevailing at the time for comparable transactions with unaffiliated companies. 12 U.S.C. § 371c-1(a)(1)(A). Section 23B applies to any transaction by a bank with a third party if an affiliate has a financial interest in the third party or if an affiliate is a participant in the transaction. *Id.* at (a)(2)(E).

[57] See Saule T. Omarova, "From Gramm-Leach-Bliley to Dodd-Frank: The Unfulfilled Promise of Section 23A of the Federal Reserve Act," *North Carolina Law Review,* Vol. 89, pgs. 1684-1769. The shadow banking system refers to a web of financial institutions that channel funds from savers to borrowers through a range of securitization and secured funding techniques. Unlike traditional banks, shadow banking institutions lack explicit access to the federal safety nets, such as the discount window and deposit insurance.

[58] Bear Stearns was one of the largest primary dealers and engaged in a broad range of activities, including investment banking, securities and derivatives trading, brokerage services, and origination and securitization of mortgage loans.

[59] The Housing and Economic Recovery Act of 2008, Pub. L. No. 110-289, 122 Stat. 2654, established the Federal Housing Finance Agency, which was authorized to be appointed conservator for the government-sponsored enterprises. §§ 1101, 1145, 122 Stat. at 2661, 2734.

[60] Under the Senior Preferred Stock Purchase Agreements program, Treasury has made funding advances to Fannie Mae and Freddie Mac to ensure that they have sufficient assets to support their liabilities.

[61] AIG is a multinational insurer that was also a significant participant in the financial derivatives market.

[62] For more information about the federal government's actions to assist AIG and the restructuring and repayment of this assistance over time, see GAO, *Troubled Asset Relief Program: Government's Exposure to AIG Lessens as Equity Investments are Sold,* GAO-12-574 (Washington, D.C.: May 7, 2012).

[63] See GAO
[64] In December 2010, Treasury sold its remaining shares of Citigroup common stock.
[65] Pub. L. No. 84-511, 70 Stat. 133 (codified at 12 U.S.C. §§ 1841-1852).
[66] For various reasons, the Bank Holding Company Act exempts from regulation certain companies that own depository institutions; these subsidiaries are not defined as banks for purposes of the act and thus the companies that own them are not considered bank holding companies and are not required to comply with the act's restrictions. 12 U.S.C. § 1841(c)(2). One type of these companies is the ILC. *Id.* at § 1841(c)(2)(H). ILCs are limited-service financial institutions that make loans and raise funds by selling certificates called "investment shares" and by accepting deposits. ILCs are distinguished from finance companies because ILCs accept deposits in addition to making consumer loans. ILCs also differ from commercial banks because most ILCs do not offer demand deposit (checking) accounts. For more information about ILCs and other exempt companies, see GAO, *Bank Holding Company Act: Characteristics and Regulation of Exempt Institutions and the Implications of Removing the Exemptions*, GAO-12-160 (Washington, D.C.: Jan. 19, 2012).
[67] On that same day, Bank of America had agreed to acquire Merrill Lynch & Co., which would become part of a bank holding company pending completion of its merger with Bank of America, a bank holding company supervised by the Federal Reserve System upon completion of the acquisition.
[68] See generally Pub. L. No. 111-203, 124 Stat. 1376 (2010).
[69] §§ 204, 210, 124 Stat. at 1454-56, 1460.
[70] §335, 124 Stat. at 1540.
[71] *Deposit Insurance Regulations; Permanent Increase in Standard Coverage Amount*, 75 Fed. Reg. 49363 (Aug. 13, 2010).
[72] §343(a), 124 Stat. at 1544.
[73] *Id.*
[74] §331(b), 124 Stat. at 1538.
[75] *Assessments, Large Bank Pricing*, 76 Fed. Reg. 10672 (Feb. 25, 2011).
[76] For more information on this rule, see GAO, *Dodd-Frank Act Regulations: Implementation Could Benefit from Additional Analyses and Coordination,* GAO-12-151 (Washington, D.C.: Nov. 10, 2011).
[77] § 1103(b), 124 Stat. at 2118.
[78] Section 23A of the Federal Reserve Act restricts the ability of banks to provide funding to their nonbank affiliates above a certain limit, and imposes collateral and other requirements for those transactions. The goals of Section 23A are to protect federally insured banks from too much exposure to riskier nonbank affiliates and to prevent the transfer of the federal subsidy to nondepository institutions.
[79] § 608(a), 124 Stat. at 1609-10.
[80] § 608(a)(1)(A), 124 Stat. at 1608. Section 23B generally requires that certain transactions between a bank and its affiliates occur on market terms; that is, on terms and under circumstances that are substantially the same, or at least as favorable to the bank, as those prevailing at the time for comparable transactions with unaffiliated companies. Section 23B applies to any transaction by a bank with a third party if an affiliate has a financial interest in the third party or if an affiliate is a participant in the transaction.
[81] § 608(a)(2), 124 Stat. at 1608.
[82] *Prohibitions and Restrictions on Proprietary Trading and Certain Interests in, and Relationships With, Hedge Funds and Covered Funds; Proposed Rule*, 77 Fed. Reg. 8332 (Feb. 14, 2012); *Prohibitions and Restrictions on Proprietary Trading and Certain Interests in, and Relationships With, Hedge Funds and Private Equity Funds; Proposed Rule*, 76 Fed. Reg. 68846 (Nov. 7, 2011).
[83] § 716(a), 124 Stat. at 1648. A swap is a type of derivative that involves an ongoing exchange of one or more assets, liabilities, or payments for a specified period. Financial and nonfinancial firms use swaps and other derivatives to hedge risk, or speculate, or for other purposes. Swaps include interest rate swaps, commodity-based swaps, and broad- based credit default swaps. Security-based swaps include single-name and narrow-based credit default swaps and equity-based swaps. Certain insured depository institutions are excluded from the definition of "swaps entity" and are therefore exempt from Section 716 restrictions. § 716(b)(2)(B).
[84] §§ 1105(a), 1106(b), 124 Stat. at 2121, 2125.
[85] For more information about the systemic risk exception, see GAO, *Federal Deposit Insurance Act: Regulators' Use of Systemic Risk Exception Raises Moral Hazard Concerns and Opportunities Exist to Clarify the Provision*, GAO-10-100 (Washington, D.C.: Apr. 15, 2010). A systemic risk determination exempts FDIC from the Federal Deposit Insurance Act's least-cost rule, which requires FDIC to use the least costly method when assisting an insured institution and prohibits FDIC from increasing losses to the Deposit Insurance Fund by protecting creditors and uninsured depositors of an insured institution.
[86] § 1105(e), 124 Stat. at 2124.
[87] § 1105(c)-(d), 124 Stat. at 2121-2122.
88 During the financial crisis, several large financial institutions became insolvent and filed for bankruptcy when no private-sector solution was found. For example, Lehman Brothers filed for Chapter 11 bankruptcy on the morning of September 15, 2008. Lehman had $639 billion in total assets and $613 billion in total liabilities as of May 31, 2008. The bankruptcy proceedings highlighted inconsistencies in laws and regulations across

countries and limitations on the ability of countries to coordinate effectively during the reorganization or liquidation of international financial institutions. Bankruptcy is a federal court procedure conducted under rules and requirements of the U.S. Bankruptcy Code. The goal of bankruptcy is to give individuals and businesses a "fresh start" from burdensome debts by eliminating or restructuring debts they cannot repay and help creditors receive some payment in an equitable manner through liquidation or reorganization of the debtor.

[89] § 204, 124 Stat. at 1454-1456.

[90] § 204(b), 124 Stat. at 1455. The factors to be addressed are set forth in Section 203(b) of the Dodd-Frank Act. § 203(b), 124 Stat. at 1451. Before the Secretary of the Treasury, in consultation with the President, makes a decision to appoint FDIC as receiver of a covered financial company, at least two-thirds of those serving on the Board of Governors of the Federal Reserve System and at least two-thirds of those serving on the Board of Directors of FDIC must vote to make a written recommendation to the Secretary of the Treasury to appoint FDIC as receiver. § 203(a), 124 Stat. at 1450. In the case of a broker- dealer, the recommendation must come from the Federal Reserve Board and the Securities and Exchange Commission, in consultation with FDIC, and in the case of an insurance company from the Federal Reserve Board and the Director of the Federal Insurance Office, in consultation with FDIC.

[91] § 204(a)(2), 124 Stat. at 1454.

[92] § 210(n), 124 Stat. at 1506.

[93] § 210(o)(1), 124 Stat. at 1509.

[94] *Certain Orderly Liquidation Authority Provisions under Title II of the Dodd-Frank Wall Street Reform and Consumer Protection Act*, 76 Fed. Reg. 41626 (July 15, 2011).

[95] Bipartisan Policy Center, *Too Big to Fail: The Path to a Solution* (Washington, D.C.: May 2013), The Clearing House, *Report on the Orderly Liquidation Authority Resolution Symposium and Simulation* (New York, N.Y.: January 2013).

[96] *See* Pub. L. No. 111-203, § 210(h)(5)(E), 124 Stat. 1376, 1499 (2010); 12 U.S.C. § 5390(b)(4)(A)(ii); 12 CFR 380.27.

[97] Barclays, *TBTF: The $83bn Question* (New York, N.Y.: July 1, 2013).

[98] § 165(d)(1), 124 Stat. at 1426.

[99] *Living Wills Required*, 76 Fed. Reg. 67323 (Nov. 1, 2011).

[100] In October 2013, the Federal Reserve Board and FDIC released the public sections of filed annual resolution plans for 11 firms. Federal Reserve Board and FDIC, Agencies Release Public Sections of the Second Submission of Resolution Plans for 11 Institutions, accessed on November 7, 2013, http://www.federalreserve.gov/newsevents/press/bcreg/20131003a.htm

[101] § 1101(a), 124 Stat. at 2113.

[102] § 1101(a)(6), 124 Stat. at 2114 (codified at 12 U.S.C. § 343(B)(ii)-(iii)).

[103] §§ 1101-1103, 124 Stat. at 2113-20. These requirements include a requirement for the Federal Reserve Board to report to Congress on any loan or financial assistance authorized under Section 13(3), including the justification for the exercise of authority; the identity of the recipient; the date, amount, and form of the assistance; and the material terms of the assistance. § 1101(a)(6) (codified at 12 U.S.C. § 343(C)(i)).

[104] § 1101(a)(6)(B)(i), 124 Stat. at 2113-14. (codified at 12 U.S.C. § 343(B)).

[105] § 1101(a)(6)(B)(i), 124 Stat. at 2113. (codified at 12 U.S.C. § 343(B)(i)).

[106] GAO

[107] See GAO

[108] §§ 165-166, 124 Stat. at 1423-32.

[109] §165(a)(1), 124 Stat. at 1423.

[110] §165(b)(1)(A)(i), 124 Stat. at 1424; *Enhanced Prudential Standards and Early Remediation Requirements for Covered Companies; Proposed Rule,* 77 Fed. Reg. 594 (Jan. 5, 2012).

[111] §165(b)(1)(A)(ii), 124 Stat. at 1424: *Enhanced Prudential Standards and Early Remediation Requirements for Covered Companies; Proposed Rule*, 77 Fed. Reg. 594 (Jan. 5, 2012).

[112] §165(e)(2), 124 Stat. at 1427.

[113] §165(h), 124 Stat. at 1429.

[114] §165(i)(1), 124 Stat. at 1430. Companies subject to enhanced prudential standards also must conduct annual or semiannual stress tests of their own, depending on their size. § 165(i)(2), 124 Stat. at 1430-31.

[115] §165(j), 124 Stat. at 1431.

[116] §166, 124 Stat. at 1432.

[117] *Supervisory and Company-Run Stress Test Requirements for Covered Companies*, 77 Fed. Reg. 62378 (Oct. 12, 2012); 12 C.F.R. §§ 252.131-136, 252.141-138.

[118] *Enhanced Prudential Standards and Early Remediation Requirements for Foreign Banking Organizations and Foreign Nonbank Financial Companies*, 77 Fed. Reg. 76628 (Dec. 28, 2012). Additionally, rules regarding single-counterparty credit limits and risk management have been proposed but not finalized. *Enhanced Prudential Standards and Early Remediation Requirements for Covered Companies*; Proposed Rule, 77 Fed. Reg. 594 (Jan. 5, 2012).

[119] *Regulatory Capital Rules: Regulatory Capital, Implementation of Basel III, Capital Adequacy, Transition Provisions, Prompt Corrective Action, Standardized Approach for Risk-Weighted Assets, Market Discipline and Disclosure Requirements, Advanced Approaches Risk-Based Capital Rule, and Market Risk Capital Rule*, 78 Fed. Reg. 62018 (Oct. 11, 2013); 78 Fed. Reg. 55340 (Sept. 10, 2013).

[120] *Id.* National banking regulators classify capital as either Tier 1—currently the highest- quality form of capital and includes common equity—or Tier 2, which is weaker in absorbing losses. Tier 1, or core, capital consists primarily of common equity. Tier 2 is supplementary capital and includes limited amounts of subordinated debt, loan loss reserves, and certain other instruments.

[121] *Regulatory Capital Rules: Regulatory Capital, Enhanced Supplementary Leverage Ratio Standards for Certain Bank Holding Companies and Their Subsidiary Insured Depository Institutions*, 78 Fed. Reg. 51101 (Aug. 20, 2013).

[122] *Id.* The Federal Deposit Insurance Corporation Improvement Act of 1991, Pub. L. No. 102-242, 105 Stat. 2236, created Sections 38 and 39 of the Federal Deposit Insurance Act to improve the ability of regulators to identify and promptly address deficiencies at depository institutions—banks and thrifts—and better safeguard and minimize losses to the deposit insurance fund. Section 38 requires regulators to classify banks into one of five capital categories and take increasingly severe actions, known as prompt corrective action, as a bank's capital deteriorates. Section 38 primarily focuses on capital as an indicator of bank health; therefore, supervisory actions under it are designed to address a bank's deteriorating capital level. Section 39 requires the banking regulators to prescribe safety and soundness standards related to noncapital criteria, including operations and management; compensation; and asset quality, earnings, and stock valuation. Section 39 allows the regulators to take action if a bank fails to meet one or more of these standards.

[123] The Federal Reserve System consists of the Board of Governors of the Federal Reserve System—a federal agency—and 12 regional Reserve Banks. The Federal Reserve Board has delegated some of its responsibilities for supervision and regulation to the Reserve Banks. The Federal Reserve Act authorizes the Reserve Banks to make discount window loans to the extent authorized by the Federal Reserve Board. Pub. L. No. 63-43, §§ 10B, 13, 38 Stat. 251 (codified at 12 U.S.C. §§ 347b(a), 343).

[124] We reviewed prior GAO work on other emergency government programs that may have provided benefits to bank holding companies or their subsidiaries. For example, Treasury's Money Market Mutual Fund Guarantee Program and the Federal Reserve System's AMLF provided support to money market mutual funds. In the absence of these programs, money market mutual funds might have reduced their purchases of money market instruments issued by bank holding companies, their subsidiaries, and other firms, thereby exacerbating funding pressures on these firms. Other significant government programs included the Term Asset-Backed Securities Loan Facility (TALF), which was created by the Federal Reserve System and Treasury to support certain securitization markets, and other programs created by Treasury under TARP authority. For more information about TALF, see GAO, *Troubled Asset Relief Program: Treasury Needs to Strengthen Its Decision-Making Process on the Term Asset-Backed Securities Loan Facility*, GAO-10-25 (Washington, D.C.: Feb. 5, 2010). For more information about CPP and other TARP programs, see GAO, *Troubled Asset Relief Program: One Year Later, Actions Are Needed to Address Remaining Transparency and Accountability Challenges*, GAO-10-16 (Washington, D.C.: Oct. 8, 2009).

[125] Pub. L. No. 63-43, § 23A, 38 Stat. 251, 272 (1913) (12 U.S.C. § 371c).

[126] See generally Pub. L. No. 111-203, 124 Stat. 1376 (2010).

[127] This report focuses on the Federal Reserve System's programs that provided the most significant direct funding support to bank holding companies and their subsidiaries. For a broader discussion of the Federal Reserve System's emergency actions during the crisis, see GAO, *Federal Reserve System: Opportunities Exist to Strengthen Policies and Processes for Managing Emergency Assistance,* GAO-11-696 (Washington, D.C.: July 21, 2011).

[128] The sudden spike in the cost of term funding followed the August 9, 2007, announcement by BNP Paribas, a large banking organization based in France, that it could not value certain mortgage-related assets in three of its investment funds because of a lack of liquidity in U.S. securitization markets. Greater reliance on overnight borrowing increased the volatility of banks' funding costs and increased "rollover" risk, or the risk that banks would not be able to renew their funding as loans matured.

[129] One basis point is equivalent to 0.01 percent or 1/100th of a percent. The Federal Reserve Board later approved further reductions in the discount rate and increased the maximum maturity of discount window loans to 90 days. In addition to the discount window changes, starting in September 2007, the Federal Open Market Committee (FOMC) announced a series of reductions in the target federal funds rate—the FOMC- established target interest rate that banks charge each other for loans.

[130] The Federal Reserve Board authorized Reserve Banks to extend credit through TAF by revising the regulations governing Reserve Bank discount window lending.

[131] Section 10B of the Federal Reserve Act provides the Reserve Banks broad authority to extend credit to depository institutions. 12 U.S.C. § 347b.

[132] Under a repurchase agreement, a borrowing institution generally acquires funds by selling securities to a lending institution and agreeing to repurchase the securities after a specified time at a given price. The securities, in

effect, are collateral provided by the borrower to the lender. In the event of a borrower's default on the repurchase transaction, the lender would be able to take (and sell) the collateral provided by the borrower. Lenders typically will not provide a loan for the full market value of the posted securities, and the difference between the values of the securities and the loan is called a margin or haircut. This deduction is intended to protect the lenders against a decline in the price of the securities provided as collateral. When the market value of assets used to secure or collateralize repurchase transactions declines, borrowers are usually required to post additional collateral.

[133] The Federal Reserve System conducts open market operations to influence the amount of money and credit available in the economy. FRBNY carries out directives from the Federal Open Market Committee—which consists of members of the Board of Governors and the FRBNY president, and four other Reserve Bank presidents who serve on a rotating basis—by engaging in purchase or sales of certain securities, typically U.S. government securities, in the secondary market. FRBNY conducts these transactions through the primary dealers.

[134] Federal Reserve Board officials noted that although TSLF was announced to address market tensions impacting many firms, some market participants concluded that its establishment was driven by specific concerns about Bear Stearns.

[135] As discussed later in this section, the Federal Reserve Board used its emergency authority to authorize an emergency overnight loan and other assistance to avoid a disorderly failure of Bear Stearns.

[136] For TSLF, previously, only Treasury securities, agency securities, and AAA-rated mortgage-backed and asset-backed securities could be pledged. For PDCF, previously, eligible collateral had to have at least an investment-grade rating. Tri-party repurchase agreements include three parties: the borrower, the lender, and a tri-party agent that facilitates the repurchase agreement transaction by providing custody of the securities posted as collateral and valuing the collateral, among other services.

[137] There are two main types of commercial paper: unsecured and asset-backed. Unsecured paper is not backed by collateral and the credit rating of the issuing institution is a key variable in determining the cost of its issuance. In contrast, Asset Backed Commercial Paper is collateralized by assets and therefore is a secured form of borrowing.

[138] These programs included the AMLF and the Term Asset-Backed Securities Loan Facility. For more information about these programs, see GAO

[139] Pub. L. No. 110-343, Div. A, 122 Stat. 3765 (codified at 12 U.S.C. §§ 5201-5261). EESA established the Office of Financial Stability within Treasury and provided it with broad, flexible authorities to buy or guarantee troubled mortgage-related assets or any other financial instruments necessary to stabilize the financial markets. *Id.* at § 101 (12 U.S.C. § 5211).

[140] A warrant is an option to buy shares of common stock or preferred stock at a predetermined price on or before a specified date.

[141] TLGP's authorization required a systemic risk determination by the Secretary of the Treasury. For more information about this determination, see GAO, *Federal Deposit Insurance Act: Regulators' Use of Systemic Risk Exception Raises Moral Hazard Concerns and Opportunities Exist to Clarify the Provision,* GAO-10-100 (Washington, D.C.: April 15, 2010).

[142] However, the quantity of funds made available in the auction could also reduce prices in the alternative market, which would provide benefits to participants and nonparticipants alike. The size of the benefit in this instance would also be difficult to measure.

[143] Our analysis focuses on the use of emergency programs by banking organizations. However, emergency programs also provided funding for some nonbank financial institutions, such as standalone broker-dealers, and for some nonfinancial companies, such as McDonald's Corp. and Harley-Davidson.

[144] The final TAF auction was held in March 2010. However, credit extended under that auction did not mature until April 2010.

[145] Treasury made TIP investments in two banking organizations, Bank of America Corporation and Citigroup, Inc., both of which are in the group of banking organizations with $250 billion or more in assets in every quarter.

[146] Some small banks repaid their CPP investments with funds from Treasury's Small Business Lending Fund (SBLF). As a result, their liability to Treasury remained following their repayment of CPP funds. SBLF is a capital support program that encourages small and midsize banks and community development loan funds to lend to small businesses.

In: Bank Holding Companies and Government Support Issues ISBN: 978-1-63463-687-2
Editor: Colleen Royce

Chapter 2

LARGE BANK HOLDING COMPANIES: EXPECTATIONS OF GOVERNMENT SUPPORT*

United States Government Accountability Office

WHY GAO DID THIS STUDY

"Too big to fail" is a market notion that the federal government would intervene to prevent the failure of a large, complex financial institution to avoid destabilizing the financial sector and the economy. Expectations of government rescues can distort investor incentives to properly price the risks of firms they view as too big to fail, potentially giving rise to funding and other advantages for these firms.

GAO was asked to review the benefits that the largest bank holding companies (those with more than $500 billion in assets) have received from perceived government support. This is the second of two GAO reports on government support for bank holding companies. The first study focused on actual government support during the 2007-2009 financial crisis and recent statutory and regulatory changes related to government support for these firms. This report examines how financial reforms have altered market expectations of government rescues and the existence or size of funding advantages the largest bank holding companies may have received due to perceived government support.

GAO reviewed relevant statutes and rules and interviewed regulators, rating agencies, investment firms, and corporate customers of banks. GAO also reviewed relevant studies and interviewed authors of these studies. Finally, GAO conducted quantitative analyses to assess potential "too-big-to-fail" funding cost advantages.

In its comments, the Department of the Treasury generally agreed with GAO's analysis. GAO incorporated technical comments from the financial regulators, as appropriate.

---

* This is an edited, reformatted and augmented version of the United States Government Accountability Office publication, GAO-14-621, dated July 2014.

WHAT GAO FOUND

While views varied among market participants with whom GAO spoke, many believed that recent regulatory reforms have reduced but not eliminated the likelihood the federal government would prevent the failure of one of the largest bank holding companies. Recent reforms provide regulators with new authority to resolve a large failing bank holding company in an orderly process and require the largest bank holding companies to meet stricter capital and other standards, increasing costs and reducing risks for these firms. In response to reforms, two of three major rating agencies reduced or removed the assumed government support they incorporated into some large bank holding companies' overall credit ratings. Credit rating agencies and large investors cited the new Orderly Liquidation Authority as a key factor influencing their views. While several large investors viewed the resolution process as credible, others cited potential challenges, such as the risk that multiple failures of large firms could destabilize markets. Remaining market expectations of government support can benefit large bank holding companies if they affect investors' and customers' decisions.

GAO analyzed the relationship between a bank holding company's size and its funding costs, taking into account a broad set of other factors that can influence funding costs. To inform this analysis and to understand the breadth of methodological approaches and results, GAO reviewed selected studies that estimated funding cost differences between large and small financial institutions that could be associated with the perception that some institutions are too big to fail. Studies GAO reviewed generally found that the largest financial institutions had lower funding costs during the 2007-2009 financial crisis but that the difference between the funding costs of the largest and smaller institutions has since declined. However, these empirical analyses contain a number of limitations that could reduce their validity or applicability to U.S. bank holding companies. For example, some studies used credit ratings which provide only an indirect measure of funding costs.

GAO's analysis, which addresses some limitations of these studies, suggests that large bank holding companies had lower funding costs than smaller ones during the financial crisis but provides mixed evidence of such advantages in recent years. However, most models suggest that such advantages may have declined or reversed. GAO developed a series of statistical models that estimate the relationship between bank holding companies' bond funding costs and their size or systemic importance, controlling for other drivers of bond funding costs, such as bank holding company credit risk. Key features of GAO's approach include the following:

- **U.S. Bank Holding Companies:** The models focused on U.S. bank holding companies to better understand the relationship between funding costs and size in the context of the U.S. economic and regulatory environment.
- **Bond Funding Costs:** The models used bond yield spreads—the difference between the yield or rate of return on a bond and the yield on a Treasury bond of comparable maturity—to measure funding costs because they are a risk-sensitive measure of what investors charge bank holding companies to borrow.
- **Extensive Controls:** The models controlled for credit risk, bond liquidity, and other variables to account for factors other than size that could affect funding costs.

- **Multiple Models:** GAO used 42 models for each year from 2006 through 2013 to assess the impact of using alternative measures of credit risk, bond liquidity, and size and to allow the relationship between size and bond funding costs to vary over time with changes in the economic and regulatory environment.
- **Credit Risk Levels:** GAO compared bond funding costs for bank holding companies of different sizes at the average level of credit risk for each year, at low and high levels of credit risk for each year, and at the average level of credit risk during the financial crisis.

The figure below shows the differences between model- estimated bond funding costs for bank holding companies with $1 trillion in assets and bank holding companies with $10 billion in assets, with average levels of credit risk in each year. Circles represent statistically significant model- estimated differences.

All 42 models found that larger bank holding companies had lower bond funding costs than smaller ones in 2008 and 2009, while more than half of the models found that larger bank holding companies had higher bond funding costs than smaller ones in 2011 through 2013, given the average level of credit risk each year. However, the models' comparisons of bond funding costs for bank holding companies of different sizes varied depending on the level of credit risk. For example, in hypothetical scenarios where levels of credit risk in every year from 2010 to 2013 are assumed to be as high as they were during the financial crisis, GAO's analysis suggests that large bank holding companies might have had lower funding costs than smaller ones in recent years. However, reforms in the Dodd-Frank Wall Street Reform and Consumer Protection Act, such as enhanced standards for capital and liquidity, could enhance the stability of the financial system and make such a credit risk scenario less likely.

This analysis builds on certain aspects of prior studies, but important limitations remain and these results should be interpreted with caution. GAO's estimates of differences in funding costs reflect a combination of several factors, including investors' beliefs about the likelihood a bank holding company will fail and the likelihood it will be rescued by the government if it fails, and cannot precisely identify the influence of each factor. In addition, these estimates may reflect factors other than investors' beliefs about the likelihood of government support and may also reflect differences in the characteristics of bank holding companies that do and do not issue bonds. Finally, GAO's estimates, like all past estimates, are not indicative of future trends.

ABBREVIATIONS

AIG	American International Group, Inc.
BHC	bank holding company
CCAR	Comprehensive Capital Analysis and Review
FDIC	Federal Deposit Insurance Corporation
FDICIA	FDIC Improvement Act of 1991
FSOC	Financial Stability Oversight Council
GSIB	global systemically important bank

IDI	insured depository institution
LTCM	Long-Term Capital Management
OCC	Office of the Comptroller of the Currency
OFR	Office of Financial Research
OLA	Orderly Liquidation Authority
S&P	Standard & Poor's
SIFI	systemically important financial institution
SPOE	Single Point-of-Entry
TARP	Troubled Asset Relief Program

***

July 31, 2014

The Honorable Sherrod Brown
Chairman
Subcommittee on Financial Institutions and Consumer Protection
Committee on Banking, Housing, and Urban Affairs
United States Senate

The Honorable David Vitter
United States Senate

"Too big to fail" refers to a market notion that the federal government would intervene to prevent the failure of a large, interconnected financial institution to avoid harm to the economy. Events during the 2007-2009 financial crisis heightened concerns that market participants had come to view several of the largest U.S. financial institutions as too big to fail. Most notably, the U.S. government intervened to provide tens of billions of dollars of capital and other support to a few large troubled financial institutions out of concern that allowing these firms to go into bankruptcy would have further disrupted troubled credit markets and damaged confidence in the U.S. financial system.[1] Market expectations of government rescues can distort the incentives of investors and counterparties to properly price and restrain the risks of firms they believe to be too big to fail, potentially giving rise to funding cost and other advantages for these firms relative to smaller competitors. For example, creditors may be willing to accept lower interest rates on debt issued by these firms if they believe the possibility of a government rescue reduces the likelihood that they could suffer losses. If creditors and other counterparties do not fully charge a firm for the risks it is taking, that firm may have incentives to take on greater risks in the pursuit of higher returns. Excessive risk-taking in response to such incentives can increase the likelihood that such a firm could become distressed and disrupt financial markets.

The Dodd-Frank Wall Street Reform and Consumer Protection Act (Dodd- Frank Act) prohibits rescues of individual failing financial institutions and provides new tools and authorities for the Federal Deposit Insurance Corporation (FDIC) to resolve a large failing financial institution in a manner that imposes losses on the firm's creditors and other investors while minimizing adverse impacts to the economy.[2] Nevertheless, market observers have continued to debate whether some of the largest and most complex financial institutions may continue to benefit from beliefs among their investors and counterparties that the government might intervene to prevent their failure.

You asked us to review any economic benefits that the largest bank holding companies (those with more than $500 billion in total consolidated assets) have received as a result of actual or perceived government support. This is the second of two reports we are issuing on this topic.[3] In this report, we review (1) what is known about how financial reforms have altered market expectations of government rescues and the relative advantages or disadvantages of being a large bank holding company and (2) the extent to which the largest bank holding companies have received funding cost advantages as a result of perceptions that the government would not allow them to fail.

Scope and Methodology

To address our first objective, we reviewed information from relevant statutory provisions and regulations and prior GAO reports to describe financial reforms that could impact market expectations of government rescues or relative advantages or disadvantages of being a large bank holding company.[4] We obtained perspectives on the potential impacts of these reforms from credit rating agencies, investment firms, and corporations that are customers of banks. Where available and relevant, we reviewed some public statements, reports, and other analyses by these groups. For example, to obtain information about credit rating agencies' assessments of the likelihood and level of government support for large bank holding companies, we reviewed relevant publications by the three largest credit rating agencies: Fitch Ratings (Fitch), Moody's Investors Service (Moody's), and Standard & Poor's (S&P). We interviewed representatives from each of these rating agencies to obtain their perspectives on factors contributing to changes in their assessments of government support over time.

We conducted interviews with representatives from 10 investment firms and six corporations to learn about (1) factors that influence their decisions to invest in or do business with bank holding companies of various sizes; (2) how they assess the risks of banks and the extent to which they rely on credit rating agencies' assessments of these risks; (3) their views on the likelihood that the federal government would intervene to prevent the failure of a large bank holding company and factors that have influenced these views over time; and (4) how, if at all, expectations of government support have impacted their decisions to invest in or do business with banks of various sizes. In selecting investment firms and large corporations for interviews, we selected nonrepresentative samples of firms. As a result, the views we present from these firms are not generalizable to the broader community of bank investors and customers and do not indicate which views are most prevalent. We selected investment firms with experience investing in debt or equity securities of banks and bank holding companies and selected different types of investment firms to obtain perspectives reflecting a range of investing strategies. Specifically, we selected three large asset management firms (each with more than $1 trillion in assets under management); three public pension funds (each with more than $50 billion in assets under management); three hedge funds; and one large insurance company. We selected U.S. corporations from different industry sectors and with a range of banking needs. We identified four of these firms and contacted them with the assistance of the U.S. Chamber of Commerce, which reached out to its members on our behalf, and selected two additional firms to achieve additional diversity across industry sectors. The corporations we interviewed included four multinational corporations (a chemical company, a delivery and logistics company, an energy company, and a technology company) and two corporations with all or close to all of their operations in the United States (a regional electric utility company and a national retail services company).

To obtain additional information and perspectives on how financial reforms or credit ratings could impact the relative advantages or disadvantages of being a large bank holding company, we reviewed relevant publicly available information in the financial statements of bank holding companies and conducted interviews with bank holding companies of various sizes, bank industry associations, public interest groups, academics, and other experts. For example, we reviewed bank holding companies' financial disclosures about how Dodd-Frank reforms could increase certain fees and how a credit rating downgrade could impact the amount of collateral required of them under certain financial contracts. We also reviewed our prior work on potential impacts of Dodd- Frank Act implementation.[5]

As part of our first objective, we reviewed regulators' efforts to assess their progress in addressing too-big-to-fail perceptions and market distortions that can result. We reviewed Dodd-Frank Act provisions that outline statutory responsibilities for the Financial Stability Oversight Council (FSOC) and reviewed relevant sections of the FSOC annual report. We interviewed officials from FSOC, the Department of the Treasury (Treasury), the Board of Governors of the Federal Reserve System (Federal Reserve Board), FDIC, and the Office of the Comptroller of the Currency (OCC) about their efforts to analyze the impacts of Dodd-Frank reforms on too-big-to-fail perceptions and to evaluate whether additional policy actions may be needed to address any remaining market distortions. We also reviewed relevant congressional testimonies and other public statements by agency officials.

To assess the extent to which the largest bank holding companies have received funding cost advantages as a result of perceptions that the government would not allow them to fail, we conducted an econometric analysis of the relationship between a bank holding company's size and its funding costs. To inform our econometric approach and understand the breadth of results and methodological approaches, we reviewed studies that estimated the funding cost difference between large and small financial institutions that could be associated with the perception that some institutions are too big to fail. We evaluated studies that met the following criteria: (1) used a comparative empirical approach that attempted to account for differences across financial institutions that could influence funding costs, (2) included U.S. bank holding companies, and (3) included analysis of data from 2002 or later. We chose these criteria to identify the most relevant and rigorous studies related to our research objective. To identify studies that met these criteria, we sought input from individuals, agencies, and groups that we interviewed, identified studies cited in an initial set of studies we had already identified, and conducted a systematic search of research databases (including Google Scholar and SSRN).

Our criteria excluded studies that used option-pricing approaches—that is, techniques that use tools for pricing stock options to estimate the value associated with possible government interventions to assist distressed banks—because these studies assume a too-big-to-fail funding cost advantage exists and only estimate its magnitude. We also excluded two studies that otherwise met our criteria, but did not attempt to control for important differences between financial institutions. We were aware of potential conflicts of interest associated with a number of studies in our review. For example, one study was conducted by researchers at a large bank holding company and two others were sponsored by a trade group representing large commercial banks. We considered the potential impact these conflicts of interest might have on their methods and results. We ultimately included 16 studies in our review that we determined were sufficiently reliable for the purposes of this report.

In reviewing these studies, we assessed what they identified as the level of funding cost differences and how that level has changed over time and we identified the strengths and limitations of the studies' approaches. Because of limitations of the methodologies of these studies, their results, while suggestive of general trends, are not definitive and thus should be interpreted with caution. We interviewed authors of selected studies, federal financial regulators, and other experts to obtain perspectives on the strengths and limitations of relevant quantitative approaches that have been used.

Taking into consideration the strengths and limitations of different methodologies, we developed our own econometric approach to evaluate the extent to which the largest bank holding companies may have received funding cost advantages as a result of perceptions that the government would not allow them to fail. In addition, we selected three experts with relevant expertise to review our econometric approach and assess its strengths and limitations. These experts reviewed our approach before we implemented it and provided comments on our methodology. In many instances, we made changes or additions to our models to address their comments, and in other instances, we disclosed additional limitations of the models. Before selecting these experts, we reviewed potential sources of conflicts of interest, and we determined that the experts we selected did not have any material conflicts of interest for the purpose of reviewing our work.

We used a multivariate regression model to estimate the relationship between bank holding companies' funding costs and their size while controlling for factors other than size that may also influence funding costs. Our general regression model is the following:

$$funding\ cost_{bq} = \alpha + \beta \cdot size_{bq} + \gamma \cdot credit\ risk_{bq} + \delta \cdot (size_{bq} \times credit\ risk_{bq}) + X'_{bq} \cdot \Theta + \varepsilon_{bq}$$

In this model, b denotes the bank holding company, q denotes the quarter, $funding\ cost_{bq}$ is the bank holding company's cost of funding in a quarter, $size_{bq}$ is a measure of the bank holding company's size at the beginning of the quarter, $credit\ risk_{bq}$ is a list of proxies for the bank holding company's credit risk—the risk that the bank holding company will not repay the funds it borrowed as agreed, X_{bq} is a list of other variables that may influence funding costs, ε_{bq} is an idiosyncratic error term, and α,β,γ,δ, and Θ are parameters to be estimated. The parameter β captures the direct relationship between a bank holding company's funding cost and its size. The parameter δ captures the indirect relationship between a bank holding company's funding cost and its size that exists if the size of a bank holding company affects the relationship between its funding cost and credit risk. If investors view larger bank holding companies as less risky than smaller bank holding companies due to beliefs that the government is more likely to rescue larger bank holding companies in distress, then either β is less than zero, δ is less than zero, or both.[6] However, the parameters β and δ may also reflect factors other than these beliefs.

We used a measure of funding costs based on bonds issued by bank holding companies. Bank holding companies use a variety of funding types from different sources, including various types of deposits, bonds, and equity. We used bond yield spreads—the difference between the yield on a bond and the yield on a Treasury bond of comparable maturity—to measure a bank holding company's cost of bond funding. Treasury securities are widely viewed as a risk-free asset, so the yield spread measures the price that investors charge a bank holding company to borrow to compensate them for credit risk and other factors. We focused on bond yield spreads because they are a measure of funding costs that is available for bank holding companies of a range of sizes, including bank holding companies with less than $10 billion in assets. Furthermore, bonds are traded in secondary markets, so changes in bond yield spreads can be publicly observed in a timely manner. Finally, bond yield spreads are a direct measure of funding costs, unlike alternatives such as credit ratings.

We used Bloomberg to identify U.S. bank holding companies with more than $500 million in assets that were operating in 1 or more years from 2006 through 2013, and to identify all plain vanilla, fixed-rate, senior unsecured bonds issued by these bank holding companies, excluding bonds with an explicit government guarantee.[7] We collected data on bond yield spreads, bank holding company size, variables associated with bank holding company credit risk, and bond characteristics from Bloomberg. We used these data to assemble a dataset with one observation for each bond in each quarter from the first quarter of 2006 through the fourth quarter of 2013. We constructed alternative measures to control for size, bond liquidity, and credit risk due to uncertainty about how to appropriately capture these important factors influencing bond yields and because the regression results may be sensitive to alternative specifications (see table 1). The numbers of bank holding companies and bonds we analyzed and summary statistics for our indicators of size, credit risk, and other factors are in appendix I.

Table 1. Overview of Variables Used in Econometric Models

Funding costs	Size	Credit risk[a]	Other bond and bank holding company characteristics
Quarterly average bond yield spreads based on prices from executed trades, executable quotes, and composites derived from executable and indicative quotes.[b] Quarterly average bond yield spreads based on executed trades only.	Total assets. Total assets and total assets squared. An indicator for whether or not a bank holding company had $50 billion or more in assets.[c] An indicator for whether or not a bank holding company was designated a globally systemically important bank in November 2013.	*Capital adequacy:* Equity capital and subordinated debt as percentages of assets and risk-weighted assets.[d] *Asset quality:* Nonperforming assets as a percentage of tangible common equity plus loan loss reserves.[e] *Earnings:* Net income as a percentage of assets. *Maturity mismatch:* Volatile liabilities minus liquid assets as a percentage of total liabilities.[f] *Volatility:* Standard deviation of equity prices over the quarter, option-implied volatility for the quarter, the standard deviation of equity returns over the quarter, the standard deviation of excess equity returns over the quarter, and the standard deviation of earnings.[g]	*Bond liquidity*: Issue size, total volume traded during a quarter, and average bid-ask spread over a quarter.[h] *Coupon rate:* The current interest rate on the bond. *Time to maturity:* The number of quarters until the bond matures. *Operating expenses:* Noninterest expense as a percentage of total assets.

Source: GAO. | GAO-14-621.

Note: Unless otherwise noted, all balance sheet and income statement variables—such as assets, liabilities, and net income—are measured as of the beginning of the quarter.

[a] Credit risk increases with higher values of our asset quality, maturity mismatch, and volatility measures and with lower values of our capital adequacy and earnings measures.

[b] Bond yield spreads are the difference between the yield on a bond and the yield on a comparable Treasury bond. Executed trades are completed transactions for which the terms have been agreed upon and assets have been exchanged. Executable quotes (or firm quotes) are prices quoted by dealers at which they would be willing to trade. Indicative quotes are prices quoted by dealers that give an indication of the price at which a bond might trade but at which they are not obligated to trade. Composite quotes or prices are derived from quantitative algorithms that aggregate information on prices from executed trades, executable quotes, and indicative quotes to give an indication of the market price of a bond.

[c] The Dodd-Frank Act requires bank holding companies with $50 billion or more in total assets to be subjected to enhanced regulatory standards and supervision. Pub. L. No. 111-203, § 165, 124 Stat. 1376, 1423 (2010) (codified at 12 U.S.C. § 5365).

[d] Regulators generally require that banks maintain certain ratios of capital as a share of assets to ensure that they have sufficient capital to absorb losses. Under the Basel approaches, banks may weight certain assets based on their risks, and use these risk-weighted assets to calculate their capital adequacy ratios.

[e] Nonperforming assets include assets in nonaccrual status, other real estate owned, restructured loans, and restructured loans in compliance. Tangible common equity is total capital minus perpetual preferred stock minus goodwill and other intangibles.

[f] Volatile liabilities include federal funds purchased and repurchase agreements, trading liabilities, other borrowed funds, foreign deposits, and jumbo deposits less derivatives with negative fair value. Liquid assets include cash, securities, federal funds sold and reverse repurchase agreements, and trading assets less pledged securities.

[g] Option-implied volatility is a measure of a security's expected volatility as reflected by the market price of traded options on that security. The theoretical price of an option is a function of the underlying price, strike price, historical volatility of the underlying, the risk-free rate, and the time to expiration. Implied volatility is calculated by using the market price of the option and solving for volatility. Excess return is a security's return minus the return from a no-risk security during the same time period.

[h] The bid-ask spread is the difference between the best buying price and the best selling price.

We developed a variety of econometric models that use alternative measures of bond liquidity, bank holding company credit risk, and the size or systemic importance of a bank holding company. We estimated the parameters for each of our models separately for each year from 2006 through 2013 to allow the relationship between bank holding company size and bond funding costs to vary over time.[8] Our baseline models used average yield spreads on senior unsecured bonds based on actual trades, executable quotes, and composites derived from executable and indicative quotes to measure bond funding costs; total assets to measure size; equity capital and subordinated debt as percentages of total assets to measure capital adequacy; and issue size and total volume to measure bond liquidity. We estimated the baseline model for each year and for each of our five measures of volatility, as well as for each year without a measure of volatility. We also estimated models that added average bid-ask spread to our baseline indicators of bond liquidity, models that used average yield spreads based only on actual trades, models that used equity capital and subordinated debt as percentages of risk-weighted assets as our indicators of capital adequacy, models that used global systemically important bank (GSIB) designation as an indicator of size, models that used the $50 billion asset threshold as an indicator of size, and models that used both total assets and the square of total assets as indicators of size.[9] Altogether, we used 42 separate models for each year from 2006 through 2013. For all models, we included indicators for each quarter to control for the influence on yield spreads of economic conditions, the regulatory environment, and other factors that vary over time but not across bank holding companies. The details of the models we estimated and the results for our baseline models for select years are in appendix I.

We used our models to compare bond funding costs for bank holding companies of different sizes, all else being equal.[10] Because our models account for the possibility that investors' beliefs about government rescues depend on the credit risk level of the bank holding company, we made comparisons for bank holding companies with the average level of credit risk that prevailed each year. In addition, we assessed the impact of credit risk on our comparisons by making comparisons at credit risk levels higher and lower than the average for each year and also while holding the level of credit risk constant over time at the average level for 2008—the year when the financial crisis peaked and credit risk for bank holding companies was high. By holding credit risk constant, we can assess the extent to which changes in average credit risk over time may have influenced changes in funding costs relative to other factors.

Our approach is limited by several factors. Investors' beliefs about the likelihood of government support are composed of several different elements, including the likelihood that a bank holding company will fail, the likelihood that it will be rescued by the government if it fails, and the size of the losses that the government may impose on investors if it rescues the bank holding company, but our methodology—like the methodologies used by other researchers—does not allow us to precisely identify the influence of each of these components. Although we have taken into account many factors that may influence bond yield spreads and that differ for bank holding companies of different sizes, our estimates of differences in bond yield spreads for bank holding companies of different sizes may reflect factors other than investors' beliefs about the likelihood of government support because our control variables are imperfect or may be incomplete. In addition, our estimates of differences in bond yield spreads for bank holding companies of different sizes may reflect differences in the characteristics of bank holding companies that choose to issue bonds. The section of this report that addresses our second objective contains a fuller discussion of the limitations associated with our empirical work.

For parts of our work that involved the analysis of computer-processed data, such as market data used in our analysis of funding cost differences, we assessed the reliability of these data by reviewing relevant documentation and conducting interviews with data providers to review steps they took to collect and ensure the reliability of the data. In addition, we electronically tested data fields for missing values, outliers, and obvious errors. We determined that these data were sufficiently reliable for our purposes.

We conducted this performance audit from January 2013 to July 2014 in accordance with generally accepted government auditing standards. Those standards require that we plan and perform the audit to obtain sufficient, appropriate evidence to provide a reasonable basis for our findings and conclusions based on our audit objectives. We believe that the evidence obtained provides a reasonable basis for our findings and conclusions based on our audit objectives.

BACKGROUND

While the 2007-2009 financial crisis highlighted concerns about the market distortions that can result from too-big-to-fail perceptions, concern about such distortions pre-dated the crisis. A key factor giving rise to the too-big-to-fail dilemma has been the emergence of financial institutions of such size, interconnectedness, and market importance that their failure could threaten to severely disrupt the financial system and damage the economy. Although the federal government's policy responses to failing financial institutions in recent decades have not formed a clear pattern in terms of the availability or structure of government support, these responses may have influenced market views on the likelihood of government support. Several observers trace too-big-to-fail concerns back to 1984 when FDIC provided support to Continental Illinois National Bank, then the sixth largest U.S. bank in terms of total assets, to prevent its failure and losses to its depositors and creditors.[11] The Federal Reserve Board's response to the near failure of a large U.S. hedge fund, Long-Term Capital Management (LTCM), in 1998 was another significant event that may have contributed to too-big-to-fail perceptions.[12] While LTCM was not itself a large bank, the Federal Reserve Board's intervention in helping to facilitate private-sector assistance to LTCM may have signaled the willingness of federal government authorities to intervene to avoid potential systemic consequences from a large, interconnected financial firm's failure. Other factors may have contributed to some ambiguity surrounding the likely recipients and circumstances of government support in the years leading up to the 2007-2009 financial crisis. For example, failures and near-failures of large financial firms had been infrequent and occurred under varying circumstances, making it difficult to discern a clear pattern of government support.

During the 2007-2009 crisis, the federal government took actions to stabilize the financial system by creating new emergency programs with broad-based eligibility and providing firm-specific assistance to prevent the failures of large financial institutions.[13] Notably, however, U.S. government authorities' initial responses to impending failures of large financial institutions did not send a clear signal about the availability of government support. In March 2008, the Federal Reserve Board authorized emergency assistance to prevent the failure of one large investment bank (Bear Stearns Companies, Inc.), but 6 months later, Federal Reserve Board officials determined that they could not assist another large failing investment bank, Lehman Brothers Holdings, Inc. (Lehman Brothers).[14] Following Lehman Brothers' bankruptcy announcement on September 15, 2008, which triggered an intensification of the financial crisis, U.S. government authorities took actions that signaled a stronger near-term commitment to prevent the failure of systemically important financial institutions. On the day after Lehman Brothers' bankruptcy announcement, the Federal Reserve Board authorized up to $85 billion of credit assistance for American International Group, Inc. (AIG) to prevent its failure.[15] In addition, on September 29, 2008, the Secretary of the Treasury invoked the systemic risk exception for the first time since the enactment of the FDIC Improvement Act of 1991(FDICIA) to authorize FDIC to provide assistance to avert the failure of Wachovia Corporation—then the fourth-largest banking organization in terms of assets in the United States—by facilitating Citigroup Inc.'s acquisition of its banking operations.[16]

At the height of the crisis in late 2008, the United States and other G7 countries announced an agreement to implement a comprehensive action plan to provide liquidity to financial markets and prevent the failure of any systemically important institution, among other objectives.[17] That month, U.S. government agencies launched two of the largest U.S. emergency initiatives: the Troubled Asset Relief Program, through which Treasury provided capital and other assistance to eligible financial institutions, and the Temporary Liquidity Guarantee Program, through which FDIC guaranteed certain uninsured deposits and newly issued unsecured debt of eligible financial institutions.[18] In late 2008 and early 2009, Treasury, the Federal Reserve Board, and FDIC authorized packages of firm- specific assistance for two of the largest U.S. bank holding companies, Citigroup Inc. and Bank of America Corporation. Foreign governments launched parallel initiatives to provide broad-based liquidity support and also took steps to prevent the failures of large financial institutions. Examples of large foreign financial institutions that received firm-specific assistance from their governments include Royal Bank of Scotland Group PLC (United Kingdom) and UBS (Switzerland).

Since the onset of the financial crisis, the largest banks have grown bigger in many major advanced economies, even as the financial sector has shrunk, and U.S. and foreign policymakers have acknowledged that crisis policy interventions raised moral hazard concerns.[19] As discussed earlier, market perceptions that some firms are too big to fail can distort market participants' incentives to properly price and restrain risk-taking by these firms. U.S. regulators have coordinated with foreign counterparts through the G20 and the Financial Stability Board to develop a policy framework for addressing the risks posed by large, complex financial institutions.[20] In November 2010, G20 leaders endorsed the Financial Stability Board's framework for addressing too-big-to-fail concerns. The framework aims to reduce the probability and impact of the failure of systemically important firms.[21] Key elements of this framework include developing effective resolution regimes and strengthening capital standards for systemically important financial institutions. FDIC, the Federal Reserve Bank of New York, and Treasury helped to develop standards the Financial Stability Board issued for effective resolution regimes in October 2011.[22] In addition, U.S. banking regulators have worked with their foreign counterparts to develop a strengthened capital regime that will require global systemically important banks to have additional loss absorbing capacity.[23] U.S. federal financial regulators are implementing these and other elements of the Financial Stability Board's framework for addressing too big to fail as part of the process of implementing relevant Dodd-Frank Act provisions.

Dodd-Frank Act Provisions

U.S. federal financial regulators have made progress in implementing Dodd-Frank Act provisions and related reforms to restrict future government support and reduce the likelihood and impacts of the failure of a systemically important financial institution (SIFI).[24] These reforms can be grouped into four general categories: (1) restrictions on regulators' emergency authorities to provide assistance to financial institutions; (2) new tools and authorities for regulators to resolve a failing SIFI outside of bankruptcy if its failure would have serious adverse effects on the U.S. financial system; (3) enhanced regulatory standards for SIFIs related to capital, liquidity, and risk management; and (4) other reforms intended to reduce the potential disruptions to the financial system that could result from a SIFI's failure.

Restrictions on Emergency Authorities. The Dodd-Frank Act revised Federal Reserve Board and FDIC emergency authorities so that emergency assistance can no longer be provided to assist a single and specific firm but rather can only be made available through a program with broad-based eligibility—that is, a program that provides funding support to institutions that meet program requirements and that choose to participate.[25]

New Tools and Authorities for Resolving SIFIs. The Dodd-Frank Act includes two key reforms intended to facilitate the orderly resolution of a large failing firm without a taxpayer-funded rescue: (1) requirements for SIFIs to formulate and submit to regulators resolution plans (or "living wills") that detail how the companies could be resolved in bankruptcy in the event of material financial distress or failure; and (2) the Orderly Liquidation Authority (OLA), through which FDIC can resolve large financial firms, and which provides an alternative to bankruptcy if resolution under the bankruptcy code would have serious adverse effects on financial stability.[26]

- *Living wills.* Title I of the Dodd-Frank Act requires bank holding companies with $50 billion or more in consolidated assets and nonbank financial companies designated by FSOC to formulate and submit to FDIC, the Federal Reserve Board, and FSOC resolution plans (or "living wills") that detail how the companies could be resolved in bankruptcy in the event of material financial distress or failure.[27] The Federal Reserve Board and FDIC have finalized rules relating to resolution plans, and the large bank holding companies that were the first firms required to prepare and submit such plans submitted these to regulators as expected in July 2012.[28] Regulators reviewed these initial plans and developed guidance on what information should be included in 2013 resolution plan submissions.[29] If FDIC and the Federal Reserve Board jointly determine that a resolution plan is not credible or would not facilitate an orderly resolution of the company under the bankruptcy code, after giving the company an opportunity to remedy the plan's deficiencies, the agencies may jointly decide to impose more stringent regulatory requirements on the company.[30]
- *Orderly Liquidation Authority.* OLA gives FDIC the authority, subject to certain constraints, to resolve large financial firms, including nonbanks, outside of the bankruptcy process.[31] This authority allows for FDIC to be appointed receiver for a financial firm if the Secretary of the Treasury determines, among other things, that the firm's failure and its resolution under applicable federal or state law, including bankruptcy, would have serious adverse effects on U.S. financial stability and no viable private-sector alternative is available to prevent the default of the financial company.[32] While the Dodd-Frank Act does not specify how FDIC must exercise this authority, FDIC is developing an approach to resolving a firm under OLA that it refers to as the Single Point-of-Entry (SPOE) approach.

  Under the SPOE approach, FDIC would be appointed receiver of the top-tier U.S. parent holding company of a financial group determined to be in default or in danger of default following the completion of the appointment process set forth under the Dodd-Frank Act. Immediately after placing the parent holding company into receivership, FDIC would transfer assets (primarily the equity and investments in subsidiaries) from the receivership estate to a bridge financial holding company. By allowing FDIC to take control of the firm at the holding company level, this approach is intended to allow subsidiaries (domestic and foreign) carrying out critical services to remain open and operating. In a SPOE resolution, at the parent holding company level, shareholders would be wiped out, and unsecured debt holders would have their claims written down to reflect any losses that shareholders cannot cover. Under the Dodd-Frank Act, officers and directors responsible for the failure cannot be retained.[33]

The new resolution authority under the Dodd-Frank Act provides a back-up source for liquidity support, the Orderly Liquidation Fund, which could provide liquidity support to the bridge financial company if customary sources of liquidity are unavailable.[34] The law requires FDIC to recover any losses arising from a resolution by collecting assessments from bank holding companies with $50 billion or more in consolidated assets, nonbank financial holding companies designated for supervision by the Federal Reserve Board, and other financial companies with $50 billion or more in consolidated assets.[35]

Enhanced Regulatory Standards. The Dodd-Frank Act also introduced a number of regulatory changes designed to reduce the risks that the largest financial institutions pose to the financial system. The act requires the Federal Reserve Board to create enhanced capital and prudential standards for SIFIs.[36] According to Federal Reserve Board officials, in implementing these reforms, the Federal Reserve Board aims to design prudential standards that will both reduce the likelihood of a covered institution's failure and create incentives for these institutions to reduce their systemic footprint. The act's provisions related to enhanced prudential standards for these covered firms include, but are not limited to, the following:

- *Risk-based capital requirements and leverage limits.* The act required the Federal Reserve Board to establish capital and leverage standards, which, as finalized, include a requirement for covered firms to develop capital plans to help ensure that they maintain capital ratios above specified standards, under both normal and adverse conditions.[37] In addition, the Federal Reserve Board has announced its intention to apply capital surcharges to some or all firms based on the risks these firms pose to the financial system.[38]
- *Liquidity requirements.* The act required the Federal Reserve Board to establish liquidity standards, which as finalized include requirements for covered firms to hold liquid assets that can be used to cover their cash outflows over short periods and in stressed conditions.[39] In addition, the Federal Reserve Board, FDIC, and OCC have issued a proposed rule that would implement a minimum liquidity requirement that is consistent with the Basel III liquidity coverage ratio and would apply to internationally active U.S. banking organizations and U.S. depository institutions with $250 billion or more in total consolidated assets.[40]
- *Risk management requirements.* Publicly traded covered firms must establish a risk committee and be subject to enhanced risk management standards.[41]
- *Stress testing requirements.* The Federal Reserve Board is required to conduct an annual evaluation of whether covered firms have sufficient capital to absorb losses that could arise from adverse economic conditions.[42]

The Federal Reserve Board has been implementing the enhanced standards required by the Dodd-Frank Act in conjunction with its implementation of Basel III, a set of risk-based capital, leverage, and liquidity standards developed by the Basel Committee on Banking

Supervision.[43] The Basel capital reforms include a risk-based capital surcharge that will apply to financial institutions that have been designated as GSIBs. Further, the U.S. banking agencies have already adopted a leverage capital surcharge that will apply to the eight U.S. banking organizations that are GSIBs.[44]

Other Reforms. The act includes other reforms that could help reduce the likelihood or impacts of a SIFI's failure.

- *Authorities related to SIFI size and complexity.* The Dodd-Frank Act grants regulators new authorities to take certain actions if they determine that a SIFI poses risks of serious adverse effects on the stability of the financial system. These include the authority for the Federal Reserve Board to require a SIFI to meet even stricter regulatory standards, the authority for the Federal Reserve Board to limit (with the approval of FSOC) the ability of a SIFI to merge with another company if it determines that the merger would pose a grave threat to U.S. financial stability, and, as noted above, the joint authority for the Federal Reserve Board and FDIC to require a firm to take steps to become more resolvable in bankruptcy.[45]
- *Volcker rule.* Section 619 of the Dodd-Frank Act (also known as the Volcker rule) generally prohibits proprietary trading by insured depository institutions and their affiliates and places restrictions on sponsorship or investment in hedge and private equity funds.[46] The Volcker rule's restrictions may have greater impacts on larger bank holding companies that have been more involved in the types of activities the rule restricts. To the extent that Volcker rule implementation prevents these large institutions from engaging in certain risky activities, it could serve to reduce the likelihood of their failure.
- *Swaps clearing and margin requirements.* Title VII of the Dodd-Frank Act establishes a new regulatory framework for swaps to reduce risk, increase transparency, and promote market integrity in swaps markets.[47] As we previously reported, requirements for swaps to be cleared through clearinghouses can reduce the vulnerability of the financial system to the failure of one or a few of the major swap dealers by transferring credit risk from the swap counterparties to the clearinghouse.[48] At the same time, experts have pointed out that clearinghouses concentrate credit risk and thus represent a potential source of systemic risk.[49] A benefit of the central clearing requirement is that clearinghouses require members to post margin for their trades and the Dodd-Frank Act also includes provisions that require regulators to develop margin requirements for uncleared swaps.[50] These new requirements could help reduce systemic risk by preventing the build-up of large, undercollateralized exposures.

Although federal financial regulators have finalized a number of rules related to these reforms, implementation of some key reforms has not yet been completed. For example, FDIC has largely completed the core rulemakings necessary to carry out its systemic resolution responsibilities, and is continuing to develop its SPOE approach. FDIC requested public comments on its SPOE resolution strategy in December 2013, and the comment period closed in March 2014.[51] In addition, regulators have not finalized certain rules that would subject SIFIs to enhanced prudential standards. For example, regulators have not finalized rules on single- counterparty credit limits.[52]

Reforms Have Reduced Expectations of Government Support among Key Market Observers and Increased Regulation for Large Institutions

While views among investment firms we interviewed and credit rating agencies varied, many believe the Dodd-Frank Act has reduced but not eliminated the possibility of a government rescue of one of the largest bank holding companies. Two of the three largest credit rating agencies cited FDIC's resolution process as a key factor in their decisions to reduce or eliminate "uplift"—an increase in the credit rating—they had assigned to the credit ratings of eight of the largest bank holding companies due to their assumptions of government support for these firms. Several representatives from large investment firms with whom we spoke told us that FDIC's resolution process makes significant progress in reducing expectations of government support, but several agreed that uncertainty around its implementation or the circumstances of its use remains. As such, some market perceptions that the government might not allow the largest bank holding companies to fail remain and can give rise to advantages for these firms if these perceptions affect decisions by investors, counterparties, and customers of these firms. For example, credit rating agencies' assignment of higher credit ratings due to assumed government support can create benefits for these firms, but because investors may rely on credit ratings to varying degrees, the impact of such benefits may vary accordingly. In addition, Dodd-Frank Act provisions and related rules subject the largest firms to higher fees and stricter regulation that may reduce their risk of failure and increase costs on them relative to smaller competitors. Officials from FSOC and some of its member agencies have stated that financial reforms have not completely removed too-big-to-fail perceptions, but have made significant progress toward doing so. They anticipate that remaining expectations of government support will decline as Dodd-Frank implementation progresses.

Some Credit Rating Agencies and Large Investors Believe Dodd- Frank Has Reduced the Likelihood of Government Rescues

While views among credit rating agencies and investment firms varied, many believe the Dodd-Frank Act has reduced but not eliminated the possibility of a government rescue of one of the largest bank holding companies. During the financial crisis, credit rating agencies assigned or increased "uplift"—or an increase in the credit rating—for several large bank holding companies' credit ratings to reflect their view that the increased possibility of government support for these firms reduced the risk that the firms' creditors would suffer losses.[53] We reviewed changes in credit rating agencies' assumptions about government support over time and interviewed credit rating agency representatives. Because large investors do not necessarily rely on credit ratings or rating agencies' assessments of government support, we obtained perspectives from representatives of large asset management firms, pension funds, hedge funds, and other investment firms that purchase debt and equity issued by bank holding companies.[54]

Citing progress in Dodd-Frank implementation and other changes, two credit rating agencies have reduced or eliminated their rating uplift for the largest bank holding companies since the end of the 2007-2009 financial crisis, and a third rating agency has noted that regulatory developments may lead it to reduce or eliminate the uplift it assigns to these bank holding companies' ratings. The three largest credit rating agencies— Fitch, Moody's, and S&P—have incorporated government support into their ratings over time, with the amount of increase in credit rating being driven by their assessment of the firm's standalone credit rating—the credit rating that assumes no government support—and the impact on the firm's creditworthiness they attribute to the likelihood of government support.[55] These three rating agencies have incorporated government support into their ratings using different approaches and under Fitch's approach, assumptions of extraordinary government support have not led to an increase in rating for U.S. bank holding companies in all cases. Fitch incorporates government support into its ratings by assigning a "support rating floor," a minimum credit rating that reflects its view about the likelihood an entity will receive company-specific government support in case of need, though the entity only receives "uplift" in its rating if its standalone credit rating is below the "support rating floor." Following the July 2010 enactment of the Dodd-Frank Act, Fitch and Moody's removed their assumptions of government support for several large regional bank holding companies and their subsidiary banks and reduced (but did not eliminate) their assumptions of support for eight of the largest U.S. bank holding companies.[56] Fitch and Moody's reports cited FDIC's new resolution authority and a reduced willingness by the U.S. government to assist a failing bank holding company as key factors influencing these changes in assumed government support. As of June 2014, S&P had not changed its level of assumed government support since the financial crisis.[57] However, in June 2013, S&P noted that regulatory developments may lead it to reassess its assumptions of government support for the eight bank holding companies.[58] The three credit rating agencies each noted that their remaining assumptions of government support reflected continued uncertainty about the ability of the U.S. government to effectively resolve one of the largest bank holding companies in OLA. In September 2013, Fitch indicated that it would conduct a global review of its support ratings and in March 2014, Fitch reported that it expects to remove its support rating floor for several of the largest U.S. bank holding companies within the next one or two years.[59] In November 2013, Moody's removed all uplift from assumed government support from its credit ratings for the remaining eight large bank holding companies.[60]

Moody's cited regulators' substantial progress in establishing the SPOE receivership framework as a main consideration in their decision to remove the uplift. They noted that the SPOE framework would allow FDIC to impose losses on the creditors of a U.S. bank holding company to recapitalize and preserve the operations of the bank's systemically important subsidiaries in a stress scenario. As a result, they believe that the holding company creditors of systemically important U.S. banks are unlikely to receive government support.

Representatives of large investment firms with whom we spoke said that they rely primarily on their own assessments of government support when investing in financial institutions, and they identified OLA and other reforms as factors influencing their views. While representatives of several firms said that Dodd-Frank reforms have significantly reduced or eliminated expectations of government rescues, others said they continue to expect that the government would rescue one of the largest bank holding companies under certain scenarios if policymakers judged the potential costs to the economy from such a failure to be too great.

Investors generally cited progress on OLA and enhanced regulatory standards for the largest bank holding companies as among the most important factors influencing their views on the likelihood of government support, and many considered living wills and other reforms to be less significant factors.

FDIC's resolution process. Investors with whom we spoke said that FDIC's progress in developing its resolution process to implement OLA as an alternative to bankruptcy has caused them to significantly reduce their expectations of government support, but uncertainty around its implementation and circumstances of its use remains. Although several investors believed that FDIC's resolution process is credible for managing a single large failure, two expressed doubts about whether it could be used to resolve multiple failing firms in a systemic crisis. They noted that if the economic costs of a large firm's failure were judged to be too high, the federal government might not want to risk using OLA if regulators believed it would destabilize markets. Two investors noted that in the event that concerns about destabilizing markets led the federal government to provide emergency assistance to a failing firm in lieu of using OLA, policymakers might face political pressure to structure the assistance in a manner that imposed losses on creditors.[61] Other factors being equal, an investor's belief that there is a possibility of incurring losses even if the government prevents a firm's failure would reduce that investor's willingness to provide funds to that firm on more favorable terms because of a too-big-to-fail perception. Because OLA is untested, some uncertainty may exist about its viability as an alternative to bankruptcy and government rescues until it is used.

Some investors identified areas where further progress is needed to enhance the credibility of OLA. First, some market observers have pointed to opportunities to further minimize the adverse market impacts that could result from resolving a firm under OLA. For example, although OLA provides for a 1-day stay on qualified financial contracts to allow for the selection of contracts to transfer to the bridge company, derivatives contracts written under the laws of other countries could allow counterparties to close out those contracts immediately, possibly posing liquidity issues for the firm and leading it to sell assets at depressed prices into the market. Some regulatory officials have said that cross- border agreements that create conformity in the treatment of derivatives contracts in resolution processes would enhance OLA's effectiveness and practicality as a resolution tool. In addition, some investors noted that progress on the Federal Reserve's planned proposal for a minimum long- term debt requirement could create greater certainty that the largest bank holding companies would have enough equity and debt to absorb losses and recapitalize their operating subsidiaries under OLA.[62]

Enhanced regulatory standards. Many investment firm representatives credited enhanced regulatory standards for the largest bank holding companies with improving the safety and soundness of these firms and reducing the likelihood that they would experience distress that could result in failure or government support. One representative from a large investment firm said that the best defense against banks needing government support is to make sure they are well-capitalized. Similarly, another investment firm representative said that higher capital ratios and strengthened balance sheets have given confidence to the markets that the institutions are more sound, in turn reducing the likelihood that they would fail and potentially receive government assistance. A representative from one large asset management firm said that enhanced capital and liquidity standards are a positive from a debt holder's perspective because increased capital provides a bigger buffer to absorb losses and increased liquidity makes a run on the firm less likely.

Living wills. Several investors said the living wills may have positive effects, but some investors have expressed doubts about the effectiveness of the plans, with one investor citing a lack of public transparency. In a public comment letter to FDIC, The Credit Roundtable, a financial industry association, noted that additional living will disclosures would improve the market's ability to gauge the level of risk under a SPOE scenario. Additionally, while the purpose of living wills is to make SIFIs resolvable in bankruptcy, several large investors said they assume that a failing SIFI would be resolved through OLA.

Remaining Market Expectations of Government Support Can Have Benefits for Large Firms

Remaining market assumptions about government support can give rise to advantages for the largest bank holding companies in three broad categories to the extent these assumptions affect decisions by investors, counterparties, and customers of these firms. Those categories are funding costs, financial contracts that reference ratings, and ability to attract customers.

Funding Costs

Market beliefs about government support could benefit a firm by lowering its funding costs. However, the extent to which this occurs depends in part on the extent to which providers of funds—such as depositors, bond investors, and stockholders—rely on credit ratings that assume government support or incorporate their own expectations of government support into their decisions to provide funds. For example, an investor that relies on credit ratings may view a firm with a rating that incorporates implied government support as having lower risk—other factors being equal—and may be more inclined to invest in the firm and accept a lower interest rate or return on the firm's obligations. These effects can be more pronounced during a financial crisis, particularly if market strains cause credit rating agencies to reduce ratings more for firms they believe the government would not rescue and if providers of funds seek to reduce their risk exposures to firms they believe are not too big to fail.

Several factors influence the extent to which investors rely on ratings. For example, an investor's reliance on credit ratings can depend on the extent to which the investor conducts its own credit analysis. While representatives of large investment firms with whom we spoke said they rely primarily on their own assessments of credit risk and do not rely on credit ratings, smaller investors lacking the resources to do their own credit analysis may rely more on credit ratings and rating agencies' assessments of the impact of possible government support on a firm's risk profile. In addition, while an investment firm's assessment of government support can be relevant to funds that it actively manages, it may not incorporate this factor into the investment decisions of funds that it manages using passive investment strategies.[63] Finally, some representatives of large investment firms said that while they do not rely on credit ratings for investment decisions, they pay attention to them when managing funds for clients whose investments must meet minimum credit rating requirements and for clients who may use credit ratings to assess their performance.

Representatives of large investment firms with whom we spoke generally said their views on the likelihood of government support do not affect their investment decisions. Some representatives of investment firms said that while they believe some probability of government rescues remains, there is too much uncertainty surrounding future government support to factor it into their current investment decisions. Several bond investors said it is difficult to distinguish any pricing impacts from market expectations of government support from the variety of other factors related to firm size that can impact debt pricing and investors' investment decisions. For example, compared to smaller institutions, large bank holding companies issue bonds more frequently and in larger amounts, which increases the liquidity of their bonds. Investors may accept lower interest rates on more liquid bonds because more liquid bonds can be sold more easily without reducing the price. In the section addressing the second objective of this report, we analyze the existence and size of potential funding cost advantages for the largest bank holding companies using quantitative approaches that control for factors outside of government support that can influence funding cost differences.

Financial Contracts That Reference Ratings

Higher credit ratings from assumed government support can also benefit firms through private contracts that reference credit ratings. For example, derivative contracts often tie collateral requirements to a firm's credit rating. Representatives of some large bank holding companies said that reduced credit ratings would require them to post more collateral. Additional collateral requirements would demand additional funds that could otherwise be used in other investments. The largest bank holding companies disclose information in their financial statements about how a credit rating downgrade could cause them to post more collateral. While estimates of these collateral impacts have varied over time and across firms, several of these firms have estimated that a downgrade in their credit rating could require them to post between $1 billion and $4 billion of additional collateral, depending on the size of the downgrade. Another way that private contracts can reference credit ratings is by setting minimum credit rating requirements. Examples of such requirements include investment funds that cannot purchase securities that are below minimum ratings requirements and counterparties that will not accept a letter of credit from a bank with a low credit rating.

Ability to Attract Customers

Corporate customers with whom we spoke expressed varying views on the degree to which expectations of government support influence their banking decisions. Two corporate customers with whom we spoke said that they believe the government would intervene to prevent the failure of the largest bank holding companies, but that potential government support is only one of several factors they consider in choosing a bank and is not necessarily a decisive factor. Several corporate treasurers identified size-related factors that are unrelated to government support that make them more inclined to use the largest banks for their banking needs. For example, treasurers of global firms noted that the largest U.S. banks have the geographic presence and ability to provide funding on the scale they need to support their operations around the world. One corporate customer noted that although the company's credit facility includes both regional banks and some of the largest banks, they tend to use the services of large banks more because of their capacity for handling large transactions and the variety of their business lines.

However, while two treasurers said that they tend to select the largest U.S. banks primarily for reasons that are unrelated to government support, their beliefs about which banks would be rescued by the government can impact how they manage their risk exposures to banks of different sizes. For example, a treasurer for a large domestic corporation said that the possibility of government rescues can be a factor when evaluating counterparty risk and the safety of deposits. She noted that in normal economic conditions, the likelihood of government support for banks is not a significant factor, but when markets become strained, her company may reduce its deposits and other exposures to regional banks they believe the government would allow to fail. Outside of these treasurers, a treasurer from a large global company said that potential government support may impact his company's banking decisions indirectly through credit ratings. He noted that the company uses credit ratings as a factor in assessing a bank's creditworthiness and adjusting its exposures to banks. For example, if a bank's credit rating falls, the company may reduce its intraday exposure to that bank by shifting deposits and other exposures away from that bank. A few corporate customers told us they do not consider the possibility of government support for large banks when they decide how to allocate their banking business.

Stricter Capital and Other Regulatory Standards May Reduce Risk of Failure and Increase Costs for Largest Firms

The Dodd-Frank Act imposes new and higher fees on large bank holding companies and requires the Federal Reserve Board to subject large bank holding companies to enhanced regulatory standards for capital, liquidity, and risk management. These enhanced standards may help to reduce the likelihood and potential market impacts of the failure of a large bank holding company. Taken together, higher fees, stricter regulatory standards, and other reforms could increase costs for the largest bank holding companies relative to smaller competitors.[64] New or revised fees and assessments impose higher direct costs on bank holding companies with more than $50 billion in total assets.

- **Deposit insurance assessments.** The Dodd-Frank Act required FDIC to change the definition of an insured depository institution's assessment base, which can affect the amount of deposit insurance assessment the institution pays into the deposit insurance fund.[65] According to FDIC, this change shifted some of the overall assessment burden from smaller banks to larger institutions that rely less on deposits but did not affect the overall amount of assessment revenue collected. The base was changed from total domestic deposits to average consolidated total assets minus average tangible equity. The largest bank holding companies generally saw the largest percentage increases in their deposit insurance assessments because they rely less on domestic deposits for their funding than smaller institutions. One of the largest bank holding companies reported that the change to the assessment calculation resulted in a $600 million increase in its deposit insurance assessments in 2011. In the quarter after the rule became effective, those banks with less than $10 billion in assets saw a 33 percent drop in their assessments (from about $1 billion to about $700 million), while those banks with over $10 billion in assets saw a 17 percent rise in their assessments (from about $2.4 billion to about $2.8 billion).

- **Fees on SIFIs.** In addition, the Dodd-Frank Act directs the Federal Reserve Board to collect fees from bank SIFIs equal to the expenses the Federal Reserve Board estimates are necessary or appropriate to carry out its supervision and regulation of those companies.[66] In addition, the Dodd-Frank Act directs Treasury to collect assessments from bank and nonbank SIFIs to fund the operations of the Office of Financial Research. These assessments totaled $137 million in 2012 and $35 million in 2013.

The Dodd-Frank Act requires the Federal Reserve Board to subject large bank holding companies to heightened standards for capital, liquidity, and stress testing, as well as other provisions, all of which could reduce the risk of their failure and the costs that their distress could impose on the financial system. Following Dodd-Frank enactment, bank SIFIs significantly increased their capital and liquidity in advance of finalization of new rules for capital, leverage, and liquidity standards. As of December 31, 2013, the six largest U.S. GSIBs had an average tier 1 common equity capital ratio of 12.1 percent, compared to the 4.5 percent minimum required under Basel III and an average of 8.4 percent among these firms as of December 31, 2009.[67] In addition, pursuant to the Dodd-Frank Act, the Federal Reserve Board conducts stress testing and evaluates the capital planning process of large bank holding companies to help ensure these firms are resilient to periods of economic or financial stress. In the most recent round of capital planning reviews, the Federal Reserve Board rejected the capital plan of one U.S. GSIB and required another to resubmit its capital plan after errors were discovered.[68] Pending approval of their revised capital plans, the Federal Reserve Board did not allow proposed actions by these firms, such as dividend increases, that would have reduced their capital. In April 2014, U.S. bank regulators adopted a new rule that strengthens the leverage ratio standards for the largest, most interconnected U.S. banking organizations.[69]

Beyond the new rules and regulatory reviews to ensure capital adequacy, the Federal Reserve Board has indicated that eight of the largest U.S. bank holding companies will be subject to a capital surcharge—an increase in their risk-based capital requirement—based on their size, complexity, and interconnectedness.[70] Federal Reserve Board officials have stated that the capital surcharge is intended to force the largest bank holding companies to internalize the costs they could impose on the financial system from their systemic footprint. Federal Reserve Board and Treasury officials said that this capital surcharge could also help to offset any funding cost advantages that remain from market perceptions that the government would not allow the largest bank holding companies to fail.

Higher capital and liquidity requirements for banks can increase their funding and other costs. For example, higher capital requirements can require banks to increase the portion of their funding that comes from equity capital rather than debt, which can increase funding costs.[71] In prior work, we have summarized the results of studies by the Bank for International Settlements and others on the benefits and costs of increasing capital requirements for banks, but these studies generally estimated cost impacts to the economy rather than the incidence of increased costs for the institutions themselves. While banks can respond to additional costs in a variety of ways, including passing on some costs to borrowers by charging higher interest rates on loans, a Federal Reserve Board official noted that costs associated with the GSIB capital surcharges—which will not apply to most banks and will not apply evenly among the GSIBs—may be more difficult for the largest bank holding companies to pass on to customers.

Dodd-Frank also imposes additional compliance costs on large bank holding companies required to comply with other Dodd-Frank provisions. For example, as previously discussed, Dodd-Frank requires SIFIs to periodically submit resolution plans to the Federal Reserve and FDIC, as well as to conduct company-run stress tests semiannually. Regulators and industry officials have stated that SIFIs have devoted significant staffing resources to developing these resolution plans. According to industry representatives, stress testing requires newly covered firms to incur significant compliance costs associated with building information systems, contracting with outside vendors, recruiting personnel, and developing stress testing models that are unique to their organization. Furthermore, changes to the market infrastructure for swaps—such as clearing and exchange-trading requirements—and real-time reporting requirements for designated major swap dealers or major swap participants will require firms to purchase or upgrade information systems. Industry representatives and regulators said that while some compliance costs of the derivatives reforms could be recurring, a large part of these costs will come from one-time upfront investments to update processes and technology. Additionally, by generally prohibiting banks from engaging in proprietary trading and limiting their ability to sponsor or invest in hedge and private equity funds, the Volcker rule restrictions could eliminate past sources of trading and fee income for some banks.

As we have noted in prior work, measuring the costs of financial regulation is challenging because of the multitude of intervening variables, the complexity of the financial system, and data limitations.[72] For example, the extent to which regulated institutions pass on a portion of their increased costs to their customers may be impacted by competitive forces or other factors. Other sources of uncertainty, such as the potential for regulatory arbitrage, add to the challenges of estimating the act's potential costs. For example, increased regulation could cause certain financial activities in the United States to move to foreign jurisdictions with less stringent regulations. U.S. regulators have acknowledged the importance of harmonizing international regulatory standards and noted that it can be advantageous for the United States to be the leader in implementing new regulatory safeguards.

Agencies See Progress in Addressing too-Big-to-Fail Perceptions and Expect Further Progress as Reforms Are More Fully Implemented

Officials from FSOC and its member agencies have stated that financial reforms have not completely removed too-big-to-fail perceptions but have made significant progress toward doing so. In a December 2013 speech, Treasury Secretary Jack Lew said there is growing recognition of the Dodd-Frank reforms and that market analysts are factoring them into their assumptions. However, he noted that there is still more work to be done.

Under the Dodd-Frank Act, FSOC is, among other things, charged with promoting market discipline by eliminating expectations on the part of shareholders, creditors, and counterparties of large bank holding companies that the U.S. government will shield them from losses in the event of failure. FSOC and its member agencies monitor progress in addressing expectations of government support primarily through monitoring progress in implementing relevant Dodd-Frank reforms. FSOC's 2014 annual report includes a discussion of progress made on OLA, enhanced prudential standards, and other relevant reforms. According to Treasury officials, several key areas require continued progress:

- **International regulatory reform.** In its 2013 annual report, FSOC writes that international coordination of financial regulation is essential to mitigate threats to financial stability. FDIC officials said they continue to work with foreign regulators to address issues related to creating a viable process for effecting the orderly resolution of a failing financial institution with significant cross-border activities. For example, FDIC is working with foreign counterparts on changes needed to ensure that derivatives contracts under other countries' laws include a stay similar to that which applies to U.S. contracts under Dodd-Frank to prevent termination of these contracts by counterparties of a firm pulled into resolution. Federal Reserve Board staff said U.S. regulators are considering steps that may be needed to help ensure that foreign regulators do not take disruptive actions with respect to foreign operations of a U.S. firm pulled into resolution. They noted that global U.S. SIFIs may need to create intragroup loss absorbency arrangements that provide clarity and assurance to foreign regulators about how loss absorbency from the U.S. holding company will be made available to support foreign operations during a resolution.
- **The Federal Reserve's long-term debt requirement.** The Federal Reserve Board has identified the implementation of a long-term debt requirement as a regulatory priority that it and other agencies are actively considering. In testimony before the Senate Banking Committee, Federal Reserve Board Governor Daniel Tarullo said that successful resolution without taxpayer assistance would be most effectively accomplished if a firm has sufficient long-term, unsecured debt to absorb additional losses and to recapitalize the business transferred to a bridge operating company.
- **General education of market participants on reforms.** Treasury officials identified the education of market participants as a key area for progress. Public outreach and education often take the form of speeches from agency officials and meetings with industry stakeholders. Regulators also solicit feedback on proposed rulemakings and regulations during public comment periods. For example, on December 18, 2013, FDIC published a public notice on the framework for a SPOE approach for resolution of failed financial institutions under OLA and solicited comments from the public through February 18, 2014, before subsequently extending the comment period through March 20, 2014.[73]

Treasury officials also monitor market trends and outside research to inform their assessment of progress in addressing too-big-to-fail perceptions. Treasury staff have looked at trends in bond prices, credit- default-swap prices, and other market data for bank holding companies of different sizes for evidence that investors have reduced their expectations of government support. Treasury staff also monitor relevant outside research, including a growing body of research by academics and others that has used quantitative approaches to analyze the existence and size of potential funding cost advantages that the largest bank holding companies could receive because of market expectations of government support. The next section of this report includes a summary of selected studies in this literature and discusses the strengths and limitations of the methods they use. FSOC and Treasury staff have reviewed these studies and noted that while the studies have limitations, their findings are consistent with a reduction in expectations of government support following the Dodd-Frank Act.

EVIDENCE SUGGESTS LARGE BANKS HAD A FUNDING COST ADVANTAGE OVER SMALL ONES DURING THE FINANCIAL CRISIS THAT MAY HAVE DECLINED OR REVERSED SINCE

Our analysis and the results of studies we reviewed provide evidence that the largest bank holding companies had lower funding costs than smaller bank holding companies during the 2007-2009 financial crisis but that differences may have declined or reversed in more recent years. To inform our econometric approach, we reviewed studies that estimated funding cost differences between large and small financial institutions that could be associated with the perception that some institutions are too big to fail. Studies we reviewed generally found that the largest financial institutions had lower funding costs during the 2007-2009 financial crisis but that the difference between the funding costs of the largest and smaller financial institutions has since declined. In some cases these findings could be interpreted as evidence of advantages driven by too-big-to-fail perceptions; however, these empirical analyses are imperfect and contain a number of limitations that could reduce their validity or applicability to U.S. bank holding companies. Our analysis, which addresses certain limitations of these studies, also provides evidence that large or systemically important bank holding companies had lower funding costs than smaller bank holding companies during the 2007-2009 financial crisis, which may have been associated with expectations of government assistance. In addition, our analysis provides some evidence that funding cost differences may have declined or reversed in recent years and that large bank holding companies may have had higher funding costs since the crisis. However, we also analyzed what funding cost differences might have been since the crisis in hypothetical scenarios where levels of credit risk in every year from 2010 to 2013 are assumed to be as high as they were during the financial crisis. This analysis suggests that large bank holding companies might have had lower funding costs than smaller bank holding companies since the crisis if levels of credit risk had remained high, indicating that changes in funding cost differences over time may be due in part to improvements in bank holding companies' financial conditions. Although our analysis improves on certain aspects of prior studies, important limitations remain and our results should be interpreted with caution.

Studies Generally Found the Largest Banks Had Lower Funding Costs during the Financial Crisis but Results Have Limitations

Studies we reviewed generally found that the largest financial institutions had lower funding costs than smaller ones during the 2007-2009 financial crisis but that the difference between the funding costs of the largest and smaller financial institutions has since declined. In some cases these findings could be interpreted as evidence of advantages driven by too-big-to-fail perceptions; however, these empirical analyses are imperfect and contain a number of limitations that could reduce their validity or applicability to U.S. bank holding companies.

We reviewed studies that estimated the funding cost difference between large and small financial institutions that could be associated with the perception that some institutions are too big to fail. We evaluated studies that met the following criteria: (1) used a comparative empirical approach that attempted to account for differences across financial institutions that could influence funding costs, (2) included U.S. bank holding companies, and (3) included analysis of data from 2002 or later. See our scope and methodology section for more information on our criteria and approach.

The 16 studies we reviewed made a wide variety of methodological decisions and came to a range of conclusions. We present the variety of methodological decisions along two key dimensions—which source of funding is analyzed (e.g., deposits, bonds) and time period of analysis—in table 2 below. The source of funding that is analyzed is an important methodological decision because investors may have differing expectations regarding the likelihood that various sources of funding might receive government support, and these expectations could differ by the size of the financial institution. Results could differ across studies because of differences in creditor priority (subordinated debt versus senior debt) or maturity (bonds that mature several years in the future versus deposits that can be demanded at any time). We also include information in table 2 on the reported affiliations of the study authors.

Studies we reviewed generally found that the largest financial institutions had lower funding costs than smaller ones during the 2007-2009 financial crisis, but that the difference between the funding costs of the largest and smaller financial institutions has since declined. For example, one study estimated that large U.S. financial institutions had roughly 100 basis points lower bond funding costs than smaller ones in 2009, but this difference had declined to around 40 basis points by 2011.[74] Similarly, a study of U.S. bank credit default swaps found that large U.S. bank holding companies had roughly 100 basis points lower funding costs in 2009, but this difference had declined to around 15 basis points in 2013.[75] In some cases these differences could be interpreted as evidence of funding cost advantages driven by too-big-to-fail perceptions. In other cases, limitations in the studies make it difficult to eliminate other explanations of why funding cost differences might exist—such as greater liquidity or diversification that could be associated with size or spurious results driven by imperfect measures of funding costs. Time period of analysis was another important difference across studies we reviewed. Few studies in our review included data beyond 2011. Therefore, most results may not reflect recent changes in the regulatory environment and market expectations discussed earlier in the report.

Table 2. Empirical Studies of Too-Big-to-Fail Funding Cost Differences

Study authors (Year)	Measure of funding cost	Time period	Affiliation category
Acharya, Anginer & Warburton (2013)	Bonds	1990-2011	Academic
Araten & Turner (2012)	Combination of funding sources	2002-2011	Private[a]
Balasubramnian & Cyree (2014)	Bonds[b]	2009-2011	Academic

Study authors (Year)	Measure of funding cost	Time period	Affiliation category
Balasubramnian & Cyree (2013)	Bonds[c]	2009-2011	Academic
Barth & Schnabel (2013)	Credit default swaps	2005-2011	Academic
Bertay, Demirgüç-Kunt & Huizinga (2013)	Combination of funding sources	1990-2011	Academic and public
International Monetary Fund (2014)	Credit ratings, credit default swaps	2005-2014	Public
Jacewitz & Pogach (2012)	Deposits	2005-2010	Public
Keppo & Yang (2013)	Bonds, deposits	1990-2011	Academic and public
Kumar & Lester (2014a)	Deposits	2006-2012	Private[d]
Kumar & Lester (2014b)	Bonds	2009-2013	Private[d]
Li et al. (2011)	Credit default swaps	2001-2010	Private
Santos (2014)	Bonds	1985-2009	Public
Tsesmelidakis & Merton (2012)	Credit default swaps	2002-2010	Academic and private
Ueda & Di Mauro (2012)	Credit ratings	2007, 2009	Academic and public

Source: GAO | GAO-14-621.

Note: We read and evaluated studies that met the following criteria: (1) used a regression or similar comparative empirical methodology to estimate any funding cost difference, (2) included U.S. bank holding companies, and (3) included analysis of data from 2002 or later. Our criteria excluded studies that used option-pricing approaches—this methodology assumes a too-big-to-fail funding cost advantage exists and only estimates its magnitude. We identified author affiliations based on information included in the papers, which may not reflect all relevant affiliations. Academic affiliation includes authors at universities or research institutes. Private affiliation includes authors at financial institutions and other private firms. Public affiliation includes authors at government and regulatory agencies (including the regional Federal Reserve banks which are private corporations), and international financial institutions such as the World Bank. We also excluded two studies that otherwise met our criteria but did not attempt to control for important differences between financial institutions. We were aware of potential conflicts of interest associated with a number of studies in our review. As with other studies we reviewed, these studies must have attempted to address factors that might account for differences in funding costs in order to be included, and we also considered the potential impact these conflicts of interest might have on their methods and results. See our scope and methodology for more details on our approach.

[a] This study was conducted by researchers at JP Morgan Chase.

[b] This study focused on subordinated bonds.

[c] This study focused on senior bonds.

[d] This study was conducted by researchers at Oliver Wyman and sponsored by the Clearinghouse Association, a trade association of the world's largest commercial banks.

Studies also varied in their approach to identifying financial institutions that might be perceived as too big to fail, using a variety of size and other thresholds. For example, some studies measured too-big-to-fail status by a bank's assets; however, the threshold between too-big-to-fail and other banks varied from $50 billion to $500 billion. Several papers estimated too-big-to-fail status by size relative to industry, such as the largest 20 banks or top

10 percent by assets. These different approaches indicate that there is no consensus within the literature on which financial institutions may be considered too big to fail for the purposes of comparing funding costs.

The studies we reviewed can be grouped into categories based on their approaches. While all studies included in our review used standard approaches and attempted to address factors that might account for differences in funding costs, these empirical analyses remain imperfect.

- **Regression.** Most studies we reviewed adopted a regression methodology in which some measure of funding costs was explained by a variety of control variables, such as risk, liquidity, and maturity, to attempt to account for differences across financial institutions. These models are standard empirical tools and are flexible in terms of the information about financial institutions and markets that they can incorporate. In some instances these models rely on a small number of indicators that may only imperfectly measure underlying default risks. As a result, some analyses may not correctly estimate the size of any too-big-to-fail advantages because they omit important factors that influence funding costs. In other studies that account for a more thorough set of factors that influence funding costs, results may be sensitive to alternative measurements of these factors.[76] For example, default risk is an underlying driver of funding costs, and studies may produce different results by using a bank's earnings volatility as an indicator for default risk as opposed to other indicators such as the quality of a bank's assets. In addition, liquidity is another important factor to account for when attempting to explain funding cost differences—investors charge banks more for less liquid sources of funding—and some studies do not adequately control for the liquidity of the funding source. Challenges similar to those involved in accurately capturing default risk arise in finding appropriate indicators for a bond's liquidity.
- **Equity-based.** Three papers we reviewed measured the difference between observed credit default swap spreads (which approximate bond funding costs) and hypothetical credit default swap spreads (which are estimated based on information implied by equity prices).[77] This approach estimates hypothetical spreads with a standard theoretical model used in finance that uses the risk of a firm's equity to estimate the risk of a firm's debt.[78] In doing so, the approach assumes that hypothetical spreads derived from equity prices are *not* influenced by any expectations of government support, but that observed credit default swap spreads *are* influenced by such expectations. By comparing the two spreads the approach can estimate the magnitude of expectations of government support. While this approach has some advantages, it relies on critical assumptions about how a limited number of factors influence the risk of default.[79] As a result, these analyses may also omit important factors that influence funding costs, such as earnings.[80]
- **Ratings-based.** Two papers used Fitch credit ratings to estimate the funding cost difference that could be associated with potential government support.[81] Models based on credit ratings offer a convenient way to incorporate all the factors the rating agency considers relevant to default risk and take advantage of the rating agency's explicit separation of the impact of expected government support through, for example, the assignment of a standalone credit rating (assuming no government

support) and a higher credit rating assuming government support.[82] However, this approach assumes that all information about market expectations of default risk and government support are incorporated into credit ratings, which is a potentially weak assumption. Credit ratings had a limited impact on the views of large investors we interviewed, as previously discussed. Moreover, funding costs vary for firms within a particular rating. As a result, these studies may estimate funding costs with considerable error. Finally, results of these studies are sensitive to the credit rating agency used—for example, results based on Moody's ratings could be quite different than other rating agencies because Moody's removed expectations of government support for U.S. bank holding companies in 2013.

In addition to the approach-specific limitations, a number of general limitations related to implementation of the various approaches exist across studies we reviewed that could reduce their validity or applicability to U.S. bank holding companies. For example, studies varied in the countries that were included in the analysis—some studies focused on the United States, while others included a broad cross-section of more than 20 countries. Studies that pooled a large number of countries in their analysis have results that may not be applicable to U.S. bank holding companies. For example, studies that included Switzerland and Iceland in their analyses may not apply to the United States because banking sectors in those countries are much larger relative to the economy. As noted above, because few studies included data past 2011, results may not reflect recent changes in the regulatory environment and market sentiment; for example, the Federal Reserve's rule for enhanced prudential standards for large bank holding companies and FDIC's proposed strategy for orderly liquidation.

As a result of the limitations associated with these methodological choices, estimates of the size of the funding cost difference associated with a too-big-to-fail advantage based on this literature—while suggestive of general trends—are not definitive and should be interpreted with caution.

GAO Analysis Suggests Large Banks Had Lower Funding Costs during the Financial Crisis but This Advantage May Have Declined or Reversed Since

We conducted our own analysis to assess the extent to which the largest bank holding companies have had lower funding costs as a result of perceptions that the government would not allow them to fail. Overall, our analysis provides some evidence that large or systemic bank holding companies had lower funding costs than smaller ones during the 2007-2009 financial crisis that may have been associated with expectations of government assistance. Our analysis provides only limited evidence that large bank holding companies had lower funding costs since the crisis and instead provides some evidence that the opposite may have been true at the levels of credit risk that prevailed in those years. However, in hypothetical scenarios where levels of credit risk in every year from 2010 to 2013 are assumed to be as high as they were during the financial crisis, our analysis suggests that large bank holding companies might have had lower funding costs than smaller bank holding companies. Although our analysis improves on certain aspects of prior studies, important limitations remain and our results should be interpreted with caution.

To conduct our analysis, we developed a series of econometric models— models that use statistical techniques to estimate the relationships between quantitative economic and financial variables—based on our assessment of relevant studies and expert views. These models estimate the relationship between bank holding companies' bond funding costs and their size, while also controlling for other drivers of bond funding costs, including credit risk and bond liquidity. Key features of our econometric approach include the following:

- **U.S. bank holding companies.** To better understand the relationship between bank holding company funding costs and size in the context of the U.S. economic and regulatory environment, we only analyzed U.S. bank holding companies. In contrast, some of the literature we reviewed analyzed nonbank financial companies and foreign companies.
- **2006-2013 time period.** To better understand the relationship between bank holding company funding costs and size in the context of the current economic and regulatory environment, we analyzed the period from 2006 through 2013, which includes the recent financial crisis as well as years before the crisis and following the enactment of the Dodd-Frank Act. In contrast, some of the literature we reviewed did not analyze data in the years after the financial crisis.
- **Bond funding costs.** We used bond yield spreads as our measure of bank holding company funding costs because they are a direct measure of what investors charge bank holding companies to borrow money and because they are sensitive to credit risk and hence expected government support. This indicator of funding costs has distinct advantages over certain other indicators used in studies we reviewed, including credit ratings, which do not directly measure funding costs, and total interest expense, which mixes the costs of funding from multiple sources.
- **Alternative measures of size.** Size or systemic importance can be measured in multiple ways, as reflected in our review of the literature. Based on that review and the comments we received from external reviewers, we used four different measures of size or systemic importance: total assets, total assets and the square of total assets, whether or not a bank holding company was designated a GSIB by the Financial Stability Board in November 2013, and whether or not a bank holding company had assets of $50 billion or more.
- **Extensive controls for bond liquidity, credit risk, and other key factors.** To account for the many factors that could influence funding costs, we controlled for credit risk, bond liquidity, and other key factors in our models. We included a number of variables that are associated with the risk of default, including measures of capital adequacy, asset quality, earnings, and volatility. We also included a number of variables that can be used to measure bond liquidity. Finally, we included variables that measure other key characteristics of bonds, such as time to maturity, and key characteristics of bank holding companies, such as operating expenses. Our models include a broader set of controls for credit risk and bond liquidity than some studies we reviewed and, as we discuss later, we directly assess the sensitivity of our results to using alternative controls on our estimates of funding costs.
- **Multiple model specifications.** In order to assess the sensitivity of our results to using alternative measures of size, bond liquidity, and credit risk discussed above, we estimated multiple different model specifications. We developed models using four

alternative measures of size, two alternative sets of measures of capital adequacy, six alternative measures of volatility, and three alternative measures of bond liquidity to assess the impact of using alternative measures on our results. In contrast, some of the studies we reviewed estimated a more limited number of model specifications.

- **Annual estimates of models.** To allow for changes in investors' beliefs about the likelihood of government rescues between the years of the financial crisis—when emergency government programs designed to assist financial institutions were available—and the years following the crisis, our models allow the relationship between bank holding company funding costs and size to vary over time. In contrast, some of the studies we reviewed assumed that the relationship between bank holding company funding costs and size was constant over time.
- **Link between size and credit risk.** To account for the possibility that investors' beliefs about government rescues affect their responsiveness to credit risk, our models allow the relationships between bank holding company funding costs and credit risk to depend on size.

Altogether, we estimated 42 different models for each year from 2006 through 2013 and then used these models to compare bond yield spreads—our measure of bond funding costs—for bank holding companies of different sizes but with the same level of credit risk.[83] Figure 1 shows our models' comparisons of the difference between bond funding costs for bank holding companies with $1 trillion in assets and average credit risk and bond funding costs for similar bank holding companies with $10 billion in assets, for each model and for each year.[84] Each circle and dash in figure 1 shows the comparison of bond funding costs for a different model. Circles show model-estimated differences that were statistically significant at the 10 percent level, while dashes represent differences that were not statistically significant at that level.[85] Circles and dashes below zero correspond to models suggesting that bank holding companies with $1 trillion in assets have lower bond funding costs than bank holding companies with $10 billion in assets, and vice versa.

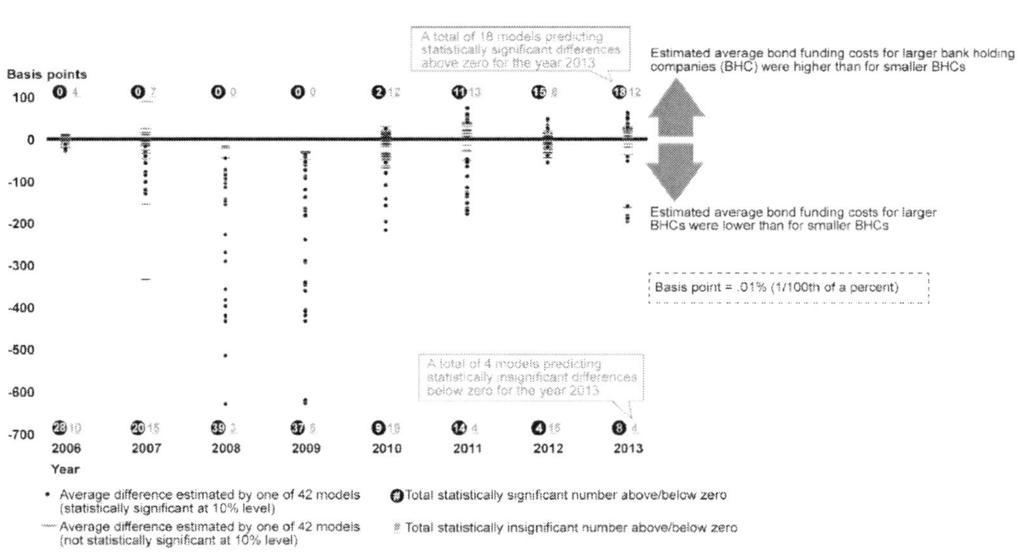

Source: GAO analysis of data from Bloomberg and the Financial Stability Board. | GAO-14-621.

Notes: We estimated econometric models of the relationship between bank holding company size and funding costs using data for U.S. bank holding companies and their outstanding senior unsecured bonds for the first quarter of 2006 through the fourth quarter of 2013. The models used bond yield spreads to measure funding costs and controlled for credit risk factors such as capital adequacy, asset quality, earnings, maturity mismatch, and volatility, as well as bond liquidity and other characteristics of bonds and bank holding companies that can affect funding costs. We estimated 42 models for each year from 2006 through 2013 to assess the sensitivity of estimated funding cost differences to alternative measures of capital adequacy, volatility, bond liquidity, and size or systemic importance. We used the models to compare bond funding costs for bank holding companies of different sizes but the same levels of credit risk, bond liquidity, and other characteristics. This figure compares bond funding costs for bank holding companies with $1 trillion and $10 billion in assets, for each model and for each year, with average levels of credit risk. Each circle and dash shows the comparison for a different model, where circles and dashes below zero suggest bank holding companies with $1 trillion in assets have lower bond funding costs than bank holding companies with $10 billion in assets, and vice versa.

Figure 1. Estimates from 42 Models of Average Bond Funding Cost Differences between Bank Holding Companies with $1 Trillion and $10 Billion in Assets, 2006-2013.

Our analysis provides evidence that the largest bank holding companies had lower funding costs during the 2007-2009 financial crisis but that differences may have declined or reversed in recent years. However, we found that the outcomes of our econometric models varied with the various controls we used to capture size, credit risk, and bond liquidity. This variation indicates that uncertainty related to how to model funding costs has an important impact on estimated funding cost differences between large and small bank holding companies. As figure 1 shows, most models found that larger bank holding companies had lower bond funding costs than smaller bank holding companies during the 2007-2009 financial crisis, but the magnitude of the difference varied widely across models, as indicated by the range of results for each year. For example, for 2008, our models suggest that bond funding costs for bank holding companies with $1 trillion in assets and average credit risk were from 17 to 630 basis points lower than bond funding costs for similar bank holding companies with $10 billion in assets. For 2009, our models suggest that bond funding costs for bank holding companies with $1 trillion in assets and average credit risk were from 30 to 628 basis points lower than bond funding costs for similar bank holding companies with $10 billion in assets.

Our models' comparisons of bond funding costs for different-sized bank holding companies for 2010 through 2013 also vary widely. For bank holding companies with average credit risk, more than half of our models suggest that larger bank holding companies had higher bond funding costs than smaller bank holding companies from 2011 through 2013, but many models suggest that larger bank holding companies still had lower bond funding costs than smaller ones during this period. For example, for 2013, our models suggest that bond funding costs for average credit risk bank holding companies with $1 trillion in assets ranged from 196 basis points lower to 63 basis points higher than bond funding costs for similar bank holding companies with $10 billion in assets (see figure 1). For 2013, thirty of our models suggest that the larger banks had higher funding costs, and 12 of our models suggest that the larger banks had lower funding costs.

Our models' comparisons were particularly sensitive to the measure of size or systemic importance we used. For example, for 2013, models that used total assets as the indicator of size or systemic importance suggest that bond funding costs for bank holding companies with $1 trillion in assets and average credit risk ranged from 23 to 59 basis points higher than bond funding costs for similar bank holding companies with $10 billion in assets (see figure 2). Models that used the GSIB designation suggest that bond funding costs for bank holding companies with $1 trillion ranged from 11 basis points lower to 36 basis points higher than bond funding costs for bank holding companies with $10 billion in assets. Models that used total assets and the square of total assets—which allows for a nonlinear relationship between size and yield spreads— suggest that bond funding costs for bank holding companies with $1 trillion in assets ranged from 52 basis points lower to 4 basis points higher than bond funding costs for bank holding companies with $10 billion in assets. Finally, models that used whether or not a bank holding company had $50 billion in assets suggest that bond funding costs for bank holding companies with $1 trillion ranged from 161 to 196 basis points lower than bond funding costs for bank holding companies with $10 billion in assets.

We also found that our models' comparisons of bond funding costs for bank holding companies of different sizes varied depending on bank holding companies' level of credit risk. For low credit risk bank holding companies, most models suggest that bond funding costs for larger bank holding companies were lower than bond funding costs for smaller bank holding companies during the 2007-2009 financial crisis and that bond funding costs for larger bank holding companies were higher than bond funding costs for smaller bank holding companies from 2010 through 2013. Depending on the year, 25 to 42 of our 42 models suggest that bond funding costs for larger, low risk bank holding companies were lower during the financial crisis, while 31 to 41 of our 42 models suggest that bond funding costs for larger low risk bank holding companies were higher following the crisis. However, for high credit risk bank holding companies, most models suggest that bond funding costs for larger bank holding companies were lower than bond funding costs for smaller bank holding companies in every year (28 to 41 of our 42 models, depending on the year).

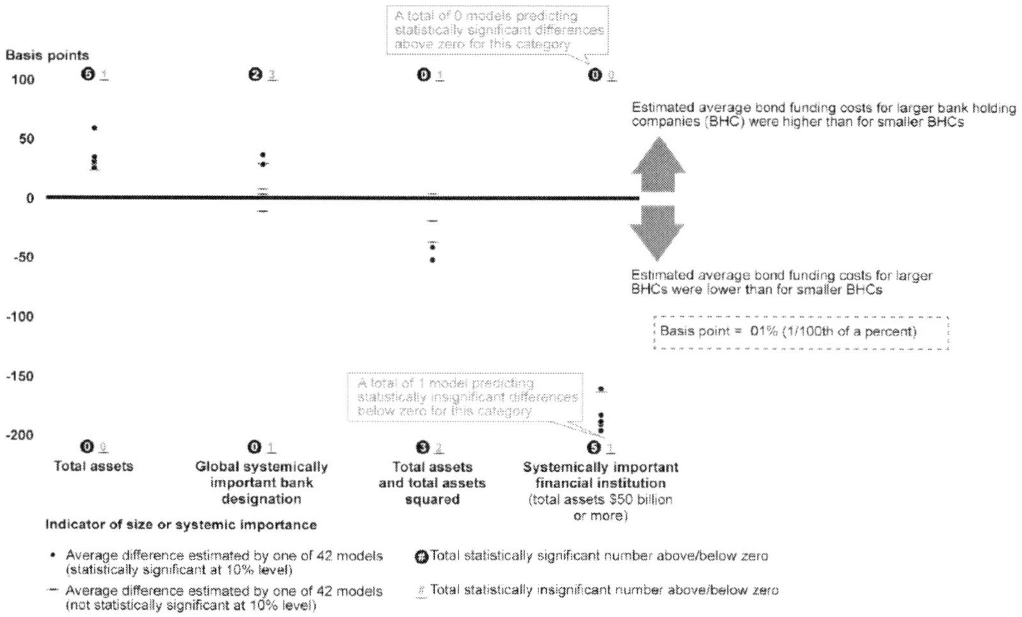

Source: GAO analysis of data from Bloomberg and the Financial Stability Board. | GAO-14-621.

Notes: We estimated econometric models of the relationship between bank holding company size and funding costs using data for U.S. bank holding companies and their outstanding senior unsecured bonds for the first quarter of 2006 through the fourth quarter of 2013. The models used bond yield spreads to measure funding costs and controlled for credit risk factors such as capital adequacy, asset quality, earnings, maturity mismatch, and volatility, as well as bond liquidity and other characteristics of bonds and bank holding companies that can affect funding costs. We estimated multiple models for each year from 2006 through 2013 to assess the sensitivity of estimated funding cost differences to alternative measures of capital adequacy, volatility, bond liquidity, and size or systemic importance. We used the models to compare bond funding costs for bank holding companies of different sizes but the same levels of credit risk, bond liquidity, and other characteristics. This figure compares bond funding costs for bank holding companies with $1 trillion and $10 billion in assets with average levels of credit risk for 2013 for models that differ in how they measure size. Each circle and dash shows the comparison for a different model, where circles and dashes below zero suggest bank holding companies with $1 trillion in assets have lower bond funding costs than bank holding companies with $10 billion in assets, and vice versa.

Figure 2. Difference in Estimated Bond Funding Costs for Average Credit Risk Bank Holding Companies with $1 Trillion versus $10 Billion in Assets by Indicator of Size or Systemic Importance, 2013.

Given that most models suggest that large bank holding companies' bond funding costs are typically lower than small bank holding companies' bond funding costs at high levels of credit risk, this suggests that size- related funding cost differences that favor large bank holding companies are more likely to emerge when the likelihood that a bank holding company will fail increases. As we discuss later, investors' overall beliefs about the likelihood of government support may have several components, including beliefs about whether or not a bank holding company will fail—which is related to its credit risk—and beliefs about whether or not a bank holding company will be supported by the government if it fails. For example, investors may believe that larger bank holding companies are more likely to be supported than smaller bank holding companies in the event of failure, but investors may also believe that all bank holding companies are relatively safe and unlikely to fail. In this case, investors' overall expectations of government support for all bank holding companies are likely to be low, and differences in funding costs due to varying expectations of government support for bank holding companies of different sizes are likely to be small or nonexistent. In contrast, if investors believe that all bank holding companies are risky and prone to fail, then investors' overall expectations of government support for larger bank holding companies are likely to be higher than for smaller bank holding companies, and differences in funding costs are likely to be greater.

To assess how investors' beliefs that the government will support failing bank holding companies have changed over time, we compared bond funding costs for bank holding companies of various sizes while holding the level of credit risk constant over time at the average for 2008—a relatively high level of credit risk that prevailed during the financial crisis.[86] In these hypothetical scenarios, most models suggest that bond funding costs for larger bank holding companies would have been lower than bond funding costs for smaller bank holding companies in most years. For example, most models for 2013 predict that bond funding costs for larger bank holding companies would be higher than for smaller bank holding companies at the average level of credit risk in that year, but would be lower at financial crisis levels of credit risk (see figure 3). These results suggest that changes over time in funding cost differences we estimated (depicted in figure 1) have been driven at least in part by improvements in the financial condition of bank holding companies.[87] At the same time, more models predict lower bond funding costs for larger bank holding companies in 2008 than in 2013 when we assume that financial crisis levels of credit risk prevailed in both years, which suggests that investors' expectations of government support have changed over time.[88] However, it is important to note that the relationships between variables estimated by our models could be sensitive to the average level of credit risk among bank holding companies, making these estimates of the potential impact of the level of credit risk from 2008 in the current environment even more uncertain. Moreover, Dodd-Frank Act reforms discussed earlier in this report, such as enhanced regulatory standards for capital and liquidity, could enhance the stability of the U.S. financial system and make such a credit risk scenario less likely. However, the extent to which such benefits will materialize depends on many factors that remain difficult to predict.

Estimates of Size-Related Funding Cost Differences Should Be Interpreted with Caution

Our estimates of the relationship between the size of a bank holding company and the yield spreads on its bonds are limited by several factors and should be interpreted with caution. These factors present challenges to using our results and the results of other studies as the basis for public policy responses to concerns about the risks posed by large financial institutions.

Investors' beliefs about the likelihood of government support are composed of several different elements, including the likelihood that a bank holding company will fail, the likelihood that it will be rescued by the government if it fails, and the size of the losses that the government may impose on investors if it rescues the bank holding company. Like the methodologies used in the literature we reviewed, our methodology does not allow us to precisely identify the influence of each of these factors. As a result, changes over time in our estimates of the relationship between bond funding costs and size may reflect changes in one or more of these components, but we cannot identify which with certainty. For example, if bond funding costs for a bank holding company with $1 trillion are less than those for a bank holding company with $10 billion but the difference decreases over time, this trend may indicate that investors believe that the larger bank holding company is relatively less likely to fail, which could be the case if the level of credit risk is falling over time, either due to market pressure, regulatory requirements, or other reasons. This trend could also indicate that investors believe that the government has become less likely to rescue the larger bank holding company if it fails or more likely to impose losses on investors in a rescue.

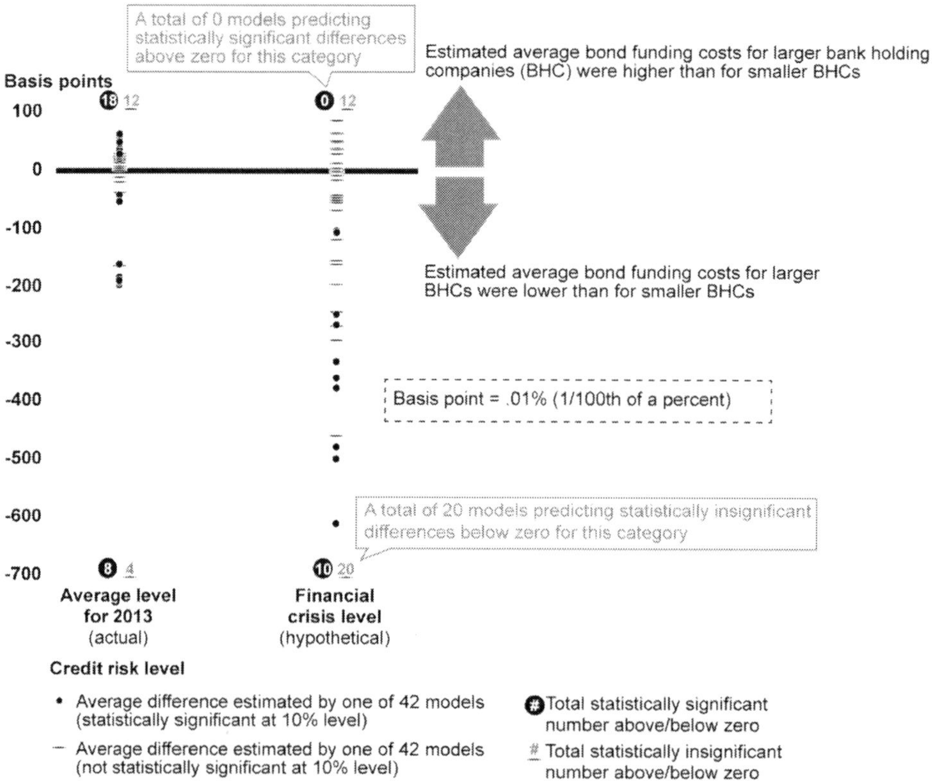

Source: GAO analysis of data from Bloomberg and the Financial Stability Board. | GAO-14-621.

Notes: We estimated econometric models of the relationship between bank holding company size and funding costs using data for U.S. bank holding companies and their outstanding senior unsecured bonds for the first quarter of 2006 through the fourth quarter of 2013. The models used bond yield spreads to measure funding costs and controlled for credit risk factors such as capital adequacy, asset quality, earnings, maturity mismatch, and volatility, as well as bond liquidity and other characteristics of bonds and bank holding companies that can affect funding costs. We estimated 42 models for each year from 2006 through 2013 to assess the sensitivity of estimated funding cost differences to alternative measures of capital adequacy, volatility, bond liquidity, and size or systemic importance. We used the models to compare bond funding costs for bank holding companies of different sizes but the same levels of credit risk, bond liquidity, and other characteristics. This figure compares bond funding costs for bank holding companies with $1 trillion and $10 billion in assets, for each model for 2013, with the average level of credit risk in 2013 and the average level of credit risk in 2008 during the financial crisis. Each circle and dash shows the comparison for a different model, where circles and dashes below zero suggest bank holding companies with $1 trillion in assets have lower bond funding costs than bank holding companies with $10 billion in assets, and vice versa.

Figure 3. Difference in Estimated Bond Funding Costs for Bank Holding Companies with $1 Trillion versus $10 Billion in Assets by Level of Credit Risk, 2013.

In addition, our estimates of differences in bond funding costs for bank holding companies of different sizes may reflect factors other than investors' beliefs about the likelihood of government support. We have taken into account many of the factors that may help explain differences in yield spreads for bank holding companies of different size, such as credit risk and bond liquidity. However, we may not have taken into account all possible factors. If a factor that we have not taken into account is associated with size, then our results may reflect the relationship between bond funding costs and this omitted factor instead of, or in addition to, the relationship between bond funding costs and bank holding company size.

Our estimates of differences in bond funding costs for bank holding companies of different sizes may also reflect differences in the characteristics of bank holding companies that choose to issue bonds. Bank holding companies that issue bonds may differ from those that do not in ways that may or may not be observable. If such differences exist and are unobservable, then our models' comparisons are likely to be consistently either too high or too low depending on the relationship between size and the relevant unobservable characteristic. However, if bank holding companies that issue bonds differ from those that do not in ways that are observable in our model, then our models' comparisons of bond funding cost differences for bank holding companies of different sizes are unlikely to be consistently either too high or too low. We found some evidence that this may be the case. Investors with whom we spoke told us that larger bank holding companies are generally more likely to issue bonds than smaller ones because they can issue a large enough quantity of debt to satisfy investors' demand for liquidity and to allow investors to make a large enough investment to cover their transaction costs. Thus, size, which is observable, may be an important difference between bank holding companies that issue bonds and those that do not. Importantly, bank holding company size matters in this case because it is associated with bond issue size, which we control for, not because it is associated with investors' beliefs about government rescues.

In general, our estimates of the impact of size on bond funding costs may reflect a relationship between size, credit risk, or other explanatory variables and the part of bond funding costs that is not explained by our model (endogeneity). This could occur if any of our control variables are influenced by bond funding costs. In this case, our estimates of the magnitude of the association between size and bond funding costs will be imperfect and our ability to infer a causal relationship between size and bond funding costs will be limited.

Historical estimates of differences in bond funding costs for bank holding companies of different sizes are not indicative of future differences. As we have discussed, our estimates of the historical relationship between bank holding company size and bond funding costs vary from year to year. Thus, it is likely that the relationship between bond funding costs and bank holding company size may change in the future. As we have noted, the Dodd-Frank Act imposes new and higher fees on large bank holding companies and requires the Federal Reserve Board to subject large bank holding companies to enhanced regulatory standards for capital, liquidity, and risk management. These enhanced standards may help to reduce the likelihood that a large bank holding company will fail, which may in turn alter investors' beliefs about the likelihood of government support and thus affect the size of any differences in yield spreads on bonds issued by large and small bank holding companies. Improvements in economic conditions, such as faster economic growth and lower unemployment, may have a similar effect. Finally, changes in the structure of financial markets, such as an increase in the share of credit provided by nonbank financial companies that reduces the systemic importance of large bank holding companies, could also lead investors to change their beliefs about government rescues in future episodes of individual or system-wide distress.

Finally, our estimates of the differences in bond funding costs for bank holding companies of different sizes do not necessarily reflect the harm that the failure of a large bank holding company could do to the economy. Bond funding costs reflect the risk that a bank holding company might fail and not be able to fully repay its investors. However, parties other than investors may be harmed if a bank holding company fails. For example, the customers of a failed bank holding company may be harmed if they have less access to credit or to specialized services provided by the bank holding company, which could be the case if the bank holding company has a large enough share of the market.

AGENCY COMMENTS AND OUR EVALUATION

We made copies of the draft report available to FDIC, the Federal Reserve Board, FSOC, OCC and Treasury for their review and comment. We also provided excerpts of the draft report for technical comment to Fitch, Moody's, Standard and Poor's, and the International Monetary Fund. All of these agencies and third parties, except for FSOC, provided technical comments, which we have incorporated, as appropriate.

In its written comments Treasury generally agreed with the results of our analysis and commented that our draft report represents a meaningful contribution to the literature. Treasury further commented that the Dodd-Frank Act makes clear that shareholders, creditors and executives—not taxpayers—will be responsible if a large company fails and that our results reflect increased market recognition that the Dodd-Frank Act ended "too big to fail" as a matter of law. While our results do suggest bond funding cost differences between large and smaller bank holding companies may have declined or reversed since the 2007-2009 financial crisis, we also report that a higher credit risk environment could be associated with lower bond funding costs for large bank holding companies than for small ones. Furthermore, as we have noted, many market participants we spoke with believe that recent regulatory reforms have reduced but not eliminated the perception of "too big to fail" and both they and Treasury officials indicated that additional steps were required to address "too big to fail." As discussed in the final section of our report on page 56, changes over time in our estimates of the relationship between bond funding costs and size may reflect changes in one or more components of investors' beliefs about government support—such as their views on the likelihood that a bank holding company will fail and the likelihood it will be rescued if it fails—but we cannot precisely identify the influence of each of these components with certainty. A decline or reversal of funding cost advantages for large bank holding companies could indicate that investors believe that the government has become less likely to rescue a large bank holding company if it fails or more likely to impose losses on investors in a rescue. This trend could also indicate that investors believe that large bank holding companies are less likely to fail.

On separate dates in July 2014, Treasury, the Federal Reserve Board, OCC and FDIC provided via email technical comments related to the draft report's analysis of funding cost differences between large and small bank holding companies. We summarize their most significant comments and our responses below.

- Treasury provided comments on our presentation of the impact of a higher credit risk environment on our analysis of bond funding costs and the statistical robustness of these results. In response to these comments, we revised text on the Highlights and in the report body to clarify that the results of this analysis reflect hypothetical scenarios and to provide greater attention to the potential impacts of regulatory reforms. With respect to the statistical robustness of these results, we note that the draft report contained clear information about the statistical significance of our results. Importantly, we note that whether one considers the estimates from all 42 models for 2013 or only the 10 models with statistically significant results, higher credit risk substantially increases (1) the number of models that suggest bond funding costs would have been lower for the largest bank holding companies than for smaller bank holding companies and (2) the size of funding cost differences in 2013. In addition, we amended the draft to clarify that our results for the hypothetical scenario for 2013 differ from our results for 2008, in which all 42 models predicted lower funding costs for larger bank holding companies.

- Treasury and the Federal Reserve Board provided comments related to the draft report's presentation of statistical significance in figures 1, 2, and 3. In response to these comments, we made formatting changes to the figures to more clearly differentiate estimates that are statistically significant from those that are not. In addition, we note that table 7 on pages 79-81 of the report contains some of the data used to create figures 1, 2 and 3 and differentiates between estimates that are statistically significant at the 1 percent, 5 percent, and 10 percent levels. Finally, while statistically insignificant estimates may be viewed as weaker evidence than statistically significant estimates and may influence how our results are interpreted, we note that statistical significance is not the only relevant characteristic of an econometric estimate and that by presenting the full range of results one can better assess their magnitude and economic significance.
- Treasury and the Federal Reserve Board also commented that in comparing bond funding costs for large and small bank holding companies, a bank holding company with \$10 billion in assets is too small to make a meaningful comparison to a bank holding company with \$1 trillion in assets. They commented that a bank holding company with at least \$50 billion in assets would provide a more relevant comparison for this analysis. While we agree that bank holding companies with \$50 billion in assets may be more similar to \$1 trillion bank holding companies than bank holding companies with \$10 billion in assets, we used a smaller size for small bank holding companies because bank holding companies with \$50 billion or more in assets may be viewed by investors as "large" and systemically important, in part because \$50 billion in assets is the size threshold for Dodd-Frank Act requirements related to enhanced regulatory standards. While we agree that bank holding companies of different sizes have different characteristics, we compared estimated funding costs for bank holding companies assuming their credit risk and other characteristics are identical. Finally, increasing the size of the small bank holding company in our comparisons would not have a substantive impact on the sign or statistical significance of our estimated differences in funding costs, nor would it change the trends in estimated differences in funding costs over time.
- The Federal Reserve Board and OCC commented that few of the estimated coefficients on the variables measuring size and size interacted with credit risk reported in table 5 were individually statistically significant, suggesting that there is little statistical evidence of a relationship between bond funding costs and size. To address this concern, we conducted hypothesis tests that the coefficients on the size and size-credit risk interaction terms are jointly equal to zero. The results of these

hypothesis tests suggest that the coefficients on the size and size-credit risk interaction terms are jointly significant at the 5 percent level, suggesting that there is statistical evidence of a relationship between bond funding costs and size. We report the results of our joint hypothesis tests in table 5 on pages 74 and 76 of the report. In addition, we note that the draft report only contains coefficient estimates for the 6 baseline models of the 42 total models for 2008 and 2013 and that those 6 models are presented as examples and do not fully reflect the impact of size in all the specifications in those years or in other years. However, we believe the regression-level detail on the 6 baseline models included in the report is sufficient to assist readers looking to understand our methodology and conclusions.

- OCC suggested that selection bias and omitted variables bias could reduce the validity of our econometric results. We agree that these biases are potential limitations of the model and are among the reasons the results should be interpreted with caution.
- OCC and FDIC commented on the endogeneity of some independent variables and the impact this could have on our results. We agree that endogeneity is a potential limitation of the model and is among the reasons the results should be interpreted with caution. In response to this comment, we added a paragraph discussing the potential impact of endogeneity on our results to the report.

Lawrance L. Evans, Jr., PhD
Director, Financial Markets and Community Investment

Appendix I. Methodology for Analysis of Funding Cost Differences between Large and Small Bank Holding Companies

To assess the extent to which the largest bank holding companies have received funding cost advantages as a result of perceptions that the government would not allow them to fail, we conducted an econometric analysis of the relationship between a bank holding company's size or systemic importance and its funding costs. Bank holding companies obtain funds from investors—such as depositors, creditors, or shareholders—which they use to finance assets, such as various types of credit. The prices that bank holding companies pay to obtain these funds are influenced by several factors, including credit risk—the likelihood that bank holding companies will repay the funds they borrowed as agreed— and other factors. Funding cost advantages may arise if investors believe that the government is more likely to support larger bank holding companies in distress than smaller bank holding companies in distress. This belief may lead investors to view larger bank holding companies as having less credit risk than smaller bank holding companies and thus charge larger bank holding companies a lower price to borrow than smaller bank holding companies.

We used a multivariate regression model to estimate the relationship between bank holding companies' funding costs and their size while controlling for factors other than size that may also influence funding costs. Our general regression model is the following:

$$funding\ cost_{bq} = \alpha + \beta \cdot size_{bq} + \gamma \cdot credit\ risk_{bq} + \delta \cdot (size_{bq} \times credit\ risk_{bq}) + X'_{bq} \cdot \Theta + \varepsilon_{bq}$$

In this model, b denotes the bank holding company, q denotes the quarter, $funding\ cost_{bq}$ is the bank holding company's cost of funding in a quarter, $size_{bq}$ is a measure of the bank holding company's size at the beginning of the quarter, $credit\ risk_{bq}$ is a list of proxies for the bank holding company's credit risk, X_{bq} is a list of other variables that may influence funding costs, ε_{bq} is an idiosyncratic error term, and $\alpha,\beta,\gamma,\delta,$ and Θ are parameters to be estimated. The parameter β captures the direct relationship between a bank holding company's funding cost and its size. The parameter δ captures the indirect relationship between a bank holding company's funding cost and its size that exists if the size of a bank holding company affects the relationship between its funding cost and credit risk. If greater values of the size measure are associated with larger bank holding companies, if greater values of the credit risk proxies are associated with greater credit risk, and if investors view larger bank holding companies as less risky than smaller bank holding companies due to beliefs that the government is more likely to rescue larger bank holding companies in distress, then either β is less than zero, δ is less than zero, or both. However, the parameters β and δ may also reflect factors other than these beliefs.

We used a measure of funding costs based on bonds issued by bank holding companies that is available for bank holding companies with a wide variety of sizes. Bank holding companies use a variety of funding types from different sources, including various types of deposits, bonds, and equity. We used bond yield spreads—the difference between the rate of return on a bond and the rate of return on a Treasury bond of comparable maturity to measure a bank holding company's cost of bond funding. Treasury securities are widely viewed as a risk-free asset, so the yield spread measures the price that investors charge a bank holding company to borrow to compensate them for credit risk and other factors. We focused on bond funding costs for several reasons. First, bonds are traded in secondary markets, so timely information about changes in their yield spreads, which reflect investors' perceptions of the credit risk of the bond's issuing bank holding company, is easily observable.[89] In contrast, some uninsured deposit products are not traded in secondary markets, so changes in the prices of those deposits, which may reflect depositors' perceptions of the riskiness of the bank holding company, may be less easy to observe. Second, bond yield spreads are a direct measure of bank holding companies' funding costs. In contrast, credit ratings are indirect measures of bank holding companies' funding costs because funding costs can vary for firms with the same rating. Similarly, total interest expense as reported on a bank holding company's balance sheet is an imperfect measure of funding costs because total interest expense may aggregate the prices of liabilities with many important differences, including term and creditor priority. Third, bonds generally rank higher in a bank holding company's capital structure than equity, so bondholders are less likely to suffer losses and more likely to be repaid if a bank holding company becomes distressed. Bondholders are thus more likely to benefit if a distressed bank holding company is rescued by the government. In contrast, equity holders generally rank lowest in a bank holding company's capital structure and are the first to suffer losses if a bank holding company becomes distressed. Shareholders are thus the least likely to benefit if a distressed bank holding company is rescued by the government. It follows that the cost of bond funding is more likely to reflect investors' beliefs about the likelihood of government support than the cost of equity funding. Fourth, bank holding companies with a wide variety of sizes issue bonds, including some with less than $10 billion in assets. In contrast, credit default swaps—the prices of which likely reflect perceptions of a bank holding company's credit risk—are available for only a small number of large bank holding companies.[90]

We used Bloomberg to identify U.S. bank holding companies with more than $500 million in assets that were active in one or more years from 2006 to 2013, and to identify all plain vanilla, fixed-rate, senior unsecured bonds issued by these bank holding companies, excluding bonds with a government guarantee.[91] See table 3 for the numbers of bank holding companies and bonds we analyzed.[92]

Table 3. Numbers of Bank Holding Companies and Bonds, 2006-2013

Year	Number of bank holding companies	Number of bank holding companies with senior unsecured bonds outstanding	Number of senior unsecured bonds outstanding
2006	1178	22	166
2007	1209	23	202
2008	1192	22	203
2009	1178	26	333
2010	1133	29	368
2011	1038	29	374
2012	1046	31	447
2013	1033	30	510

Source: GAO analysis of Bloomberg data. | GAO-14-621.

Notes: We used Bloomberg to identify U.S. bank holding companies that reported positive average assets as of the end of at least one year from 2006 to 2013, where average assets consist of the quarterly average for total assets, less goodwill, other disallowed intangible assets, disallowed deferred tax assets, and any other assets that are deducted in determining Tier 1 capital in accordance with the capital standards issued by the reporting bank's primary federal supervisory authority and are reported on form FR Y-9C. Only bank holding companies with $500 million in assets or more are required to file form FR Y-9C. We also used Bloomberg to identify all plain vanilla, fixed- rate, senior unsecured bonds issued by these bank holding companies, where "plain vanilla" bonds are bonds without any derivative or equity features. We excluded bonds guaranteed by either the Federal Deposit Insurance Corporation (FDIC) or the U.S. government.

We collected data on bond yield spreads, bank holding company size, other variables associated with bank holding company credit risk, and bond characteristics from Bloomberg and used these data to assemble a dataset with one observation for each bond in each quarter from the first quarter of 2006 to the fourth quarter of 2013.

Yield spreads. For each bond, we collected daily data on its yield spread based on prices from executed trades, executable quotes, and composites derived from executable and indicative quotes.[93] For each bond and for each quarter from 2006 to 2013, we calculated the average yield spread for each bond based on (1) executed trades, executable quotes, and composites derived from executable and indicative quotes; and (2) actual trades only.[94]

Size. We constructed four alternative indicators of a bank holding company's size or systemic importance: (1) total assets as of the beginning of the quarter; (2) an indicator for whether or not a bank holding company had $50 billion or more in assets, i.e., is a systemically important financial institution (SIFI), as of the beginning of the quarter, which captures those bank holding companies that are subject to enhanced prudential standards under the Dodd-Frank Wall Street Reform and Consumer Protection Act (Dodd-Frank Act); (3) an indicator for whether or not the Financial Stability Board designated a bank holding company a global systemically important bank (GSIB) in November 2013 based on its size, interconnectedness, lack of readily available substitutes or financial institution infrastructure, global (cross-jurisdictional) activity, and complexity; and (4) total assets and total assets squared.[95]

Credit risk. For each bank holding company, we constructed several indicators of credit risk, including indicators of capital adequacy, asset quality, earnings, maturity mismatch, and volatility.[96]

- **Capital adequacy.** Capital absorbs losses, promotes public confidence, helps restrict excessive asset growth, and provides protection to creditors. We constructed two alternative sets of indicators of capital adequacy: (1) equity capital and subordinated debt as percentages of assets as of the beginning of the quarter, and (2) equity capital and subordinated debt as percentages of risk- weighted assets as of the beginning of the quarter.
- **Asset quality.** Asset quality reflects the quantity of existing and potential credit risk associated with a bank holding company's loan and investment portfolios and other assets, as well as off-balance sheet transactions. It also reflects the ability of management to identify and manage credit risk. We used the Texas ratio—nonperforming assets as a percentage of tangible common equity plus loan loss reserves—as of the beginning of the quarter as an indicator of asset quality, where nonperforming assets include assets in nonaccrual status, other real estate owned, restructured loans, and restructured loans in compliance and tangible common equity is total capital minus perpetual preferred stock minus goodwill and other intangibles. The Texas ratio can indicate a bank holding company's likelihood of failure by comparing its troubled loans to its capital. The higher the ratio, the more likely the institution is to fail because more of its capital could be eroded by realized losses on these troubled loans.
- **Earnings.** Earnings are the initial safeguard against the risks of engaging in the banking business and represent the first line of defense against capital depletion that can result from declining asset values. We used net income as a percentage of assets as of the beginning of the quarter as an indicator of earnings.
- **Maturity mismatch.** Maturity mismatch reflects a bank holding company's ability to obtain funds at a reasonable price within a reasonable time period to meet obligations as they come due. We used the difference between volatile liabilities—liabilities that may quickly or unexpectedly come due–and liquid assets—assets that can easily be converted to cash to cover liabilities—as a percentage of total liabilities as of the beginning of each quarter as an indicator of maturity mismatch. Volatile liabilities include federal funds purchased and repurchase agreements, trading liabilities, other borrowed funds, foreign deposits, and jumbo deposits less

derivatives with negative fair value. Liquid assets include cash, securities, federal funds sold and reverse repurchase agreements, and trading assets less pledged securities.[97]

- **Volatility.** Volatility reflects how much the value of a bank holding company fluctuates over a given amount of time and the possibility that the value will fall below a given threshold for default. We constructed five alternative indicators of volatility: (1) the standard deviation of equity prices over the quarter, (2) option implied volatility for the quarter, (3) the standard deviation of equity returns over the quarter, (4) the standard deviation of excess equity returns over the quarter, and (5) the standard deviation of earnings over the past 16 quarters as alternative indicators of volatility.

Other factors. We also collected data on several other factors that may influence bond yield spreads, including bonds' coupon rates, times to maturity, and liquidity, and bank holding companies' operating expenses. We used three alternative indicators of a bond's liquidity: (1) issue size, (2) total volume traded during a quarter, and (3) average bid-ask spread over a quarter.[98] Finally, we used a bank holding company's noninterest expenses as a percentage of total assets as an indicator of its operating expenses.[99] Table 4 shows summary statistics for bank holding companies with senior unsecured bonds outstanding in 2008 and 2013 and for senior unsecured bonds outstanding in 2008 and 2013.

Table 4. Summary Statistics for Bank Holding Companies and Bonds Analyzed, 2008 and 2013

	Mean	Standard deviation	Minimum	Maximum
Bank holding companies with senior unsecured bonds outstanding, 2008				
Total assets (dollars in billions)	403.974	640.816	7.685	2134.499
Operating expense/assets (%)	1.067	0.801	0.576	4.451
Equity capital/assets (%)	10.602	5.226	5.916	31.332
Equity capital/risk-weighted assets (%)	14.340	9.326	7.688	52.366
Subordinated debt/assets (%)	3.308	1.353	0	6.010
Subordinated debt/risk-weighted assets (%)	4.157	1.412	0	6.364
Earnings/assets (%)	0.110	0.440	-1.032	1.349
Maturity mismatch (%)	17.869	18.000	-53.133	34.162
Texas ratio (%)	16.287	10.946	0.011	40.211
Equity price volatility (%)	88.156	31.924	48.106	180.773
Option implied volatility (%)	66.246	14.459	43.573	97.816
Equity return volatility (%)	5.079	0.899	3.508	6.962
Excess equity return volatility (%)	3.723	0.969	2.231	5.817
Earnings volatility (%)	6.108	4.353	0.460	23.510
GSIB designation (indicator)	0.273	—	0	1
Assets $50 billion or more (indicator)	0.818	—	0	1
Senior unsecured bonds outstanding, 2008				
Average bond yield spread calculated using prices from executed trades, executable quotes, and composites of executable and indicative quotes (bps)	456.407	305.194	15.066	1479.019
Average bond yield spread calculated using prices from executed trades (bps)	474.809	342.013	15.066	1479.019

	Mean	Standard deviation	Minimum	Maximum
Bond issue size (dollars in millions)	1004.746	1028.839	0.143	5500.000
Total trade volume (dollars in millions)	160456.800	225838.100	0	1663766.000
Average bid-ask spread, all pricing sources (%)	1.535	1.621	0.0156	14.224
Time to maturity (quarters)	17.177	19.706	0	119.000
Coupon (%)	5.461	1.219	2.000	12.500
Bank holding companies with senior unsecured bonds outstanding, 2013				
Total assets (dollars in billions)	413.488	672.505	4.563	2412.823
Operating expense/assets (%)	0.986	0.598	0.613	3.899
Equity capital/assets (%)	10.993	2.375	7.207	19.144
Equity capital/risk-weighted assets (%)	16.206	4.358	10.676	31.576
Subordinated debt/assets (%)	1.602	0.996	0	4.137
Subordinated debt/risk-weighted assets (%)	2.402	1.205	0	5.171
Earnings/assets (%)	0.280	0.150	0.040	0.766
Maturity mismatch (%)	-1.044	20.512	-53.133	47.001
Texas ratio (%)	17.523	12.061	0.812	38.690
Equity price volatility (%)	20.629	3.280	12.952	28.572
Option implied volatility (%)	23.996	3.656	15.788	30.250
Equity return volatility (%)	1.311	0.202	0.828	1.758
Excess equity return volatility (%)	1.003	0.200	0.630	1.478
Earnings volatility (%)	3.936	4.771	0.355	23.510
GSIB designation (indicator)	0.267	—	0	1
Assets $50 billion or more (indicator)	0.700	—	0	1
Senior unsecured bonds outstanding, 2013				
Average bond yield spread calculated using prices from executed trades, executable quotes, and composites of executable and indicative quotes (bps)	140.684	69.252	15.066	500.750
Average bond yield spread calculated using prices from executed trades (bps)	132.952	71.563	15.066	796.406
Bond issue size (dollars in millions)	1042.622	1107.804	0.350	5500.000
Total trade volume (dollars in millions)	161367.900	293879.200	0	33334868.000
Average bid-ask spread, all pricing sources (%)	0.537	0.474	0.003	2.819
Time to maturity (quarters)	24.548	24.729	0	126.000
Coupon (%)	4.320	1.712	0.800	10.000

Source: GAO analysis of Bloomberg and Financial Stability Board data. | GAO-14-621.

We estimated a variety of models for each year from 2006 to 2013 to address uncertainty about how to appropriately control for bond liquidity, bank holding company credit risk, and the size or systemic importance of a bank holding company and also to allow the relationship between bank holding company size and bond funding costs to vary over time. In our baseline specifications, we measured bond funding costs using average yield spreads on senior unsecured bonds based on executed trades, executable quotes, and composites derived from executable and indicative quotes; size using total assets; capital adequacy using equity capital and subordinated debt as percentages of total assets; and bond liquidity using issue size and total volume. We estimated the parameters for each year and for each of our five volatility variables, as well as for each year without controlling for volatility. We also estimated the parameters of the following variations of the baseline specifications for senior unsecured bonds:

- **Bid-ask specification.** We measured bond liquidity using issue size, total volume, and average bid-ask spread.
- **Trade Reporting and Compliance Engine specification.** We measured bond funding costs using average yield spreads based only on actual trades reported in the Trade Reporting and Compliance Engine database.
- **Risk-weighted assets specification.** We measured capital adequacy using equity capital and subordinated debt as percentages of risk-weighted assets.
- **GSIB specification.** We measured size using the indicator for whether or not a bank holding company was designated a GSIB in November 2013.
- **Systemically important financial institution (SIFI) specification.** We measured size using the indicator for whether or not a bank holding company had $50 billion or more in assets.
- **Total assets and total assets squared specification.** We measured size using both total assets and the square of total assets.

Altogether, we estimated the parameters of 42 separate specifications for each year from 2006 to 2013. For all specifications, we included indicators for each quarter to control for the influence on yield spreads of economic conditions, the regulatory environment, and other factors that vary over time but not across bank holding companies. We also adjusted the standard errors of our parameter estimates to allow for the possibility that they are not identically distributed and to allow for arbitrary correlation between observations on bonds issued by the same bank holding company. Table 5 shows the estimates of the parameters for our baseline regressions for 2008 and 2013.

Our econometric models allow the size of a bank holding company to influence its bond yield spreads both directly and indirectly through the relationships between yield spreads and each indicator of credit risk, i.e., through the interaction term. To summarize the overall relationship between yield spreads and size reflected in each specification, we predicted yield spreads on senior unsecured bonds for bank holding companies of different sizes and credit risk levels using our estimates of the parameters for each specification for each year. Specifically, for each year, we predicted bond yield spreads for bank holding companies with $10 billion, $50 billion, $100 billion, $250 billion, $500 billion, and $1 trillion in assets assuming that all bank holding companies had the average level of credit risk each year, a low level of credit risk each year, a high level of credit risk each year, and the average level of credit risk for 2008.[100]

Table 6 shows all of the differences between predicted bond yield spreads for bank holding companies with $50 billion, $100 billion, $250 billion, $500 billion, and $1 trillion in assets and predicted bond yield spreads for bank holding companies with $10 billion in assets for our baseline regressions for 2008 and 2013 assuming bank holding companies have the average level of credit risk each year.

Table 5. Parameter Estimates for Baseline Regressions, 2008 and 2013

Dependent variable = average bond yield spreads calculated using prices from executed trades, executable quotes, and composites of executable and indicative quotes (basis points)						
2008						**Volatility variable**
	Equity price volatility	**Option implied volatility**	**Equity return volatility**	**Excess equity return volatility**	**Earnings volatility**	**No volatility variable**
Time to maturity	-1.269* (0.614)	-1.187* (0.641)	-1.255* (0.606)	-1.255* (0.611)	-1.232** (0.570)	-1.267** (0.590)
Coupon	30.982 (20.589)	29.042 (21.853)	30.547 (20.257)	30.517 (20.379)	29.479 (19.355)	29.876 (20.006)
Operating expenses	-92.810** (37.956)	-202.517*** (60.420)	-89.526** (36.812)	-70.820* (35.180)	-138.984** (55.786)	-111.772*** (34.104)
Issue size	0.000 (0.023)	0.004 (0.024)	0.000 (0.023)	0.003 (0.023)	0.002 (0.022)	-0.000 (0.022)
Total trade volume	-0.000 (0.000)	-0.000 (0.000)	-0.000 (0.000)	-0.000 (0.000)	-0.000 (0.000)	-0.000 (0.000)
Total assets	0.124 (0.144)	0.064 (0.139)	0.124 (0.129)	0.130 (0.104)	0.055 (0.133)	0.063 (0.129)
Equity capital	19.526** (6.944)	23.180** (10.197)	18.946** (7.655)	17.337** (6.725)	18.710** (8.084)	19.686*** (6.863)
Equity capital x total assets	0.013 (0.023)	-0.022 (0.026)	0.012 (0.024)	0.017 (0.018)	0.021 (0.020)	0.020 (0.021)
Subordinated debt	7.918 (31.859)	14.153 (29.805)	6.180 (31.162)	0.322 (26.788)	10.856 (29.995)	11.004 (32.695)
Subordinated debt x total assets	-0.099 (0.065)	-0.025 (0.046)	-0.090 (0.065)	-0.092* (0.053)	-0.108 (0.064)	-0.103 (0.065)
Earnings	-167.831* (96.274)	-108.627 (97.037)	-143.709 (99.636)	-146.072 (84.756)	-177.705 (108.083)	-163.593* (93.830)
Earnings x total assets	0.068 (0.138)	0.169 (0.138)	0.045 (0.130)	0.060 (0.106)	-0.000 (0.130)	0.013 (0.125)
Maturity mismatch	-5.968** (2.466)	-8.608*** (2.105)	-5.385** (2.422)	-4.915** (2.181)	-7.370*** (2.349)	-6.829** (2.535)
Maturity mismatch x total assets	0.003 (0.002)	0.007*** (0.002)	0.003 (0.002)	0.002 (0.002)	-0.001 (0.003)	0.003 (0.002)
Texas ratio	6.512* (3.526)	0.258 (1.979)	6.320* (3.453)	4.985 (3.813)	7.060* (3.514)	7.531* (3.615)
Texas ratio x total assets	-0.002 (0.002)	-0.000 (0.001)	-0.002 (0.002)	-0.002 (0.002)	-0.002 (0.002)	-0.003 (0.002)
Equity price volatility		0.586 (0.396)				
Equity price volatility x total assets		-0.000 (0.000)				
Option implied volatility			1.696 (1.463)			
Option implied volatility x total assets			0.000 (0.001)			
Equity return volatility				34.178* (17.628)		
Equity return volatility x total assets				-0.005 (0.010)		
Excess equity return volatility					48.818** (18.522)	
Excess equity return volatility x total assets					-0.017* (0.009)	
Earnings volatility						7.787 (10.992)

Table 5. (Continued)

Dependent variable = average bond yield spreads calculated using prices from executed trades, executable quotes, and composites of executable and indicative quotes (basis points)						
2008	**Volatility variable**					
	Equity price volatility	**Option implied volatility**	**Equity return volatility**	**Excess equity return volatility**	**Earnings volatility**	**No volatility variable**
Earnings volatility x total assets						0.014 (0.011)
Number of observations	478	428	478	478	478	478
Adjusted R-squared	0.628	0.606	0.631	0.638	0.624	0.622
Akaike Information Criteria	5917	5254	5913	5904	5922	5927
Schwartz Information Criteria	6000	5323	5997	5988	6005	6010
Number of bank holding companies	21	18	21	21	21	21
Hypothesis test that the coefficients on total assets and the total assets-credit risk interaction terms are jointly equal to zero:						
F-statistic	3.579	3.792	2.972	4.486	2.983	4.207
Probability of observing F-statistic if hypothesis is true	0.012	0.012	0.026	0.004	0.026	0.007
2013	**Volatility variable**					
Time to maturity	0.788*** (0.093)	0.775*** (0.087)	0.794*** (0.095)	0.798*** (0.095)	0.857*** (0.120)	0.878*** (0.128)
Coupon	9.497*** (2.079)	8.455*** (1.742)	9.453*** (2.047)	9.197*** (1.926)	8.396*** (2.459)	10.085*** (2.511)
Operating expenses	5.749 (8.154)	0.972 (6.588)	6.741 (8.190)	7.736 (8.433)	-10.274** (4.296)	-13.639** (5.668)
Issue size	-0.013*** (0.004)	-0.010** (0.004)	-0.013*** (0.004)	-0.013*** (0.004)	-0.013*** (0.004)	-0.016*** (0.004)
Total trade volume	0.000 (0.000)	0.000 (0.000)	0.000 (0.000)	0.000 (0.000)	0.000 (0.000)	0.000 (0.000)
Total assets	0.013 (0.032)	0.017 (0.022)	0.010 (0.034)	0.013 (0.033)	0.269*** (0.077)	-0.037 (0.048)
Equity capital	6.763* (3.856)	7.444** (3.428)	6.072 (3.923)	3.375 (3.965)	5.487 (3.716)	0.470 (4.559)
Equity capital x total assets	-0.005 (0.005)	-0.009* (0.005)	-0.004 (0.005)	-0.002 (0.005)	-0.011 (0.007)	0.012** (0.005)
Subordinated debt	-29.137** (13.149)	-29.108*** (9.968)	-29.921** (13.257)	-31.370** (13.438)	-19.769 (16.353)	-25.283* (14.168)
Subordinated debt x total assets	0.052** (0.019)	0.057*** (0.017)	0.054** (0.020)	0.057** (0.021)	0.065* (0.033)	0.030 (0.023)
Earnings	-69.186 (49.502)	-44.545 (44.445)	-71.544 (49.088)	-74.556 (47.102)	-32.870* (17.759)	-48.299** (21.803)
Earnings x total assets	0.027 (0.041)	0.044 (0.028)	0.026 (0.042)	0.018 (0.038)	-0.070*** (0.022)	-0.048 (0.034)
Maturity mismatch	0.522 (0.695)	1.136* (0.593)	0.559 (0.714)	0.555 (0.706)	1.062 (0.779)	2.244*** (0.531)
Maturity mismatch x total assets	-0.001* (0.001)	-0.001*** (0.000)	-0.001* (0.001)	-0.001 (0.001)	-0.002* (0.001)	-0.003*** (0.001)

Dependent variable = average bond yield spreads calculated using prices from executed trades, executable quotes, and composites of executable and indicative quotes (basis points)						
2008						**Volatility variable**
	Equity price volatility	**Option implied volatility**	**Equity return volatility**	**Excess equity return volatility**	**Earnings volatility**	**No volatility variable**
Texas ratio	3.207*** (1.114)	2.961*** (0.933)	3.270*** (1.108)	2.826** (1.055)	4.106*** (1.463)	3.447** (1.464)
Texas ratio x total assets	-0.003*** (0.001)	-0.003*** (0.001)	-0.003*** (0.001)	-0.004*** (0.001)	-0.008*** (0.002)	-0.006*** (0.001)
Equity price volatility	5.959*** (1.434)					
Equity price volatility x total assets	0.000 (0.001)					
Option implied volatility		9.397*** (1.818)				
Option implied volatility x total assets		0.000 (0.001)				
Equity return volatility			98.615*** (25.234)			
Equity return volatility x total assets			-0.001 (0.014)			
Excess equity return volatility				124.829*** (32.956)		
Excess equity return volatility x total assets				-0.020 (0.017)		
Earnings volatility					12.388*** (3.559)	
Earnings volatility x total assets					-0.029*** (0.007)	
Number of observations	1446	1446	1446	1446	1535	1535
Adjusted R-squared	0.521	0.563	0.519	0.519	0.521	0.469
Akaike Information Criteria	15083	14951	15090	15090	16221	16378
Schwartz Information Criteria	15199	15067	15206	15206	16338	16484
Number of bank holding companies	30	30	30	30	31	31
Hypothesis test that the coefficients on total assets and the total assets-credit risk interaction terms are jointly equal to zero:						
F-statistic	3.027	3.907	3.009	4.477	7.309	5.258
Probability of observing F-statistic if hypothesis is true	0.016	0.004	0.017	0.002	<0.001	0.001

Source: GAO analysis of Bloomberg and Financial Stability Board data. | GAO-14-621.

Notes: We estimated econometric models of the relationship between bank holding company size and funding costs using data for U.S. bank holding companies and their outstanding senior unsecured bonds for the first quarter of 2006 through the fourth quarter of 2013. The models used bond yield spreads to measure funding costs and controlled for credit risk factors such as capital adequacy, asset quality, earnings, maturity mismatch, and volatility, as well as bond liquidity and other characteristics of bonds and bank holding companies that can affect funding costs. We estimated multiple models for each year from 2006 through 2013 to assess the sensitivity of our results to alternative measures of capital adequacy, volatility, bond liquidity, and size or systemic importance. This table shows estimates of the parameters of models for 2008 and 2013 that used average bond yield spreads calculated using prices from executed trades, executable quotes, and composites of executable and indicative quotes to measure bond funding costs; total assets to measure bank holding company size; issue size and total trade volume to measure bond liquidity; equity capital and subordinated debt as percents of assets to measure capital adequacy; and each of equity price volatility, option implied volatility, equity return volatility, excess equity return volatility, and earnings volatility to measure volatility, as well as a model with no volatility measure. Other explanatory variables include coupon, time to maturity, Texas ratio, maturity mismatch, and operating expenses. Standard errors clustered by bank holding company are in parentheses. *=statistically significant at the 10 percent level. **=statistically significant at the 5 percent level. ***=statistically significant at the 1 percent level.

Table 6. Baseline Comparisons of Bond Yield Spreads for Bank Holding Companies of Different Sizes by Year, 2008 and 2013 (basis points)

2008, credit risk equal to average for 2008	**Comparison from baseline model with volatility variable:**					
Comparison	**Equity price volatility**	**Option implied volatility**	**Equity return volatility**	**Excess equity return volatility**	**Earnings volatility**	**No volatility variable**
$50 billion vs. $10 billion in assets	-3.860*** (1.175)	-1.867** (0.770)	-4.124*** (1.186)	-3.590*** (1.181)	-4.353*** (1.235)	-4.011*** (1.256)
$100 billion vs. $10 billion in assets	-8.686*** (2.644)	-4.201** (1.734)	-9.278*** (2.669)	-8.078*** (2.658)	-9.794*** (2.779)	-9.026*** (2.827)
$250 billion vs. $10 billion in assets	-23.161*** (7.050)	-11.204** (4.623)	-24.742*** (7.118)	-21.541*** (7.088)	-26.119*** (7.410)	-24.069*** (7.537)
$500 billion vs. $10 billion in assets	-47.288*** (14.394)	-22.874** (9.439)	-50.515*** (14.532)	-43.980*** (14.471)	-53.326*** (15.128)	-49.140*** (15.389)
$1 trillion vs. $10 billion in assets	-95.541*** (29.081)	-46.215** (19.070)	-102.061*** (29.360)	-88.858*** (29.237)	-107.739*** (30.565)	-99.284*** (31.092)
2013, credit risk equal to average for 2013	**Comparison from baseline model with volatility variable:**					
Comparison	**Equity price volatility**	**Option implied volatility**	**Equity return volatility**	**Excess equity return volatility**	**Earnings volatility**	**No volatility variable**
$50 billion vs. $10 billion in assets	1.152** (0.446)	1.011*** (0.365)	1.239** (0.463)	1.388*** (0.498)	0.930 (0.861)	2.365*** (0.727)
$100 billion vs. $10 billion in assets	2.591** (1.004)	2.276*** (0.820)	2.787** (1.042)	3.123*** (1.120)	2.093 (1.936)	5.322*** (1.635)
$250 billion vs. $10 billion in assets	6.910** (2.676)	6.068*** (2.187)	7.432** (2.778)	8.329*** (2.985)	5.582 (5.164)	14.19*** (4.359)
$500 billion vs. $10 billion in assets	14.107** (5.464)	12.389*** (4.465)	15.174** (5.673)	17.006*** (6.095)	11.397 (10.542)	28.977*** (8.900)
$1 trillion vs. $10 billion in assets	28.502** (11.039)	25.031*** (9.022)	30.658** (11.461)	34.358*** (12.315)	23.027 (21.30)	58.546*** (17.982)

2013, credit risk equal to average for 2008	Comparison from baseline model with volatility variable:					
Comparison	Equity price volatility	Option implied volatility	Equity return volatility	Excess equity return volatility	Earnings volatility	No volatility variable
$50 billion vs. $10 billion in assets	1.976 (3.253)	2.541 (2.414)	1.465 (2.899)	-0.639 (2.598)	-0.087 (1.704)	-1.971 (1.750)
$100 billion vs. $10 billion in assets	4.447 (7.319)	5.717 (5.431)	3.296 (6.523)	-1.437 (5.846)	-0.195 (3.835)	-4.435 (3.937)
$250 billion vs. $10 billion in assets	11.859 (19.517)	15.245 (14.483)	8.789 (17.395)	-3.833 (15.589)	-0.519 (10.226)	-11.828 (10.499)
$500 billion vs. $10 billion in assets	24.212 (39.848)	31.126 (29.570)	17.943 (35.514)	-7.826 (31.828)	-1.060 (20.879)	-24.148 (21.436)
$1 trillion vs. $10 billion in assets	48.918 (80.509)	62.888 (59.743)	36.253 (71.754)	-15.812 (64.305)	-2.142 (42.183)	-48.789 (43.309)

Source: GAO analysis of Bloomberg and Financial Stability Board data. | GAO-14-621.

Notes: We estimated econometric models of the relationship between bank holding company size and funding costs using data for U.S. bank holding companies and their outstanding senior unsecured bonds for the first quarter of 2006 through the fourth quarter of 2013. The models used bond yield spreads to measure funding costs and controlled for credit risk factors such as capital adequacy, asset quality, earnings, maturity mismatch, and volatility, as well as bond liquidity and other characteristics of bonds and bank holding companies that can affect funding costs. We estimated multiple models for each year from 2006 through 2013 to assess the sensitivity of estimated funding cost differences to alternative measures of capital adequacy, volatility, bond liquidity, and size or systemic importance and then used the models to compare bond funding costs for bank holding companies of different sizes but the same levels of credit risk, bond liquidity, and other characteristics. This table shows bond funding cost comparisons from models for 2008 and 2013 that used average bond yield spreads calculated using prices from executed trades, executable quotes, and composites of executable and indicative quotes to measure bond funding costs; total assets to measure bank holding company size; issue size and total trade volume to measure bond liquidity; equity capital and subordinated debt as percents of assets to measure capital adequacy; and each of equity price volatility, option implied volatility, equity return volatility, excess equity return volatility, and earnings volatility to measure volatility, as well as a model with no volatility measure. Other explanatory variables include coupon, time to maturity, Texas ratio, maturity mismatch, and operating expenses. *=statistically significant at the 10 percent level. **=statistically significant at the 5 percent level. ***=statistically significant at the 1 percent level.

Table 7 shows the difference in predicted bond yield spreads for bank holding companies with $1 trillion and $10 billion in assets for all specifications for 2008 and 2013 assuming bank holding companies have the average level of credit risk each year. Table 7 also shows the difference in predicted bond yield spreads for bank holding companies with $1 trillion and $10 billion in assets for all specifications for 2013 assuming bank holding companies have the average level of credit risk in 2008.

Table 7. Comparisons of Bond Yield Spreads for Bank Holding Companies with $1 trillion versus $10 billion in Assets, All 42 Models, 2008 and 2013 (basis points)

2008, credit risk equal to average for 2008	Comparison from model with volatility variable:					
	Equity price volatility	**Option implied volatility**	**Equity return volatility**	**Excess equity return volatility**	**Earnings volatility**	**No volatility variable**
Baseline model[a]	-95.54*** (29.08)	-46.22** (19.07)	-102.06*** (29.36)	-88.86*** (29.24)	- 107.74*** (30.57)	-99.28*** (31.09)
Add bid-ask spreads to bond liquidity measures	-98.52*** (32.98)	-21.30 (15.94)	-104.08*** (31.57)	-88.60** (32.09)	-106.98** (37.49)	-104.99** (37.40)
Measure size using GSIB designation	-148.78** (60.01)	-115.16*** (35.69)	-157.00** (60.78)	-143.10** (58.73)	-145.12** (55.21)	-148.98** (57.39)
Measure size using total assets and total assets squared	-382.78*** (119.13)	-629.74*** (82.69)	-422.24*** (101.56)	-270.29** (113.61)	-228.54* (127.27)	-291.43** (120.81)
Measure capital adequacy using equity capital and subordinated debt as percents of risk-weighted assets	-86.43** (30.87)	-44.90 (32.54)	-96.96*** (31.12)	-77.63** (29.26)	-96.79*** (32.30)	-92.96** (34.10)
Measure size using an indicator of whether a bank holding company has assets of $50 billion or more	-432.86*** (90.04)	-397.28** (146.06)	-420.42*** (67.65)	-357.57*** (30.33)	- 515.38*** (133.82)	-357.49*** (73.88)
Measure bond yield spreads using prices from executed trades only	-79.73** (31.77)	-16.75 (20.62)	-89.17** (32.85)	-73.39** (32.98)	-93.21** (34.18)	-85.16** (35.49)
2013, credit risk equal to average for 2013						
Baseline modela	28.50** (11.04)	25.03*** (9.02)	30.66** (11.46)	34.36*** (12.31)	23.03 (21.30)	58.55*** (17.98)
Add bid-ask spreads to bond liquidity measures	32.80*** (10.95)	29.63*** (8.431)	34.86*** (11.35)	38.49*** (12.41)	25.87 (21.28)	62.60*** (17.88)
Measure size using GSIB designation	3.07 (11.43)	-11.18 (11.32)	7.49 (11.10)	28.13*** (9.52)	36.07** (14.40)	28.97 (20.42)
Measure size using total assets and total assets squared	-51.80** (23.50)	-41.43** (18.95)	-52.43** (23.06)	-36.89 (22.97)	-19.01 (52.29)	3.73 (43.74)
Measure capital adequacy using equity capital and subordinated debt as percents of risk-weighted assets	23.17** (10.53)	20.33** (7.790)	24.33** (11.00)	28.05** (11.91)	0.264 (15.62)	45.88** (17.03)
Measure size using an indicator of whether a bank holding company has assets of $50 billion or more	-183.08** (81.39)	-195.76*** (59.77)	-190.95** (80.21)	-160.67* (85.47)	- 188.38*** (66.17)	-163.51 (100.2)
Measure bond yield spreads using prices from executed trades only	17.32 (14.24)	13.21 (12.66)	20.06 (14.78)	24.87 (15.86)	13.39 (25.28)	49.02*** (17.37)
Baseline model[a]	48.92 (80.51)	62.89 (59.74)	36.25 (71.75)	-15.81 (64.31)	-2.14 (42.18)	-48.79 (43.31)

2008, credit risk equal to average for 2008	Comparison from model with volatility variable:					
	Equity price volatility	Option implied volatility	Equity return volatility	Excess equity return volatility	Earnings volatility	No volatility variable
Add bid-ask spreads to bond liquidity measures	64.91 (76.62)	86.12 (54.27)	51.00 (66.88)	3.65 (62.80)	-0.28 (42.16)	-43.14 (44.27)
Measure size using GSIB designation	-290.72 (210.512)	-264.12** (103.19)	-266.26 (197.211)	-118.16 (184.807)	-41.328 (55.122)	28.798 (54.296)
Measure size using total assets and total assets squared	-455.05 (279.97)	-327.16** (141.48)	-494.45* (253.52)	-473.93* (242.11)	-241.81 (195.99)	-160.75 (153.44)
Measure capital adequacy using equity capital and subordinated debt as percents of risk-weighted assets	-54.12 (68.63)	-7.73 (71.92)	-67.52 (58.98)	-102.48** (47.92)	-45.56 (35.37)	-105.58*** (37.02)
Measure size using an indicator of whether a bank holding company has assets of $50 billion or more	-194.56 (144.1)	-606.39* (307.14)	-373.43* (195.44)	-355.84*** (107.35)	-246.16* (143.55)	-154.46 (144.58)
Measure bond yield spreads using prices from executed trades only	38.47 (87.83)	35.45 (61.70)	36.14 (75.85)	-1.00 (64.28)	12.43 (35.46)	-50.39 (41.98)

Source: GAO analysis of Bloomberg and Financial Stability Board data. | GAO-14-621.

Notes: We estimated econometric models of the relationship between bank holding company size and funding costs using data for U.S. bank holding companies and their outstanding senior unsecured bonds for the first quarter of 2006 through the fourth quarter of 2013. The models used bond yield spreads to measure funding costs and controlled for credit risk factors such as capital adequacy, asset quality, earnings, maturity mismatch, and volatility, as well as bond liquidity and other characteristics of bonds and bank holding companies that can affect funding costs. We estimated multiple models for each year from 2006 through 2013 to assess the sensitivity of estimated funding cost differences to alternative measures of capital adequacy, volatility, bond liquidity, and size or systemic importance and then used the models to compare bond funding costs for bank holding companies of different sizes but the same levels of credit risk, bond liquidity, and other characteristics. This table shows bond funding cost comparisons from models for 2008 and 2013 for bank holding companies with the average level of credit risk for those years, and from models for 2013 for bank holding companies with the average level of credit risk for 2008.

*=statistically significant at the 10 percent level. **=statistically significant at the 5 percent level. ***=statistically significant at the 1 percent level.

[a] The baseline model used average bond yield spreads calculated using prices from executed trades, executable quotes, and composites of executable and indicative quotes to measure bond funding costs; total assets to measure bank holding company size; issue size and total trade volume to measure bond liquidity; equity capital and subordinated debt as percents of assets to measure capital adequacy; and each of equity price volatility, option implied volatility, equity return volatility, excess equity return volatility, and earnings volatility to measure volatility, as well as a model with no volatility measure. Other explanatory variables include coupon, time to maturity, Texas ratio, maturity mismatch, and operating expenses.

Figure 4 shows estimated bond funding costs for bank holding companies with $1 trillion in assets versus those with $10 billion in assets by model and year, assuming that all bank holding companies have the average level of credit risk in each year.

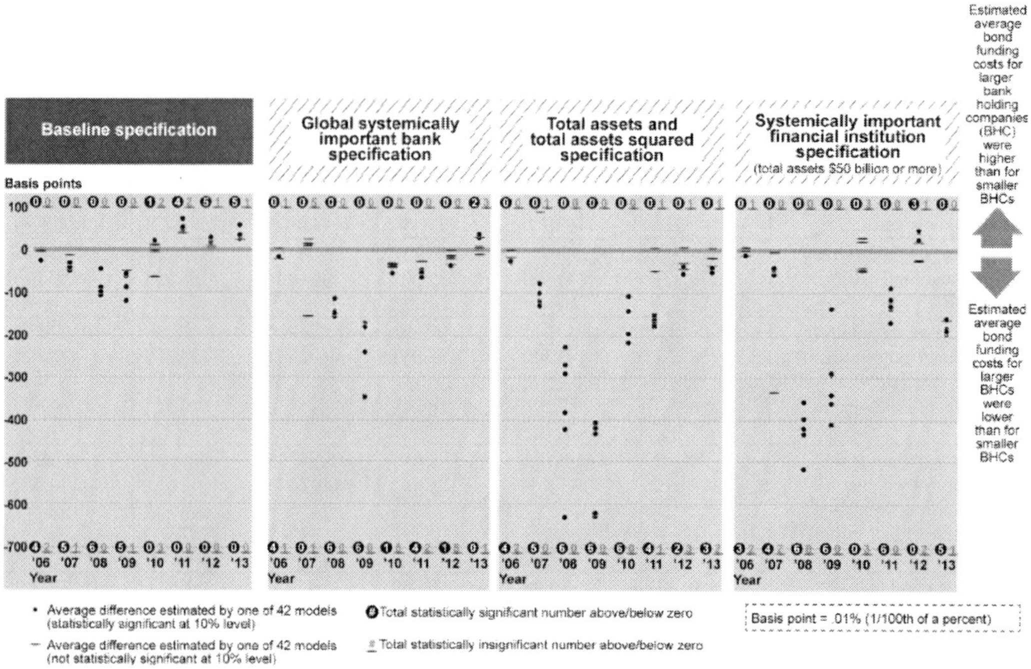

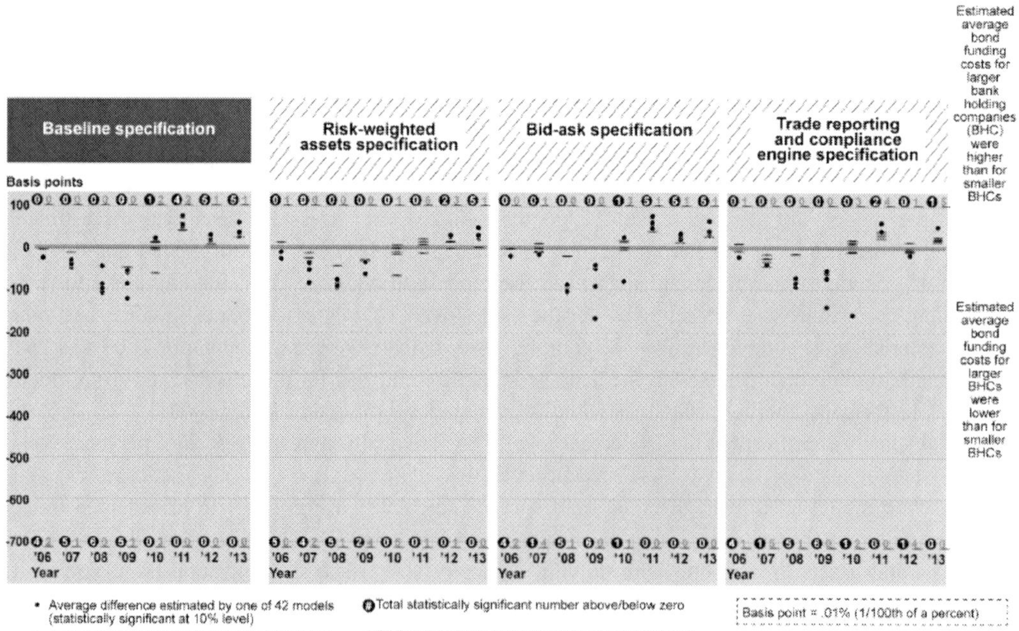

Source: GAO analysis of data from Bloomberg and the Financial Stability Board. | GAO-14-621.

Notes: We estimated econometric models of the relationship between bank holding company size and funding costs using data for U.S. bank holding companies and their outstanding senior unsecured bonds for the first quarter of 2006 through the fourth quarter of 2013. The models used bond yield spreads to measure funding costs and controlled for credit risk factors such as capital adequacy, asset quality, earnings, maturity mismatch, and volatility, as well as bond liquidity and other characteristics of bonds and bank holding companies that can affect funding costs. We estimated 42 models for each year from 2006 through 2013 to assess the sensitivity of estimated differences in funding costs to alternative measures of capital adequacy, volatility, bond liquidity, and size or systemic importance. We used the models to compare bond funding costs for bank holding companies of different sizes but the same levels of credit risk, bond liquidity, and other characteristics. This figure compares bond funding costs for bank holding companies with $1 trillion and $10 billion in assets, for each model and for each year, with average levels of credit risk. Each circle and dash shows the comparison for a different model, where circles and dashes below zero suggest bank holding companies with $1 trillion in assets have lower bond funding costs than bank holding companies with $10 billion in assets, and vice versa.

Figure 4. Difference in Estimated Bond Funding Costs for Average Credit Risk Bank Holding Companies with $1 Trillion versus $10 Billion in Assets by Model Specification, by Year, 2006-2013.

BIBLIOGRAPHY

Acharya, Viral V., Deniz Anginer, & Joseph Warburton, A. (2013). "The End of Market Discipline? Investor Expectations of Implicit State Guarantees." *Social Science Research Network Working Paper*. December.

Araten, Michel & Christopher M. Turner. (2012). "Understanding the Funding Cost Differences between Global Systemically Important Banks (G-SIBs) and Non-G-SIBs in the United States." *Social Science Research Network Working Paper.* March.

Balasubramnian, Bhanu & Ken Cyree. (2014), "Has Market Discipline on Banks Improved after the Dodd-Frank Act?" *Journal of Banking & Finance*, vol. *41*, 155-166.

Balasubramnian, Bhanu & Ken Cyree. (2012). "The End of Too-Big-to-Fail? Evidence from Senior Bank Bond Yield Spreads around the Dodd-Frank Act." *Social Science Research Network Working Paper*. June.

Barth, Andreas & Isabel Schnabel. (2013). "Why Banks are Not Too Big To Fail—Evidence from the CDS Market." *Economic Policy*, vol. *28*, no. 74. April, 335-369.

Bertay, Ata Can, Aslı Demırgüç-Kunt, & Harry Huizinga. (2013). "Do We Need Big Banks? Evidence on Performance, Strategy and Market Discipline." *Journal of Financial Intermediation*, vol. *22*, 532-558.

International Monetary Fund. (2014). "How Big is the Implicit Subsidy for Banks Considered Too Important to Fail?" *Global Financial Stability Report*, Ch. 3 (Washington, D.C.: 2014).

Jacewitz, Stefan & Jonathan Pogach. (2012) "Deposit Rate Advantages at the Largest Banks." *Social Science Research Network Working Paper*. September.

Keppo, Jussi & Jing Yang. (2013). *The Value of Too-Big-To-Fail Subsidy*. Unpublished working paper. September 2013.

Kumar, Aditi and John Lester. *Do Deposit Rates Show Evidence of Too Big To Fail Effects? An Updated Look at the Empirical Evidence through 2012 among US Banks* (Oliver Wyman, Inc., 2014).

Kumar, Aditi & John Lester. (2014). *Do Bond Spreads Show Evidence of Too Big To Fail Effects? Evidence from 2009-2013 among US Bank Holding Companies* (Oliver Wyman, Inc., 2014).

Li, Zan, Shisheng Qu & Jing Zhang. (2011). *Quantifying the Value of Implicit Government Guarantees for Large Financial Institutions* (Moody's Analytics, 2011).

Santos, João. (2014). "Evidence from the Bond Market on Banks' 'Too Big To Fail' Subsidy." *Federal Reserve Bank of New York Economic Policy Review*, vol. *20*, no. 2. March.

Tsesmelidakis, Zoe & Robert, C. (2012). Merton. "The Value of Implicit Guarantees." *Social Science Research Network Working Paper*. September.

Ueda, Kenichi, & Weder di Mauro, B. (2013). "Quantifying Structural Subsidy Values for Systemically Important Financial Institutions," *Journal of Banking & Finance*, vol. 37, no. 10. October 2013: 3830–3842.

Völz, Manja & Michael Wedow. (2009). "Does Banks' Size Distort Market Prices? Evidence for Too-Big-To-Fail in the CDS Market." *Deutsche Bundesbank Discussion Paper*, Series 2: Banking and Financial Studies, no. 6.

End Notes

[1] Bankruptcy is a federal court procedure conducted under rules and requirements of the U.S. Bankruptcy Code. The goal of bankruptcy is to give individuals and businesses a "fresh start" from burdensome debts by eliminating or restructuring debts they cannot repay and helping creditors receive some payment in an equitable manner through liquidation or reorganization of the debtor.

[2] Pub. L. No. 111-203, 124 Stat. 1376 (2010).

[3] In November 2013, we issued the first report, which examined (1) actual government support for banks and bank holding companies during the financial crisis and (2) recent statutory and regulatory changes related to government support for banks and bank holding companies. See GAO, *Government Support for Bank Holding Companies: Statutory Changes to Limit Future Support Are Not Yet Fully Implemented*, GAO-14-18 (Washington, D.C.: Nov. 14, 2013). At a January 2014 hearing, we provided testimony based on this report. See GAO, *Government Support for Bank Holding Companies: Statutory Changes to Limit Future Support Are Not Yet Fully Implemented*, GAO-14-174T (Washington, D.C.: Jan. 8, 2014).

[4] For example, we reviewed GAOwhich describes Dodd-Frank Act provisions intended to place limits on agency authorities to provide emergency assistance to financial firms and strengthen regulatory oversight of large bank holding companies. We also reviewed prior GAO work on potential impacts of the Dodd-Frank Act. See GAO, *Financial Regulatory Reform: Financial Crisis Losses and Potential Impacts of the Dodd-Frank Act*, GAO-13-180 (Washington, D.C.: Jan. 16, 2013).

[5] See GAO

[6] Negative values of β and δ are consistent with these beliefs as long as greater values of the size measure are associated with larger bank holding companies and greater values of the credit risk proxies are associated with greater credit risk.

[7] Plain vanilla bonds refer to bonds that pay interest at regular intervals and return the principal at maturity with no additional features such as convertibility to stock or options to redeem the bond before maturity. Such bonds are also known as straight bonds.

[8] We estimated the parameters of our models using the least squares estimator, which is a standard statistical and econometric technique that calculates the values of the parameters of our regression model that minimize the sum of the squared errors—the differences between bond funding costs observed in the data and bond funding costs predicted by the model.

[9] The Dodd-Frank Act requires bank holding companies with $50 billion or more in total assets to be subjected to enhanced regulatory standards and supervision. Pub. L. No. 111-203, § 165, 124 Stat. 1376, 1423 (2010) (codified at 12 U.S.C. § 5365). In addition, the Financial Stability Board designated 29 GSIBs, including eight U.S. bank holding companies, for the purpose of identifying firms that should be subject to resolution planning requirements and heightened regulatory supervision. The GSIBs generally comprise the largest and most complex internationally active financial firms. The bid-ask spread is the difference between the best buying price and the best selling price.

[10] Our models allow the size of a bank holding company to influence its bond funding costs directly and also indirectly through the interactions between size and the credit risk variables. As a result, no single parameter is sufficient to describe the relationship between bond funding costs and size. To summarize the overall relationship between bond funding costs and size reflected in each specification, we calculated bond funding costs for bank holding companies of different sizes and credit risk levels using our estimates of the parameters for each specification for each year. See appendix I for more details on the calculations.

[11] For more information about the government rescue of Continental Illinois National Bank, see GAO, *Financial Markets and Institutions: Views on the Federal Rescue of the Continental Illinois National Bank and Trust Co,* Testimony by the Comptroller General of the U.S. before the Subcommittee on Financial Institutions Supervision, Regulation, and Insurance of the Committee on Banking, Finance and Urban Affairs of the U.S. House of Representatives (Washington, D.C.: Dec. 14, 1984); and GAO, *Financial Crisis Management: Four Financial Crises in the 1980s*, GAO/GGD-97-96 (Washington, D.C.: May 1, 1997).

[12] For more information on the near-collapse of Long-Term Capital Management and broader issues it raised, see GAO, *Long-Term Capital Management: Regulators Need to Focus Greater Attention on Systemic Risk*, GAO/GGD-00-3 (Washington, D.C.: Oct. 29, 1999).

[13] For more discussion of the federal government's emergency actions to assist the financial sector, see GAO

[14] At the time, Bear Stearns was one of the largest investment banks. For further discussion of this assistance, see GAO, *Federal Reserve System: Opportunities Exist to Strengthen Policies and Processes for Managing Emergency Assistance*, GAO-11-696 (Washington, D.C.: July 21, 2011). During the weekend of September 13-15, 2008, government officials met with leaders of major financial firms to devise a private-sector solution to Lehman Brothers' likelihood of defaulting on its obligations, but they were unable to find a solution. While the Federal Reserve Board was able to provide liquidity to Lehman Brothers against collateral through its emergency credit programs, according to the Federal Reserve Board Chairman at that time, neither the Federal Reserve Board nor any other agency had the authority to provide the capital or unsecured guarantee of its obligations that they believed Lehman Brothers needed to avert failure. See Ben S. Bernanke, Board of Governors of the Federal Reserve System, "Lessons from the Failure of Lehman Brothers" (testimony before the Committee on Financial Services, U.S. House of Representatives, Washington, D.C., Apr. 20, 2010).

[15] Subsequent to the announcement of the $85 billion credit assistance, Treasury and the Federal Reserve provided new forms of assistance and restructured the assistance package for AIG over time. For more information about the federal government's assistance to AIG, see GAO, *Troubled Asset Relief Program: Status of Government Assistance Provided to AIG*, GAO-09-975 (Washington, D.C.: Sept. 21, 2009).

[16] A few days after the announcement of the proposed Citigroup acquisition, Wachovia announced that it would instead merge with Wells Fargo in a transaction that would include all of Wachovia's operations and require no FDIC assistance. As a result, the FDIC loss-sharing agreement on Wachovia assets was not implemented. FDICIA included a systemic risk exception to the requirement that FDIC resolve failed banks using the least costly method. Pub. L. No. 102-242, § 141, 105 Stat. 2236, 2275 (codified at 12 U.S.C. § 1823(c)(4)(G)). Under this exception, FDIC could provide assistance to a failing bank if compliance with its requirements to resolve the bank using the least costly approach would have "serious adverse effects on economic conditions or financial stability"—that is, would cause systemic risk—and if such assistance would "avoid or mitigate such adverse effects." *Id.* FDIC could act under the exception only under a process that included recommendations from the FDIC Board of Directors and Federal Reserve Board and approval by the Secretary of the Treasury. The Dodd-Frank Act restricts FDIC's authority to provide open bank assistance to an individual failing bank outside of receivership and replaces it with a new authority, subject to certain restrictions and a joint resolution of congressional approval, to create a debt-guarantee program with broad-based eligibility. Pub. L. No. 111-203, § 1105(a), 124 Stat. 1376, 2121 (2010) (codified at 12 U.S.C. §§ 5612(a) and 5613(b)).

[17] The G7 is an informal forum of coordination among Canada, France, Germany, Italy, Japan, the United Kingdom, and the United States.

[18] For more about the Troubled Asset Relief Program, see GAO, *Troubled Asset Relief Program: One Year Later, Actions Are Needed to Address Remaining Transparency and Accountability Challenges*, GAO-10-16 (Washington, D.C.: Oct. 8, 2009). For more about the Temporary Liquidity Guarantee Program, see GAO, *Federal Deposit Insurance Act: Regulators' Use of Systemic Risk Exception Raises Moral Hazard Concerns and Opportunities Exist to Clarify the Provision*, GAO-10-100 (Washington, D.C.: Apr. 15, 2010).

[19] The share of total bank assets held by the five largest global banks has increased in many advanced countries and highlights concerns about too big to fail.

[20] The G20, established in 1999, is a forum for international cooperation on important issues of the global economic and financial agenda. Its members include 19 countries and the European Union. The G20 leaders established the Financial Stability Board as the successor to the Financial Stability Forum and made it responsible for coordinating and promoting the implementation of the G20 reform commitments.

[21] Financial Stability Board, "Reducing the Moral Hazard Posed by Systemically Important Financial Institutions – FSB Recommendations and Time Lines," October 20, 2010. In September 2013, the Financial Stability Board issued a report providing an update on progress in implementing this framework. See Financial Stability Board, "Progress and Next Steps Towards Ending 'Too-Big-to-Fail' (TBTF) – Report of the Financial Stability Board to the G20," September 2, 2013.

[22] Financial Stability Board, "Key Attributes of Effective Resolution Regimes for Financial Institutions," October 2011.

[23] For more information about the U.S. role in international financial reform efforts, including the development of international financial standards, see GAO, *International Financial Reforms: U.S. and Other Jurisdictions' Efforts to Develop and Implement Reforms*, GAO-14-261 (Washington, D.C.: Apr. 3, 2014).

[24] While the Dodd-Frank Act does not use the term "systemically important financial institution," this term is commonly used by academics and other experts to refer to bank holding companies with $50 billion or more in total consolidated assets and nonbank financial companies designated by FSOC for Federal Reserve supervision and enhanced prudential standards.

[25] Pub. L. No. 111-203, §§ 1101 and 1105, 124 Stat. 1376, 2113 and 2121 (2010) (codified at 12 U.S.C. §§ 343(3)(A) and 5612). For more information about changes to these authorities, see GAO

[26] § 165(d), 124 Stat. at 1426 (codified at 12 U.S.C. § 5365(d)); § 204, 124 Stat. at 1454-56 (codified at 12 U.S.C. § 5384). During the financial crisis, several large financial institutions became insolvent and filed for bankruptcy when no private-sector solution was found. For example, Lehman Brothers filed for Chapter 11 bankruptcy on September 15, 2008. Lehman had $639 billion in total assets and $613 billion in total liabilities as of May 31, 2008. The bankruptcy proceedings highlighted inconsistencies in laws and regulations across countries and limitations on the ability of countries to coordinate effectively during the reorganization or liquidation of international financial institutions.

[27] § 165(d)(1), 124 Stat. at 1426 (codified at 12 U.S.C. § 5365(d)(1)).

[28] Resolution Plans Required, 76 Fed. Reg. 67323 (Nov. 1, 2011).

[29] In October 2013, the Federal Reserve Board and FDIC released the public sections of filed annual resolution plans for 11 firms. "Federal Reserve Board and FDIC, Agencies Release Public Sections of the Second Submission of Resolution Plans for 11 Institutions," accessed on November 7, 2013, http://www.federalreserve.gov/ newsevents/press/bcreg/20131003a.htm.

[30] § 165(d)(4)-(5), 124 Stat. at 1426-27 (codified at 12 U.S.C. § 5365(d)(4)-(5)). Further, if, after 2 years following the imposition of the more stringent standards, the resolution plan still does not meet the statutory standards, FDIC and the Federal Reserve Board may, in consultation with FSOC, direct a company to divest certain assets or operations. *Id.*

[31] § 204, 124 Stat. at 1454-1456 (codified at 12 U.S.C. § 5384).

[32] § 204(b), 124 Stat. at 1455 (codified at 12 U.S.C. § 5384(b)). The factors to be considered by the Secretary of the Treasury are set forth in Section 203(b) of the Dodd- Frank Act. § 203(b), 124 Stat. at 1451 (codified at 12 U.S.C. § 5383(b)). Before the Secretary of the Treasury, in consultation with the President, makes a decision to seek the appointment of FDIC as receiver of a financial company, at least two-thirds of those serving on the Board of Governors of the Federal Reserve System and at least two-thirds of those serving on the Board of Directors of FDIC must vote to make a written recommendation to the Secretary of the Treasury to appoint FDIC as receiver.

§203(a)(1)(A), 124 Stat. at 1450 (codified at 12 U.S.C. § 5383(a)(1)(A)). In the case of a broker-dealer, the recommendation must come from the Federal Reserve Board and the Securities and Exchange Commission, in consultation with FDIC, and in the case of an insurance company, from the Federal Reserve Board and the Director of the Federal Insurance Office, in consultation with FDIC. § 203(a)(1)(B)-(C), 124 Stat. at 1450 (codified at 12 U.S.C. § 5383(a)(1)(B)-(C)).

[33] § 204(a)(2), 124 Stat. at 1454 (codified at 12 U.S.C. § 5384(a)(2)).

[34] § 210(n), 124 Stat. at 1506 (codified at 12 U.S.C. § 5390(n)).

[35] § 210(o)(1), 124 Stat. at 1509 (codified at 12 U.S.C. § 5390(o)(1)).

[36] §165(a)(1), 124 Stat. at 1423 (codified at 12 U.S.C. § 5365(a)(1)).

[37] §165(b)(1)(A)(i), 124 Stat. at 1424; Enhanced Prudential Standards for Bank Holding Companies and Foreign Banking Organizations; Final Rule, 79 Fed. Reg. 17240 (Mar. 27, 2014) (codified at 12 C.F.R. pt. 252).

[38] The Federal Reserve Board plans to issue a proposal to impose graduated common equity risk-based capital surcharges on U.S. bank holding companies designated as global systemically important banks (GSIB). The Federal Reserve Board has said this proposal will be based on the GSIB capital surcharge framework developed by the Basel Committee, under which the size of the surcharge for an individual GSIB would vary from 1 percent to 2.5 percent, depending on the firm's systemic importance.

[39] §165(b)(1)(A)(ii), 124 Stat. at 1424 (codified at 12 U.S.C. § 5365(b)(1)(A)(ii)). Enhanced Prudential Standards for Bank Holding Companies and Foreign Banking Organizations; Final Rule, 79 Fed. Reg. 17240 (Mar. 27, 2014) (codified at 12 C.F.R. pt. 252).

[40] Liquidity Coverage Ratio: Liquidity Risk Measurement, Standards, and Monitoring; Proposed Rule, 78 Fed. Reg. 71818 (Nov. 29, 2013).The requirement is designed to promote the short-term resilience of the liquidity risk profile of internationally active banking organizations, thereby improving the banking sector's ability to absorb shocks arising from financial and economic stress. *Id.*

[41] §§ 165(b)(1)(A)(iii) and 165(h), 124 Stat. at 1424 and 1429 (codified at 12 U.S.C. §§ 5365(b)(1)(A)(iii) and 5365(h)).

[42] §165(i)(1), 124 Stat. at 1430 (codified at 12 U.S.C. § 5365(i)(1)). Companies subject to enhanced prudential standards as well as regulated financial firms with more than $10 billion in consolidated assets also must

conduct their own semiannual or annual stress tests, respectively. § 165(i)(2), 124 Stat. at 1430-31 (codified at 12 U.S.C. § 5365(i)(2)).

[43] The Basel Committee has developed international standards for bank capital for its member economies since the 1980s. In recent years, U.S. federal banking regulators have worked with other members of the Basel Committee to strengthen the regulatory capital regime for internationally active banks and develop a framework for a risk-based capital surcharge for the world's largest, most interconnected banking companies. The new regime, known as Basel III, seeks to improve the quality of regulatory capital and introduces a new minimum common equity requirement. Basel III also raises the numerical minimum capital requirements and introduces capital conservation and countercyclical buffers to require banking organizations to hold capital in excess of regulatory minimums. In addition, Basel III establishes for the first time an international leverage standard for internationally active banks. Federal banking regulators recently finalized capital reforms in the United States that are generally consistent with Basel III. The Federal Reserve Board will separately implement consistent capital and liquidity standards for nonbank financial companies designated for enhanced supervision by FSOC.

[44] Regulatory Capital Rules: Regulatory Capital, Enhanced Supplementary Leverage Ratio Standards for Certain Bank Holding Companies and Their Subsidiary Insured Depository Institutions, 79 Fed. Reg. 24528 (May 1, 2014).

[45] § 121(a)(1), 124 Stat. at 1410 (codified at 12 U.S.C. § 5331(a)(1)); § 165(a)(1), 124 Stat. at 1423 (codified at 12 U.S.C. § 5365(a)(1)); § 165(d)(4)-(5), 124 Stat. at 1426-27 (codified at 12 U.S.C. § 5365(d)(4)-(5)).

[46] § 619, 124 Stat. at 1620-31 (codified at 12 U.S.C. § 1851). Proprietary trading includes trading activities conducted by banking entities for their own account as opposed to those of their clients.

[47] A swap is a type of derivative that involves an ongoing exchange of one or more assets, liabilities, or payments for a specified period. Financial and nonfinancial firms use swaps and other over-the-counter derivatives to hedge risk, or speculate, or for other purposes.

[48] See GAOCounterparty credit risk is the risk to each party in an over-the- counter derivatives contract that the other party will not perform the contractual obligations. Technically, the clearing house members interact with the counterparties.

[49] FSOC has identified certain clearinghouses as systemically important financial market utilities, which are subject to risk management and other enhanced supervisory and prudential requirements under the Dodd-Frank Act and may be afforded access to collateralized emergency liquidity from Federal Reserve Banks in unusual or exigent circumstances.

[50] In May 2011, OCC, the Federal Reserve Board, FDIC, the Farm Credit Administration, and the Federal Housing Finance Agency issued a notice of proposed rule-making on margin and capital requirements for covered swap entities. Margin and Capital Requirements for Covered Swap Entities; Proposed Rule, 76 Fed. Reg. 27564 (May 11, 2011).

[51] Resolution of Systemically Important Financial Institutions: The Single Point of Entry Strategy, 78 Fed. Reg. 243 (Dec. 18, 2013); Resolution of a Systemically Important Financial Institution: The Single Point of Entry Strategy, 79 Fed. Reg. 9899 (Feb. 21, 2014).

[52] In March 2014, the Basel Committee published a standardized approach to measuring counterparty credit risk exposures. This standardized approach will take effect starting on January 1, 2017.

[53] For example, in December 2008, S&P introduced government support as a factor that could affect a financial institution's ratings. Moody's had assigned uplift in ratings for some bank holding companies before the financial crisis and during the crisis increased the amount of uplift for these firms and began to assign uplift to several other financial institutions.

[54] As explained earlier in this report's scope and methodology section, we selected nonrepresentative samples of investment firms for interviews. As a result, the views of investment firm representatives we interviewed are not generalizable to the broader universe of investors.

[55] A firm with a lower standalone credit rating may receive a bigger increase in its rating from government support than a firm with a stronger standalone rating.

[56] These eight companies were Bank of America Corporation, Bank of New York Mellon, Citigroup Inc., Goldman Sachs Group, JPMorgan Chase & Co., Morgan Stanley, State Street Corporation, and Wells Fargo & Company. While Fitch continued to assign a support rating floor to eight bank holding companies, only 3 of these companies had standalone credit ratings below the support rating floor and thus received a higher credit rating from Fitch as a result of assumed government support. These three companies were Bank of America Corporation, Citigroup Inc., and Morgan Stanley. Following a March 2014 upgrade to Citigroup Inc.'s rating, only Bank of America Corporation and Morgan Stanley continued to have a standalone rating below the support rating floor.

[57] In a July 2013 report, S&P noted that regulatory developments may lead it to reassess its assumptions of extraordinary government support on the holding company ratings of the eight systemically important banks, but it was not considering removing such support assumptions at the subsidiary level.

[58] Accordingly, S&P revised its rating outlook on the holding company of JPMorgan Chase & Co. to negative from stable, while maintaining negative rating outlooks on the holding companies of the other seven bank holding

companies. S&P noted that it is monitoring FDIC's progress in developing a resolution mechanism that aims to ensure that market confidence will not erode with the failure of a big bank and its resolution through Title II of Dodd-Frank. Furthermore, it indicated that it would consider the required level of long-term debt at the holding company as another factor in removing government support from those ratings.

[59] In March 2014, Fitch revised its outlook on Bank of America Corporation from "stable" to "negative," reflecting its expectation that its assumption of weakening sovereign support is likely to result in a downgrade. Fitch also upgraded Citigroup Inc.'s standalone rating, after which only Bank of America Corporation and Morgan Stanley—which Fitch noted was likely to be upgraded—had standalone ratings below the support rating floor and thus benefitted from an uplift.

[60] While Moody's removed rating uplift at the holding company level, it retained uplift in its ratings for the senior and subordinated debt of bank subsidiaries of these bank holding companies. Moody's did not change its assignment of uplift for bank-level senior debt, explaining that it continued to believe that the disorderly failure of one of these large bank subsidiaries would create the risk of contagion to the broader financial system. In contrast, Moody's reduced but did not eliminate uplift for subordinated debt of these banks' subsidiaries. Moody's attributed differences in its assessment of uplift for senior and subordinated debt to potential differences in the level of government support for senior and subordinated creditors. Moody's noted that it expects support for bank-level creditors to come primarily from the protection provided by holding company creditors, who take losses before the bank-level creditors under the SPOE framework. However, if imposing losses on holding company creditors does not prove sufficient to ensure the viability of the bank subsidiary, Moody's believes it is unlikely that bank-level subordinated creditors would receive direct government support. In contrast, in such a scenario, Moody's believes senior creditors might still be supported by the government.

[61] While the Dodd-Frank Act contains provisions that prohibit rescues of individual failing institutions, a few investment firm representatives believed that, under certain scenarios, the federal government might intervene to provide capital injections to distressed bank holding companies, which would require an act of Congress. These representatives said they did not know what form a government intervention would take, but indicated that elected officials could face pressure to intervene as the U.S. Congress did in October 2008 when it passed legislation authorizing TARP. One representative of a large asset management firm said that while the political cost to elected officials of rescuing large financial institutions would be high, the costs to the economy of not intervening could also be high.

[62] In his February 6, 2014, testimony to the Senate Banking Committee, Federal Reserve Governor Daniel Tarullo said that in the event that the equity of a financial firm is wiped out, successful resolution without taxpayer assistance would be most effectively accomplished if a firm has sufficient long-term, unsecured debt to absorb additional losses and to recapitalize the business transferred to a bridge operating company. In a public comment to FDIC on OLA's single-point-of-entry framework, former FDIC Chair Sheila Bair identified the long-term debt requirement as a key component to ensure that a firm in OLA has sufficient loss-absorbing capacity.

[63] For example, an investment firm may employ a passive investment strategy by managing the selection and allocation of investments in a particular fund with the goal of matching the returns of a benchmark index. In contrast, the firm may actively manage other funds by choosing investments with the goal of generating returns that outperform a benchmark index.

[64] In this report, we do not attempt to quantify the extent to which such higher costs for the largest firms could offset benefits they receive as a result of expectations of government support. For example, we did not attempt to determine the differential impacts of various Dodd-Frank Act provisions on bank holding companies of different sizes. Implementation of some Dodd-Frank Act provisions specifically targets only SIFIs, while other provisions affect both SIFIs and non-SIFIs. Representatives of community banks and other non-SIFIs have noted that while some Dodd-Frank Act provisions—such as the Volcker rule— were intended to target activities at the largest bank holding companies, smaller banks can still face burdens associated with ensuring they comply with these rules. Federal financial regulators have acknowledged the importance of minimizing regulatory burdens for financial institutions and particularly for smaller banks, whose fixed costs arising from regulatory compliance must be spread over a smaller base of revenues.

[65] Pub. L. No. 111-203, § 331(b), 124 Stat. 1376, 1538 (2010).

[66] § 318(c), 124 Stat. at 1527. In addition to these fee assessments related to Federal Reserve Board supervision, in April 2014 OCC proposed increasing the assessments it collects for national banks and federal savings associations with more than $40 billion in total assets. Assessment of Fees, 79 Fed. Reg. 23297 (Apr. 28, 2014). Under the proposal, the assessment increases would range from 0.32 percent to 14 percent, depending on the total assets of the institution reflected in its June 30, 2014, call report. *Id.* The proposed rule presented estimates of the size of the increase for institutions of various sizes. For example, a national bank with assets of $2 trillion would see its semiannual assessment increase by an estimated $9.3 million, or 14 percent.

[67] National banking regulators classify capital as either Tier 1—currently the highest-quality form of capital and includes common equity—or Tier 2, which is weaker in absorbing losses. Tier 1, or core, capital consists

primarily of common equity. Tier 2 is supplementary capital and includes limited amounts of subordinated debt, loan loss reserves, and certain other instruments.

68 On March 26, 2014, the Federal Reserve Board announced that it approved the capital plans of 25 bank holding companies participating in its Comprehensive Capital Analysis and Review (CCAR) program. It objected to the capital plans of 5 bank holding companies, including Citigroup Inc., one of the U.S. GSIBs. On April 28, 2014, the Federal Reserve Board announced that it was requiring Bank of America Corporation to resubmit its capital plan and to suspend planned increases in dividend distributions. The decision related to the disclosure by Bank of America that it incorrectly reported data used in the calculation of regulatory capital ratios and submitted as inputs for the most recent stress tests conducted by the Federal Reserve. The Federal Reserve Board can require a banking organiztion that is part of the annual CCAR program to resubmit its capital plan at any time if there has been or likely will be a material change in a firm's capital position. 12 C.F.R. § 225.8(d)(4)(i)(C)(2).

69 Regulatory Capital Rules: Regulatory Capital, Enhanced Supplementary Leverage Ratio Standards for Certain Bank Holding Companies and Their Subsidiary Insured Depository Institutions, 79 Fed. Reg. 24528 (May 1, 2014). The final rule applies to U.S. bank holding companies with more than $700 billion in consolidated total assets or more than $10 trillion in assets under custody (covered BHCs) and their insured depository institution (IDI) subsidiaries. Covered BHCs must maintain a leverage buffer greater than 2 percentage points above the minimum supplementary leverage ratio requirement of 3 percent, for a total of more than 5 percent, to avoid restrictions on capital distributions and discretionary bonus payments. IDI subsidiaries of covered BHCs must maintain at least a 6 percent supplementary leverage ratio to be considered "well capitalized" under the agencies' prompt corrective action framework. The final rule, which has an effective date of January 1, 2018, currently applies to eight large U.S. banking organizations that meet the size thresholds and their IDI subsidiaries.

70 As noted earlier in this report, the Federal Reserve Board has said its proposal will be based on the G-SIB capital surcharge framework developed by the Basel Committee, under which the size of the surcharge for an individual G-SIB would vary from 1 percent to 2.5 percent, depending on the firm's systemic importance.

71 In theory, increasing the required proportion of equity funding relative to debt funding should not affect a firm's overall cost of funding as it reduces the risk that the firm will fail, thereby reducing the returns demanded by both equity and debt holders. However, certain government policies make equity financing (such as through issuing stock to investors) more expensive for financial institutions than debt financing. For example, interest on debt is tax deductible, while dividends on equity securities are not. In addition, bank deposits benefit from federal guarantees and the interest rates a bank pays on its insured deposits may not fall as capital levels and the perceived safety of the firm increases.

72 See GAO

73 Resolution of Systemically Important Financial Institutions: The Single Point of Entry Strategy, 78 Fed. Reg. 243 (Dec. 18, 2013); Resolution of a Systemically Important Financial Institution: The Single Point of Entry Strategy, 79 Fed. Reg. 9899 (Feb. 21, 2014).

74 A basis point is one one-hundredth of a percentage point. Viral V. Acharya, Deniz Anginer and A. Joseph Warburton, "The End of Market Discipline? Investor Expectations of Implicit State Guarantees," *Social Science Research Network Working Paper* (December 2013).

75 International Monetary Fund, "How Big is the Implicit Subsidy for Banks Considered Too Important to Fail?" *Global Financial Stability Report*, Ch. 3 (Washington, D.C.: 2014).

76 Results of these models will also be sensitive to the typical assumption that the impact of variables on funding costs is linear—that is, changes in credit risk and liquidity have a constant and proportional impact on funding costs.

77 International Monetary Fund, "How Big is the Implicit Subsidy for Banks Considered Too Important to Fail?" *Global Financial Stability Report*, Ch. 3 (Washington, D.C.: 2014), Zoe Tsesmelidakis and Robert C. Merton, "The value of implicit guarantees," *Social Science Research Network working paper*, September 1, 2012, and Zan Li, Shisheng Qu and Jing Zhang, *Quantifying the Value of Implicit Government Guarantees for Large Financial Institutions* (Moody's Analytics, 2011).

78 This approach can be referred to as a "Merton model" based on Robert C. Merton, "On the pricing of corporate debt: the risk structure of interest rates," *Journal of Finance* vol. 29, 1974. Holders of equity and debt in a bank both face a risk of loss. Equity holders face a higher risk because they are the first to take losses in a failure (i.e., debt holders have higher priority). However, the risk that a debt holder will take a loss is likely to be proportional to—but smaller than—the risk facing an equity holder. As a result, one can estimate the risk of default on a debt based in part on the volatility of the stock price of the bank.

79 Another weakness of this model is that the market pricing of credit default swaps may not be reliable during a crisis.

80 See Sreedhar T. Bharath and Tyler Shumway, "Forecasting default with the Merton distance to default model," *Review of Financial Studies,* vol. 21, no. 3, May 2008.

81 International Monetary Fund, "How Big is the Implicit Subsidy for Banks Considered Too Important to Fail?" *Global Financial Stability Report*, Ch. 3 (Washington, D.C.: 2014), and Kenichi Ueda and Beatrice Weder di

Mauro, "Quantifying structural subsidy values for systemically important financial institutions," *Journal of Banking & Finance* vol. 37, no. 10, October 2013.

[82] In assessing the creditworthiness of bank holding companies, all three major rating agencies discuss the extent to which a rating is influenced by potential government support, though the specific approach differs by rating agency. By comparing a bank holding company's credit rating—with and without expected government support—to the average historical funding cost for corporations at those ratings, one can estimate the benefit of the amount of government support associated with the rating uplift.

[83] Our models allow the size of a bank holding company to influence its bond funding costs directly and also indirectly through the interaction between size and credit risk. As a result, no single parameter is sufficient to describe the relationship between bond funding costs and size. To summarize the overall relationship between bond funding costs and size reflected in each specification, we calculated bond funding costs for bank holding companies of different sizes and credit risk levels using our estimates of the parameters for each specification for each year. See appendix I for more details on these calculations.

[84] We also compared funding costs for bank holding companies with $50 billion, $100 billion, $250 billion, and $500 billion in assets to bank holding companies with $10 billion in assets. See appendix I.

[85] Many of the estimates that were statistically significant at the 10 percent level were also statistically significant at the 5 percent or 1 percent level. See table 5 in appendix I.

[86] Although higher, credit risk in 2008 was not outside the range of credit risk in 2013 in every dimension. Specifically, the average values of the credit risk variables for 2008 were less than the maximum values of the credit risk variables for 2013, with the exceptions of the variables measuring equity price volatility, option implied volatility, equity return volatility, and excess equity return volatility.

[87] As discussed earlier in this report, many investment firm representatives with whom we spoke credited enhanced regulatory standards with improving the safety and soundness of the largest bank holding companies and reducing the likelihood that they would experience distress that could result in failure or government support.

[88] To see this, compare the 2008 estimates in figure 1 to the "financial crisis level" estimates for 2013 in figure 3. Both sets of estimates are derived assuming that the level of credit risk is equal to the average for 2008.

[89] Secondary markets are markets where investors purchase securities or assets from other investors, rather than from issuing companies themselves.

[90] A credit default swap is a credit derivative in which two parties enter into an agreement whereby one party pays the other a fixed periodic coupon for the specified life of the agreement and the other party makes no payments unless a credit event relating to a predetermined reference asset occurs. If such an event occurs, the party will then make a payment to the first party and the swap will terminate. The size of the payment is usually linked to the decline in the reference asset's market value following the determination of the occurrence of a credit event.

[91] A plain vanilla bond, also known as a straight bond, is a bond that pays interest at regular intervals and at maturity pays back the principal that was originally invested. These bonds are debt instruments because they are essentially loaning money (creating debt) to an entity, which promises to pay the interest on the debt and at maturity pay back the original loan.

[92] Our sample includes only bank holding companies, so it excludes companies like Goldman Sachs and Morgan Stanley before they became bank holding companies. Similarly, our sample excludes other financial companies that were never bank holding companies.

[93] Executed trades are trades that have been completed. Executable quotes are quotes provided by bond dealers at which they are willing to trade. Indicative quotes are quotes provided by bond dealers to give an indication of the price at which a bond might trade, but at which they are not obligated to trade. Composites are aggregates of quotes from multiple sources that are suggestive of the price at which a bond might trade.

[94] The correlation between the two measures of bond yield spreads was 0.96.

[95] A bank holding company's total assets may change from one quarter to the next. Similarly, a bank holding company may have less than $50 billion in assets in some quarters and more than $50 billion in assets in others. An alternative measure of a bank holding company's size or systemic importance is whether or not it participated in the Federal Reserve's Comprehensive Capital Analysis and Review (CCAR). However, the measure of size based on CCAR participation is highly correlated with the measure of size based on whether or not a bank holding company had $50 billion or more in assets, so these two measures of size are not substantively different.

[96] Credit risk increases with higher values of our asset quality, maturity mismatch, and volatility measures and with lower values of our capital adequacy and earnings measures.

[97] Several components of volatile liabilities, such as federal funds purchased, repurchase agreements, and demand deposits, have relatively short maturities and may not be rolled over by the creditor when they mature. Maturity mismatch measures the bank holding company's capacity to cover these liabilities if the creditor chooses to not roll them over.

[98] The bid-ask spread is the difference between the best buying price and the best selling price. We expressed the bid-ask spread as a percentage of the midpoint between the bid price and the ask price.

[99] Some studies suggest that there may be economies of scale or scope in banking. For example, see Joseph P. Hughes and Loretta J. Mester, "Who Said Large Banks Don't Experience Scale Economies? Evidence From a Risk-Return-Driven Cost Function," Journal of Financial Intermediation 22 (2013), pp. 559-585. We include noninterest expense as a percentage of total assets to control for a channel through which economies of scale may affect bond funding costs. Other channels through which economies of scale or scope may affect bond funding costs are profitability, which is captured in our earnings variable, and riskiness, which is captured in our volatility variable.

[100] For predictions at average levels of credit risk, we set variables equal to the unweighted average for the sample used to estimate the regression for each year. For predictions at low levels of credit risk, we set variables measuring asset quality, maturity mismatch, and volatility equal to their 25th percentiles for each year and we set variables measuring capital adequacy and earnings equal to their 75th percentiles for each year. For predictions as high levels of credit risk, we set variables measuring asset quality, maturity mismatch, and volatility equal to their 75th percentiles for each year and we set variables measuring capital adequacy and earnings equal to their 25th percentiles for each year.

Index

D

E

J

L

M

N

O

P

Q

R

S

Y